LET'S PLAY A BIBLE GAME!

48
Reproducible Scripture
Games and Puzzles
for the Overhead Projector

ED DUNLOP

MERIWETHER PUBLISHING LTD.
Colorado Springs, Colorado

Meriwether Publishing Ltd., Publisher
P.O. Box 7710
Colorado Springs, CO 80933

Editor: Rhonda Wray
Typesetting: Sharon E. Garlock
Cover design: Steve Hunziker, Fundamental Design
Illustrations on pages 97-100, 113-114, and 126: Rebecca Dunlop. Other illustrations from clip art sources: Zedcor, Inc., Dover Publications and Corel.
Interior photographs: Norman Abshire, Rick Brooks, Pastor Harold Coe, Evangelist Dale Grisso, Louise Petersen, Gary Pruett and Jerry Short

© Copyright MCMXCV Meriwether Publishing Ltd.
Printed in the United States of America
First Edition

All rights reserved. No part of this publication, except when specifically noted, may be reproduced, stored in a retrieval system, or transmitted in any form or by any means, electronic, mechanical, photocopying, recording or otherwise, without permission of the publishers. Permission to photocopy and reproduce copies of the masters on pages 85-141 and 153-192 is granted with the purchase of this book. These photocopies are for the use of the purchaser and the purchasing organization only.

All Scripture is taken from the King James Version.

Library of Congress Cataloging-in-Publication Data

Dunlop, Ed, 1955-
    Let's play a Bible game : 48 reproducible scripture games and puzzles for the overhead projector / by Ed Dunlop.
    p. cm.
    ISBN 1-55608-013-4
    1. Games in Christian education. 2. Bible games and puzzles.
I. Title.
BV1536.3.D85 1996
261'.432----dc20   95-36395
                                                                           CIP
                                                                            AC

*To my favorite kids —
Rebecca, Steven, and Phillip.*

Contents

PART ONE
The Exciting World of Bible Games 1
- Introduction 3
- Why Teach With Bible Games? 7
- Using Bible Games Effectively 13
- Making and Storing the Bible Games 19

PART TWO
Sixteen Bible Games That Will Bring Your Class to Life 25
- Bible Games 27
- Cooties! 29
- Surprise Ending! 33
- Jonkenpon 37
- Capture the Flag! 41
- Pirate Treasure 45
- Smiles and Ladders 49
- Air Battle 53
- Apple Picking 57
- Bible Football 59
- Sea Battle 63
- Bible Tic-Tac-Toe 67
- Operation Spy Trap 69
- Rattlesnake! 73
- Matchit! 77
- Space Race 79
- The Bermuda Triangle 81
- Game Masters 85

PART THREE
Thirty-Two Scripture Puzzles That Your Class Will Love 143
- Scripture Puzzles 145
- Puzzle Masters 153
- Puzzle Solutions 193

A Final Word 197
About the Author 199

PART ONE
THE EXCITING WORLD OF BIBLE GAMES

Introduction

It was Sunday evening at a large church in Southern California. As the setting sun cast long shadows across the complex of educational buildings, the cheerful sounds of young voices raised in enthusiastic song could be heard from the Primary classroom.

At exactly five minutes after six, the door to the Junior classroom opened, and the large figure of a man appeared on the sidewalk. Shadowy figures lurking in the bushes along the side of the building crouched even lower as he passed.

The man, unaware that his every move was being monitored by watchful eyes in the shrubbery, strode purposefully to the door of the Primary classroom and flung it open. Peering inside, he growled, "Come on, let's go!"

Reluctantly, several children followed him from the room. As the door to the Junior classroom closed behind the sullen group, figures stirred again in the bushes. "Come on!" urged a voice in a loud whisper. "The coast is clear! Let's go!"

The bushes came alive with movement as the group of Juniors scrambled from their hiding places, then headed for the class of Primaries. As the latecomers took their seats, the Primary teacher acknowledged their presence with a smile. He didn't have the heart to insist that they go to their own class.

But wait a minute — what's going on here? Why would fourth, fifth and sixth grade kids even want to be in with a group of first, second, and third graders? Why would they go to such lengths to be in a class of younger kids, instead of staying with their own age group? To find the answer, let's take a look at the two classes.

In the Primary class, the teacher — a college student in his late teens — taught with enthusiasm and earnestness. He used a variety of visual aids, role-playing, Scripture-search games, and other methods of student participation. He loved his students and was willing to spend the time required to prepare for each class session. The children responded with enthusiasm. The forty-five minutes spent in class each Sunday evening just weren't enough.

In the Junior class, things were quite different. The teachers — a couple in their late thirties — were too busy to be bothered with much preparation. Class time was made up of two basic ingredients: lots and lots of half-hearted, sullen singing, and an ill-prepared lesson that made Sunday evening seem like an eternity. The students responded by hiding in the bushes.

Week after week, I watched the Juniors go to great lengths to avoid a class that they detested, and I sympathized with their attempts to be included in a class they enjoyed. I talked with students from both classes. The kids attending the Primary class all had the same complaint: "It's too short." The Juniors repeatedly voiced their opinion of their own class: "It's boring!" My heart went out to the kids who were thrust into a class with teachers who didn't care enough to prepare.

In my ministry, I talk with thousands of children every year. All too often, I hear the complaint: "Sunday school is boring. Children's church is a drag. I wouldn't go if my parents didn't make me."

Teacher, be honest with yourself. If you were a Junior age student (or a Primary, or a Junior High, or whatever age group you happen to teach), would you enjoy your own class? Would you find it exciting, challenging, or just — boring?

If you teach children the Word of God, I challenge you to

If you were a Junior age student (or a Primary, or a Junior High, or whatever age group you happen to teach), would you enjoy your own class?

find ways to make your class lively and exciting for your students. Make it so enjoyable that they'll actually look forward to the time they spend in your room.

Perhaps this book can help. In the pages that follow, you'll find sixteen Bible review games that will bring your Primaries or Juniors to life. You'll find thirty-two Scripture puzzles that will intrigue even the coolest of students. The games and puzzles are designed for use on the overhead projector. They can be made in seconds on any plain paper copier or thermofax machine.

I've used each of these games and puzzles in my own ministry, and response from the students has been tremendous. These games have been "kid-tested" in many different teaching situations — kids' crusades, summer camps, Awana clubs, Christian school chapels, backyard Bible clubs, even public school assemblies!

Grab a box of transparency film and get started today. You'll be amazed at how easily the games are made, and at how much fun you and your students will have playing them. As your class comes to life and your students begin to really enjoy your class, you'll rediscover just what a joy teaching young people can be.

> *You'll be amazed at how easily the games are made, and at how much fun you and your students will have playing them.*

Why Teach With Bible Games?

One Sunday afternoon I stood in the doorway, saying good-bye to "my kids" as they filed out of children's church. A hug here, a handshake there. Bending down to listen to a whispered prayer request. Placing a gentle hand on the shoulder of a troublesome student and saying softly, "Michael, I'm glad you were here today. I'm gonna come to your house this week to see you, OK?"

One timid little seven-year-old hung back until all the other kids were gone, then approached shyly. As I bent down to her, I suddenly found her arms around my neck. "I liked the Bible game," she whispered, then followed the others to the buses.

Perhaps you teach children, and yet you've never used a Bible game in your ministry with the kids. Allow me to give you several reasons why Bible games are so effective in teaching God's Word to young people.

1. *Bible games make learning fun and exciting!* Do your students enjoy your class? Do they tell their parents and

Many times when I talk with kids, I am dismayed to find that they think of Sunday school and church as being dull and boring.

friends about your teaching? Do they look forward to it each week? Many times when I talk with kids, I am dismayed to find that they think of Sunday school and church as being *dull* and *boring*. Where would they ever get that idea? The sad truth is, many times our classes *are* dull and boring, and the students have no desire to be there.

A recent *Calvin and Hobbes* cartoon pictured Calvin sitting in class, eyes half closed, about ready to drift off to sleep. Suddenly he sits upright and screams out, "BORING!" The next frame shows him on his way to the principal's office. Calvin has a discipline problem, of course, but wait just a minute — the teacher has a problem, too. She needs to find ways to make her class interesting for her students.

If Calvin sat with your group of wigglers next Sunday, what would be his evaluation of your class?

Why should we ever bore a child with the Word of God? It's up to us as teachers to find ways to make our classes interesting and exciting for the students, and profitable for their lives. Bible games can bring that kind of life to your teaching situation.

2. Bible games can get students to participate. Every class seems to have at least one Joe Cool. You know, the kid who sits in the back row, never sings, never reads the Scripture along

> *Why should we ever bore a child with the Word of God? It's up to us as teachers to find ways to make our classes interesting and exciting for the students, and profitable for their lives.*

with the other kids, never participates in any way. Maybe in your class of girls it's a Josie Cool.

But watch Joe when you start a Bible game! He'll sit there for the first couple of questions, just watching. But notice what happens on the third or fourth question. Joe's hand is up! He's actually participating!

I've seen it happen time after time. The child who sits there like a zombie week after week, showing no interest in what goes on in class, suddenly gets drawn out of his shell and begins to participate in a Bible game. I think it even catches the student himself by surprise!

A couple of things to keep in mind the first time Joe responds during a Bible game: first, don't show surprise when he responds, and second, be sure to call on him. As you open the door for him to respond during the game, you'll be delighted to find him responding and participating in other class activities as well.

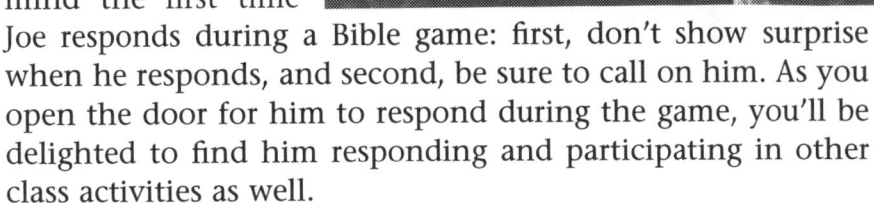

3. *Bible games can involve the entire class*. Recently I conducted a drug and alcohol assembly in a public school. There were about 350 students present, kindergarteners through fifth-graders. To conclude the assembly and review the material I had presented, we played *Cooties*. The entire group was involved, with every student hoping to be the one to answer the next question!

I've used Bible games in just about every teaching situation you can imagine. I've used them with tiny groups of five or six kids, and I've used them with groups of more than 600! The Bible games get the entire class participating.

4. *Bible games are an excellent method of review*. Do you as a teacher understand the importance of review? The educa-

> *I've used Bible games in just about every teaching situation you can imagine. I've used them with tiny groups of five or six kids, and I've used them with groups of more than 600!*

tion experts tell us that one-third of our teaching time should be spent in review. *One-third!* Think of it! If you have a thirty-minute teaching period, twenty minutes should be spent teaching new material and ten minutes should be spent in review. If you have forty-five minutes, you should spend fifteen of them in review. That's amazing, isn't it?

Perhaps your past attempts at review have been met by groans of dismay. Why not announce, "Today we're going to play *Operation Spy Trap!*" Your class will respond with an enthusiasm that will make your day!

Review is very important, yet so often we teachers don't even plan any time for review as we teach God's Word. Get started on Bible games, and they will quickly become your favorite method of review.

Do you as a teacher understand the importance of review?

5. ***Bible games can help evaluate our teaching.*** How many times I've walked out of class thinking, "My, that went well! The kids really listened!" That evening, a parent corners me after church. "What did you teach today about communion? Lisa told me that you said..." And then, to my dismay, I hear some "strange doctrine," supposedly from my own teaching, but edited by a child's understanding and memory. Ever try to explain your way out of one of those situations?

The problem with teaching is this — we rely on words to convey our message to our young students. Words can have so many different meanings and be so easily misunderstood, especially by a child. Bible games give us the opportunity to discover, in the students' own words, just what they are learning from our teaching.

6. ***Bible games can correct wrong impressions.*** Recently we were holding a kids' crusade in Rossville, Georgia. On Thursday evening there were over 200 kids in the audience. After the message, we played *Pirate Treasure*. During the game I asked the question, "Why

should we live for Jesus?"

A second-grader named Tonya responded, and here is her answer, word for word: "So we can get eternal life, and so we can go to heaven."

Here was a girl with a wrong impression, even though she had just heard a message teaching just the opposite. I took the opportunity right then to explain to her, and the rest of the crowd, that a person does not receive eternal life or go to heaven by living for Jesus. A person receives eternal life by receiving Jesus as Savior by faith.

7. Bible games can be used to stress important points. After you have finished teaching the lesson, use a Bible game to re-emphasize the important teaching points of the lesson. How do you accomplish that? Simply write out your Bible game questions in advance, drawing many of the questions from the main points of application in your Bible story or lesson.

When I began using Bible games in my first children's church, I used general Bible knowledge questions. "How many books are in the Old Testament?" "Who wrote the book of Acts?" "Where was Jesus born?" Then the Lord showed me that the Bible games could be a very effective way to review the lesson I had just taught. They could be used to re-emphasize the truths of the lesson. I have used Bible games that way ever since.

If you teach boys and girls, I trust that you'll begin using Bible games this week. You and your students will soon be as excited about them as I am. And you'll soon agree with me that Bible games are a very effective and exciting teaching

Bible games give us the opportunity to discover, in the students' own words, just what they are learning from our teaching.

tool! Your class time will come to life!

In the next chapter, I'll show you how to use Bible review games most effectively.

Using Bible Games Effectively

Let's consider some ways to use Bible games effectively in your teaching. A Bible game may be utilized at the beginning of class time to review a lesson or series of lessons that have been taught in a previous week. But experience has taught me that it is most effective to use a Bible game at the close of the class period to review the lesson that has just been taught.

Briefly, here's how a Bible game is played. At the conclusion of the lesson, announce the Bible game for the day and explain the rules.

Designate one of your students as the "starter" for the game. After each question, the starter will ring a bell, honk a bicycle horn, or strike a note on the piano as the signal for the other students to respond to your question.

When the students stand in response to the starter's signal, you or another adult worker choose the first child to stand after the signal. If that student can answer your question correctly after being recognized by the adult spotter, he comes to the overhead projector to play the game and attempts to score points for his team. Using a pencil as a pointer, he selects game pieces from the game, which you remove to reveal the points scored.

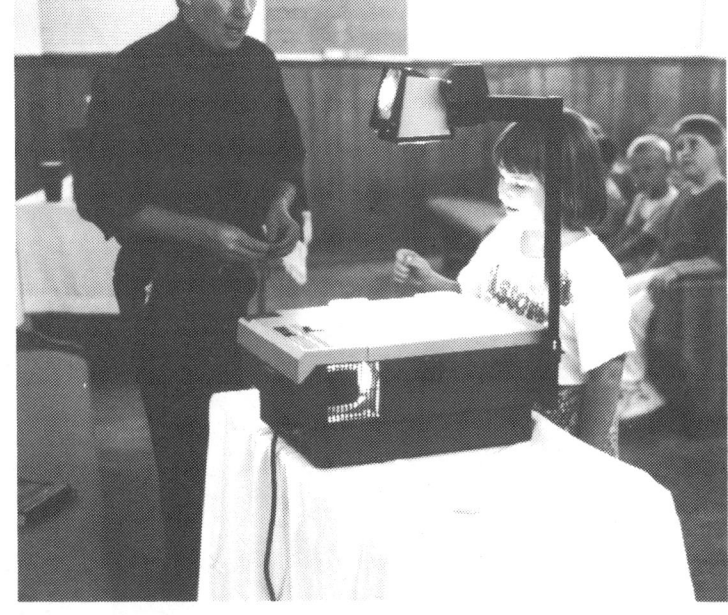

The teams may be boys against girls (there's some fierce competition there), or you may divide the class by grade levels, age, or whatever other method is quick and easy for you. Spend as little time as possible dividing your teams.

If the student cannot answer the question, or answers incorrectly, repeat the question and allow another student to answer. This second student may be from either team.

It's usually best for an adult to keep score. As the game concludes, announce the scores, then lead the victorious team in a quick cheer.

Here are a few guidelines to follow when using Bible games:

1. Make them fun and exciting! Announce the game time with excitement and enthusiasm in your voice. Relax your class rules ever so slightly as the students play the game. Enter into the students' excitement — cheering when they score points, and showing disappointment when they don't. Allow the kids to enjoy the game.

2. Ask simple questions that are easy to understand. There's no need for trick questions here. Remember your objectives in playing a Bible game — to review the Bible lesson and re-emphasize the main points of application, to evaluate your students' comprehension, and to correct any wrong impressions.

Plan your questions carefully, and write them out before coming to class. Keep them simple and concise.

3. Ask questions that relate to the lesson. The Bible game is *not* just a fun time or a "time-filler." Use it to review the lesson. Always write questions that relate to that day's lesson, or to a series of lessons that you have just finished.

Let's say that today's lesson is on King Saul's disobedience, taken from I Samuel 15. Draw each of your Bible game questions from chapter 15, perhaps with a few questions reviewing Saul's earlier life in chapters 10 through 14.

> *Enter into the students' excitement — cheering when they score points, and showing disappointment when they don't.*

4. Use both factual and Bible principle questions. The Bible questions that you write should be of two types — questions regarding the bare facts of the lesson, and questions from the lesson application.

Back to the lesson from I Samuel 15. You'll use questions that deal with just the facts stated in the Scripture text: Who was the king of Israel at this time? What army did Israel fight against? What instructions from God did Samuel give King Saul?

Then you'll want to ask questions that deal with the Bible principles taught in the lesson, or what we usually call the application: Why did Saul disobey God? Why did God reject Saul as king of Israel? What are the results of disobedience in our lives today?

Again, plan your questions carefully, and write them out in advance. Poor questions are confusing to the children and won't accomplish your objectives.

5. Address questions to the entire class. Ask the question first, then direct it to one particular team or student. When handled this way, each student answers the question in his or her own mind, hoping to be the one to answer aloud.

6. Accept only correct answers. This should be completely obvious, yet many times I observe teachers accepting incorrect answers to spare a child's feelings. But stop and think — when you accept an incorrect answer, you are actually teaching your class that the answer was correct!

Always be gracious to the child who gives an incorrect answer, and never allow the other students to make fun. Gently inform the student that the answer was incorrect, then allow another student to answer the question.

> *Poor questions are confusing to the children and won't accomplish your objectives.*

7. Repeat the correct answer so that all can hear. As I write this, we are conducting a kids' crusade in a rural area of Arkansas. Sunday night as we played the Bible game, a little girl in the second row answered one of the questions. Even though I was standing less than six feet from her, I could not hear her answer. She repeated it twice before I finally heard her. I knew that the rest of the crowd had not heard her answer, so I repeated it before the girl came to the projector to play the game.

> **Remember that you are teaching Bible truths as you play the game.**

Remember that you are teaching Bible truths as you play the game. You want your entire class to hear each correct answer. This is more important than the game itself.

Occasionally you may ask a question that no one in the entire class is able to answer, even when you rephrase it. Always be sure to give the correct answer before you go on to the next question.

8. Don't allow one or two students to answer every question. In my children's church in Tennessee, I taught a brilliant fourth-grade boy named Wayne, Jr. I don't think I ever asked a question that Wayne couldn't answer. When we played a Bible game, he was always the first one on his feet, ready to answer every question. I had to teach my workers that when they served as spotter for the Bible games, they couldn't call on Wayne for every question. They had to allow the rest of the group a chance to participate, too.

If you use one of your adult workers as the game spotter, instruct him or her to choose kids from the front of the room, the back, the sides, the middle. Get the entire group involved in the game! Many times I'll have a game spotter who wants to choose only the kids on the front row, question after question after question. When that happens, I always have to instruct the spotter to choose from the other sections of the room or auditorium as well.

9. Set a time limit. To be sure, the Bible games are exciting, but you want to bring each game to a close while the interest is still at a peak level. Conclude the game while the students are still enjoying it and wanting more.

I suggest about a dozen questions for each game. Ten or twelve questions, including the time at the projector playing the game, will involve about ten or twelve minutes. You do not want the game to go beyond that, even if you have unlimited time.

10. Use a variety of games. The first Bible game I ever made was *Bible Football*, with a 3' x 6' playing field of green felt. (You'll find the overhead version in this book.) We played *Bible Football* every week for about six months straight! Finally I realized the truth — the kids were tired of *Bible Football!*

I began to search for some other games, and the Lord gave us a number of new ideas. Now we use a Bible game in Sunday school or children's church for two or three weeks, then put it away for a year or so. The next time we play the game it will be new and fresh, and the students will respond with enthusiasm.

This book contains the masters for sixteen different Bible games. You'll notice that most of the games have at least three versions of the same game. Make all the different versions, and play a different one each week. This will keep your students from memorizing where the different points and jeopardies are. The *Sea Battle* game has two different ship overlays. These may be flipped when placed on the projector, giving you four different combinations. The overlay for games such as *Surprise Ending!* and *Operation Spy Trap* can be rotated or flipped, with eight different combinations possible!

One more suggestion. If the boys win a particular game one week and the girls win it the next, be sure to play the same game for the third week. And plan for a very exciting game!

Simply announce, "The boys' team won *Capture the Flag!* this week, and the girls won it last week! Next week will be the *Capture the Flag!* championship game! Which team will win the championship?" Needless to say, the *Capture the Flag!*

> *Conclude the game while the students are still enjoying it and wanting more.*

> *We use a Bible game in Sunday school or children's church for two or three weeks, then put it away for a year or so.*

championship game will be exciting!

I trust that by now you are excited about using Bible games in your class! The next chapter will give you some details on making and storing the games, and then we'll take a look at the games themselves.

Making and Storing the Bible Games

If you are as busy as the average teacher, you'll quickly learn to appreciate two things about the overhead Bible games: they are easy to make and easy to store.

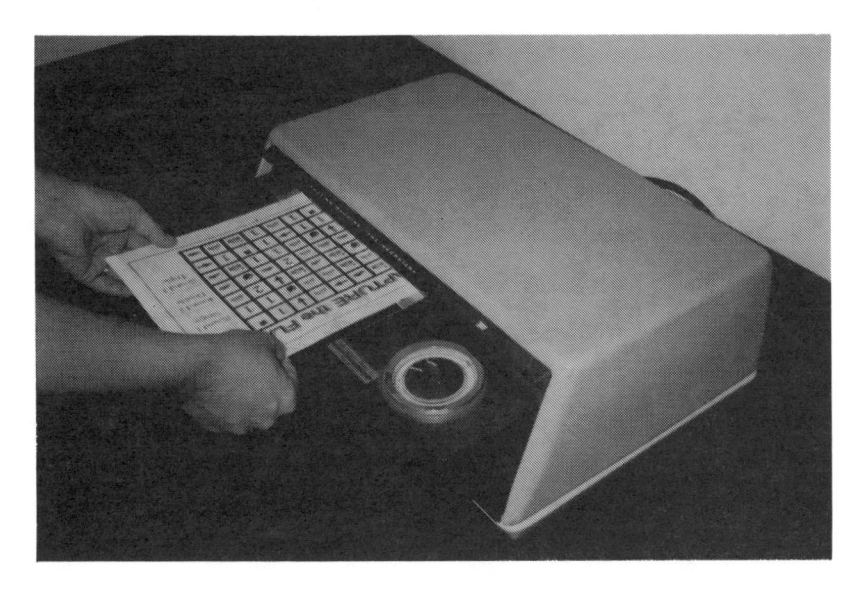

The pages of this book were designed to serve as masters for making the games on transparencies. To make a Bible game on a plain paper copier, carefully place the master in the proper position on your copier. Insert a sheet of transparency film (designed for copiers) in the paper tray, then make the copy. You have your first Bible game! It's that simple! The copier gives you a black image on a clear or colored transparency, depending on which film you use. The films, available at any office supply store, come in red, yellow, green, blue, and clear.

An infrared or thermal process machine (thermofax) can give you colored images on clear transparencies, or black images on color, again depending on the film. To make a thermofax transparency, follow these steps. Remove the master from the book and make a good, clear photocopy, then use the copy as your master for the thermofax transparency. Simply place the transparency film on top of the master, select the transparency setting on the machine, then insert the film and master together into the entrance slot. The machine does the rest!

If you are as busy as the average teacher, you'll quickly learn to appreciate two things about the overhead Bible games: they are easy to make and easy to store.

I recommend 3M brand transparency films. These come in a variety of colors for use with the plain paper copier or thermofax copier, and are available at any office supply retailer. To locate the 3M dealer nearest you, call:

1-800-328-1371.

No matter what brand of film you use, be sure that

the film you purchase is compatible with your copier. Check with your dealer to be sure, giving him the make and model number of your machine. (I once made 500 game transparencies using a film that was not designed for the photocopier I was using. The images did not fuse properly to the transparencies, and the games were useless!)

It's easy to make beautiful, multicolored transparencies for your games. They take just a bit longer, but the results on the screen are well worth the extra effort. Let's say that you want to make *Surprise Ending!* in three colors. (My own personal game has purple headline lettering, a green playing grid, and red question marks along the sides.) Here's how to do it.

Take the *Surprise Ending!* game master and make three crisp, clear copies on regular paper. With a razor blade or X-Acto knife, cut out the question marks and playing grid from the first copy, leaving only the headline and the border. Run this through the thermofax machine with a purple image film, and your headline and border are imaged in purple.

From the second copy, remove the headline, question marks, and border, leaving only the playing grid. Run this new master through the thermofax with a green image film.

On the third copy, remove everything but the question marks, then use a red image film as you run the master through the thermofax.

You now have three separate transparencies — one purple, one red, one green. Tape these one by one to a transparency frame (available at your office supply store), and the three transparencies are now combined to form one three-color game!

Your church doesn't have a thermal copier (thermofax)? Ask around. You can probably find one at a local school, another church, the local library, or even a college or university library. Once the people in charge know that you work with children, they'll usually allow you access to their machine. They may even sell you the transparency film on a sheet-by-sheet basis.

(I live near Tennessee Temple University. Its library has two thermofax machines, and it stocks the transparency films in a variety of colors. I can make a transparency on the library's machines for forty-five cents.)

Perhaps you don't even have access to a copier. Check out your local quick-service print shop. Most of them can make transparencies for you at minimal cost, even if they don't have a variety of colors available.

You may be saying, "Wait! I like the games, but our church doesn't even have an overhead projector! I have a small class — six kids — and we wouldn't even have room in our classroom for a projector!"

No projector? Small class? No problem! Simply duplicate the games on brightly colored paper and play them as table games with your class! As many as ten or twelve kids can feasibly play the games this way.

The one drawback of using the overhead projector is that the transparencies are made of plastic and often get scratched. Here are a few ways to protect your games and get the maximum use from each one.

Use cardboard transparency frames. These frames for mounting the transparencies are available from any office supply store. They are easy to use and relatively inexpensive. Simply tape each transparency to a frame for protection and ease of handling.

For maximum protection of your transparencies, first tape a sheet of clear acetate (write-on film) to the frame, then tape the game transparency over that, centering the game in the frame opening. Next, tape a second sheet of clear film over the game transparency. Your transparency is now safely sandwiched between the two clear sheets of film. When the game accumulates a few scratches, simply replace the protective sheets of film!

An even simpler but more expensive way to protect the transparency games is to use 3M's Flip-Frame Transparency Protectors. Each protector consists of two clear plastic sheets with an opening at one end and opaque flip-out borders on two sides.

To use the protectors, simply slip a transparency into the open side of the protector. The transparency stays flat on the projector stage, and the clear plastic sheets provide two-sided protection. The flip-out borders serve to frame the transparency and block out distracting light from the projector stage and presentation screen. There's even a multipunch strip

You may be saying, "Wait! I like the games, but our church doesn't even have an overhead projector!"

along the left edge to allow storage and transportation of your games in any ring binder. The transparency protectors are easy to use, but there is a drawback — they cost several times as much as the cardboard frames.

If you don't use cardboard frames or flip-frame protectors, consider Faith Venture Visuals' Insta-Frame. This handy device consists of a durable plastic frame around a piece of tempered glass. Once the Insta-Frame is in position on the projector, transparencies may be placed into it, and they are instantly aligned perfectly on the screen. No more turning to check the screen! I use my Insta-Frame with all my lesson transparencies, as well as my Bible games.

The Insta-Frame may be ordered from:

>Faith Venture Visuals, Inc.
>P.O. Box 423
>Lititz, PA 17543-0423

or by calling:

>1-800-233-3866.

Perhaps you want the ease of using the Insta-Frame, but also want to protect your transparencies by framing them. The transparency frames will not fit into the Insta-Frame, but here's one way to do it — make your own frames out of 8½" x 11" sheets of white poster board. Each transparency is sandwiched between two sheets of clear film as I mentioned earlier, and you can still use the Insta-Frame. The transparencies may then be stored in 8½" x 11" boxes purchased inexpensively at a local print shop.

You are about to enter the exciting world of Bible games! Your class may never be the same.

If you don't take the time to mount your transparencies on frames or use transparency protectors, at least protect the transparencies when transporting them to your classroom. Buy a number of letter-sized file folders at your local office supply store. Tape the two sides of each folder shut with Scotch tape, leaving the top open. Fold a single sheet of 11" x 17" paper in half (you can buy just a few sheets at any print shop), and insert it into the folder. Label the folder with the name of the game, and you're in business! You have a folder to protect the game as you transport it to class, and you can store it at home in a file cabinet or desk drawer.

Many of the games use number cards or small transparency pieces (the footballs, for instance). These are easily stored in small envelopes. (Use offering envelopes, pay envelopes, whatever.) Wrap a rubber band around the cards to keep them together. Drop them together with any playing pieces into the envelope, labeling the outside with the name of the game. Store the envelopes in a shoe box.

Ready? Let's take a look at the Bible games themselves. You are about to enter the exciting world of Bible games! Your class may never be the same.

PART TWO
SIXTEEN BIBLE GAMES THAT WILL BRING YOUR CLASS TO LIFE

Bible Games

The following games have been thoroughly "kid-tested." They have been used with both large and small groups in every teaching situation imaginable.

I am presenting the games in the same way that they have been effective in our ministry. Each game works well as it is presented here. However, every group of children is unique. You know your own students. Feel free to experiment — changing a rule here, adding a detail there. You may be able to improve some of the games so they will be even more effective for your class!

Feel free to experiment — changing a rule here, adding a detail there.

Thousands and thousands of kids and teens have played the games that you will find in this book. I trust that you will be able to use some of the Bible games you find here, and that the kids you minister to will enjoy them as much as "my kids" have!

Get started! Make that first Bible game today!

COOTIES!

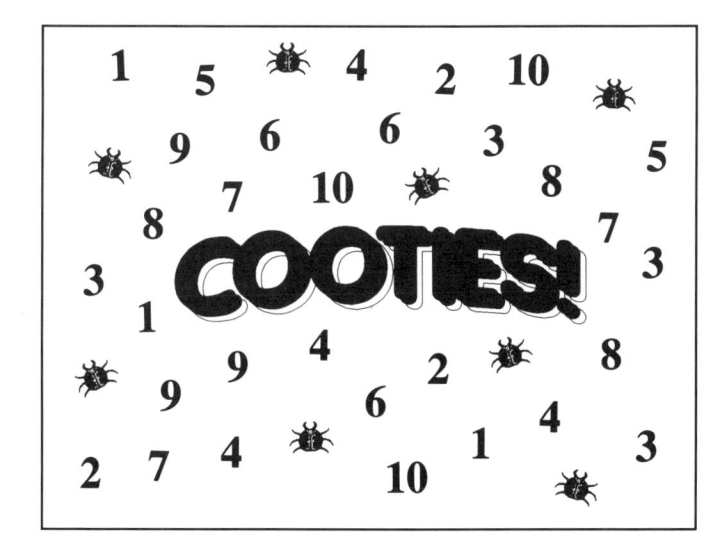

Here's an exciting game that appeals to just about all age groups. I've used it with Primaries, Juniors, and Junior High, and the response has been tremendous.

Briefly, here's how *Cooties!* is played. The student answering the Bible question correctly comes to the overhead projector and chooses one of forty pennies covering the secret numbers on the transparency. The teacher removes the penny for the student, revealing a number between one and ten. The number revealed is the number of points scored for that student's team.

When a child is at the projector, he may choose as many pennies as he desires! However, if a penny is removed to reveal a "cootie," the child's turn ends immediately, and he loses all the points from his turn!

Making the Game

There are three different masters for the *Cooties!* game. I suggest making each version of the game on a different color of transparency film to keep them straight.

To make the *Cooties!* game, simply copy a master from pages 85, 86, or 87 onto a transparency with your plain paper copier. It's that simple! Or make a regular copy of the master on your copier, then use the copy as a master in a thermofax copier.

Mount the *Cooties!* game to a transparency frame, get forty pennies to use as cover tabs, and your Bible game is ready to play!

Playing the Game

If possible, set up the *Cooties!* game before the students arrive. If you are using the overhead for your lesson or your song time, lead your class in a song while you set up the game following your lesson. *Cooties!* takes about sixty seconds to set up. Place the game transparency on the projector stage. Before turning the projector on, cover each of the numbers and "cooties" with a penny.

When you are ready to play *Cooties!*, divide your teams, then choose a student as the starter, handing her the horn or bell. The starter can give the signal from her own seat. Select one of your workers as the game spotter, or act as the spotter yourself. It is usually best not to allow a child to serve as spotter.

Introduce the game and explain the rules. "Today, class, we are going to play a brand-new Bible game called *Cooties!* It's boys against the girls! Which team will win?

"As you probably already know, a 'cootie' is a tiny, microscopic creature, smaller than a bug, but larger than a germ. Girls are born with them, but if a girl gets too close to a boy, the cooties will jump onto the boy! I did a scientific study of cooties, and I found in my research that the maximum distance that a cootie can jump is six inches. Boys, as long as you stay at least six inches from the girls, you are safe from cooties!

"Just kidding, girls. But our Bible game today really is called *Cooties!*

"Listen closely as I explain the rules. I will ask questions from our Bible lesson today. Timothy will honk this horn at the end of each question. The horn sounds like this." (Pause while Timothy honks the horn.) "Mr. Bernard will be our game spotter today. He will choose the first student to stand after the horn sounds. If you stand up before the horn, Mr. Bernard will not call on you.

"When Mr. Bernard calls on you, if you answer the question correctly, you may come to the projector and choose one penny by pointing to it. I will remove the penny for you. The number that is revealed when we move the penny is the number of points that you score for your team!

"Now, when you come to the projector, you may choose as many pennies as you want!" (Pause) "But — if I remove one of your pennies and you see a funny-looking little bug, you have chosen a cootie! If you get a cootie, you have to stop, and you lose all the points from your turn! So, when you come to the projector, choose a few pennies, but stop before you get a cootie!"

As the child chooses pennies from the projector, add his score in your head, and announce his total after each penny. He decides after each penny if he wants to stop or continue. Once the student decides to stop, announce his score and write it down, or have an adult scorekeeper record it.

Once a child stops and the score is written down, the points are permanent. Another child finding a cootie later in the game does not erase the points on the score sheet.

For added excitement at the close of the game, have a final question just for the boys and one just for the girls. Double the points on these two final questions.

Suggestions and Variations

1. When the student comes forward to play the game, hand him a pencil to use as a pointer, suggesting that he select a penny by pointing to it, but not touching it. You remove the pennies for him, announcing his score after each selection.

2. As the *Cooties!* game progresses and the score is recorded, do not announce the total scores until the end of the game. This helps build suspense. The students can add the points in their heads, of course, but very few do.

3. Never tell the students how many cooties are in the game. (The fewest is seven, the most is nine.)

4. On occasion, you may want to remove a few of the cooties, just to reduce the students' chances of getting one. Simply cut out or white out two, three, or four cooties on the master before you make the transparency, or simply leave a couple of cooties uncovered when you start the game.

5. Variation — *Jeopardy Cooties!* Color two or three cooties with a transparency marker pen, or make a second transparency with two or three cooties of another color. These are the "jeopardy cooties." If a student chooses a jeopardy cootie, she not only loses her points, but the points go to the other team!

SURPRISE ENDING!

This unusual game delivers just what the name promises — a surprise ending! Students answering the Bible questions come to the projector and place colored squares on the game grid, but nobody has any idea who has won until the last split-second of the game! Here's how it's played.

The *Surprise Ending!* game has a grid of twenty-five empty squares. If a boy answers a Bible question correctly, he places two transparent blue squares on the grid, anywhere he chooses. A girl would place two red squares on the grid. The game continues with each student placing two squares of their team's color until only one square is left. At that point, the teacher places an opaque overlay on the game transparency, which blots out all but nine squares. Any red square still showing scores for the girls, and the blue squares still visible score for the boys. The team with the greatest number of colored "windows" wins the game!

Making the Game

On your copier, make a clear transparency of the *Surprise Ending!* game master on page 88. Mount the transparency on a frame for durability and ease in handling.

Cut 14 1" squares from a sheet of red transparency film,

This unusual game delivers just what the name promises — a surprise ending!

and 14 1" squares from a sheet of blue. (If the colored film is unavailable in your area, any school supply store will have colored acetate report covers. Simply cut these into 1"squares.)

Duplicate the *Surprise Ending!* overlay on page 89 onto paper, then cut out the large square. With an X-Acto knife or single-edge razor blade, carefully remove the centers of the nine squares indicated.

Playing the Game

Place the game transparency on your projector. Have the red and blue squares and the overlay handy. Turn on the projector and explain the game to your class.

"Today, class, we are playing another brand-new Bible game! It's called *Surprise Ending!* Which team will win?

"Have you ever read a book with a surprise ending? Maybe it was a mystery. Everyone in the book is trying to figure out who has been committing a particular crime, and you know all along that the butler is guilty. But, on the very last page of the story, you find out that it wasn't the butler after all! It was the grandmother's pet goldfish! That's known as a surprise ending!

"Our game today has a surprise ending. Listen carefully as I explain the rules. As I ask Bible questions from our lesson, Lisa will honk the horn, and Miss Wilma will be the game spotter. Remember — don't stand up until you hear the horn! If you stand up before the horn, Miss Wilma will not choose you!

"When Miss Wilma calls on you, if you answer the question correctly, you may come to the projector to play *Surprise Ending!*

"If you are a girl, I will give you two red squares. If you are a boy, you will receive two blue squares. You may place your two squares anywhere you want to on the game grid. We will continue playing until nearly all the squares are filled."

Display the *Surprise Ending!* overlay. "At the end of the game, I will place this overlay on the game board. This overlay will tell us which team wins!" (Place the overlay in place on the game grid, but flip it upside-down and turn it ninety degrees to the right to keep the students from seeing which squares will be chosen. This will expose different squares, rather than the ones which will actually count in the game.)

"At the end of the game, only the colored squares showing

through my little windows will count for your team. Ready? Let's play *Surprise Ending!*"

Suggestions and Variations

1. It is usually best if you have the students point to the squares they choose and you lay the colored squares down for them. This will keep your transparencies from getting scratched so easily.

2. The *Surprise Ending!* overlay may be placed on the game grid in eight different positions, giving you eight different scoring combinations. Simply mark the top edge of the overlay, then place it on the grid right side up the first time you play the game. For the second game, turn the overlay to the right so the marked edge now lines up with the right side of the playing grid. When you have used all four positions, flip the overlay face down, and you can now use it in four new positions.

3. For greater durability, make the overlay from a piece of white poster board. Make a copy of the overlay master, then fasten the copy to a piece of poster board with three or four small dots of rubber cement. As you cut out the squares on the overlay pattern, cut deeply enough to slice through the poster board. Peel the paper master away, and you have a durable overlay.

4. Play with *double* and *triple* squares! Type the words "double" and "triple" twice each on a sheet of paper, with some space between the words. Make a clear transparency from this master, then cut out the words, leaving each word in the center of a 1¼" transparency square. Tape these squares in place over four of the windows in the overlay.

5. In the event of a tie, carefully lift the overlay from the projector stage, rotate it ninety degrees, then reposition it on the grid. This should change the score completely.

6. On occasion, play *Surprise Ending!* with number values. Using a nonpermanent overhead marker in any dark color other than red or blue, number the twenty-five squares on the game grid with numerals from one to four. At the conclusion of the game, any square showing through the overlay scores that number of points for the appropriate team.

JONKENPON

Here's a classic children's finger game that has been around for decades! You probably played it as a child, even if you didn't call it by its correct name, *Jonkenpon*. Your students will enjoy seeing it on the screen as a Bible game.

The student answering the Bible question correctly comes to the projector and selects a penny from a group of twenty on his side of the game, revealing scissors, paper, or rock. He then selects a penny from the other team's side, again revealing scissors, paper, or rock. Just as in the finger game, scissors wins over paper, paper over rock, and rock over scissors. Excitement and fun are built right into this game!

Excitement and fun are built right into this game!

Making the Game

Make a transparency from any of the *Jonkenpon* masters in the book (pages 90, 91, or 92). Mount the transparency, obtain forty pennies, and you are ready to play *Jonkenpon!*

Playing the Game

If possible, set up *Jonkenpon* before your students enter your classroom. Place the game on the projector, then use your forty pennies to cover the forty small symbols on the game before turning the projector on. Select your game starter and spotter, then introduce the game.

"Today we are playing a new Bible game known as *Jonkenpon!* How many of you have ever played *Jonkenpon* before?" (Usually no hands go up.) "Perhaps you have played *Jonkenpon* before, but you didn't call it by that name." (Turn the projector on, allowing the kids to see the game.) "You probably called it 'scissors, paper, rock'! This game actually came from the Orient, but over there they call it *Jonkenpon*.

"Listen carefully as I explain the rules for the game. I will ask questions from today's Bible lesson, and Mr. Wiggins will be our spotter. Make sure that you do not stand before the horn sounds, as Mr. Wiggins will not call on you if you do.

"When you answer a question correctly, you may come to the projector and choose a penny from your side of the game. This is the boys' side, and this is the girls'." (Indicate the left side of the screen as the boys' side, and the right as belonging to the girls.) "Underneath your penny, you'll find one of three things: scissors, paper, or a rock. Then you choose a penny from the other team's side, again finding scissors, paper, or a rock.

"As you know, scissors wins over paper, paper wins over rock, and rock wins over scissors. Let's say that a boy finds scissors on his side, then finds paper on the girls' side. Both pennies would go to the boys' side for 2,000 points! But if the boys get scissors, then find a rock on the girls' side, both pennies go to the girls' side for 2,000 points!"

(At this point, your class "question box" is sure to raise his hand.) "What happens if we find scissors on both sides, and it's a tie?"

"No problem, Gary. The student finding a tie would then choose two more pennies. The winning side would get all four pennies, for 4,000 points!"

The hand goes up again. "What if it's another tie?"

"Then you choose again, and one side would get 6,000 points!"

"What if it's a tie again?"

"Gary, let's just play the game. You'll see! Ready, class? Let's play *Jonkenpon!*"

Suggestions and Variations

1. Keep score by placing the pennies won on each turn to the side of the game, on the side of the team that won them.

2. It's usually best for the teacher to remove the pennies rather than the student, to avoid scratching the transparency.

CAPTURE THE FLAG!

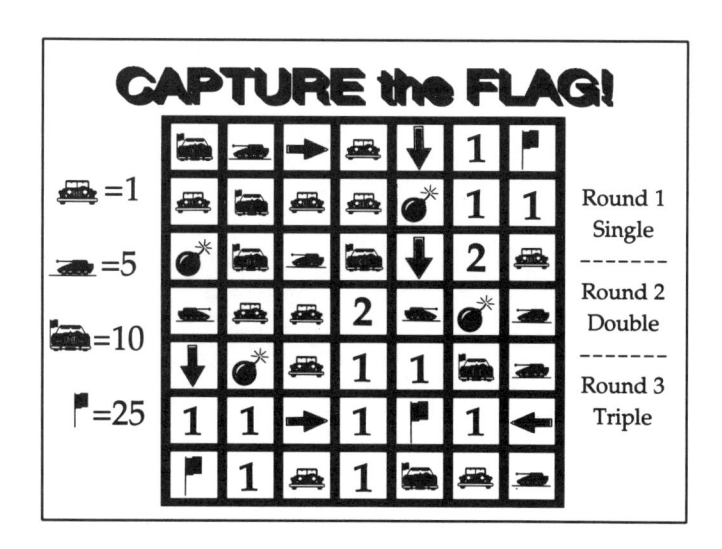

Looking for a game that will intrigue your Juniors, or maybe even your Junior Highers? *Capture the Flag!* will quickly capture the attention of your students!

Forty-nine pennies on a game grid hide three flags, a number of military vehicles, flag indicators, and a few bombs. The student answering the Bible question correctly draws a *Capture the Flag!* card, allowing her to choose one, two, three or four pennies. Each revealed vehicle scores points for the student's team, but the flags score highest of all. When the first flag is found, the game enters round two, and all points are doubled. The second flag discovery signals the beginning of round three and triple points. A bomb brings the student's turn to an abrupt end. Tension mounts as the teams scramble to figure out the location of the flags before their opponents.

Making the Game

Remove one of the three *Capture the Flag!* masters from the book (found on pages 93, 94, or 95) and make a transparency. Mount the game on a transparency frame for durability and ease of handling.

> *Looking for a game that will intrigue your Juniors, or maybe even your Junior Highers? Capture the Flag! will quickly capture the attention of your students!*

Duplicate the capture cards (page 96) on brightly colored paper, then cut the twelve cards apart with a paper cutter or a straight edge and razor blade. Cut 12 2½" x 3" cards from white poster board. Using a glue stick, paste the colorful capture cards to the flat finish side of the white poster board cards. (If you have a large class of thirty students or more, enlarge the game cards for this and other games on a photocopier for greater visibility.) Many of today's photocopiers will handle card stock. For simplicity, you may want to duplicate the capture cards onto colored card stock, rather than pasting paper cards to poster board.

Make sure that you have forty-nine pennies, and *Capture the Flag!* is ready to play!

Playing the Game

Place the *Capture the Flag!* game in proper position on your projector. Cover the forty-nine grid squares with the pennies before you turn the projector on. Spread the twelve capture cards face down on a nearby table or chair. Select a game starter and spotter, and explain the rules to your class.

"Here's a new Bible game called *Capture the Flag!* I think you'll find it to be an exciting game! Here are the rules. The first student to stand after the bell sounds will have the opportunity to answer the Bible question. If you answer the question correctly, you will draw one capture card, allowing you to select one, two, three, or four pennies from the projector.

"When I lift your penny, if you have captured a jeep, you score one point for your team. A tank scores five points, and, if you capture the general's car, you score ten points. When you capture the flag, you score twenty-five points! When someone captures the first flag, the game automatically enters round two, and all points from then on are doubled. The capture of the second flag signals round three, and all points are tripled!

"An arrow tells you that there is a flag on that row, and a numeral 1 or 2 tells you that a flag is that many squares away, but it doesn't tell you what direction. If you find a bomb, your turn ends immediately, and you lose all the points from your turn! Ready? Let's play *Capture the Flag!*"

Suggestions and Variations

1. At the conclusion of the game, have a bonus question for each team. Set the capture cards aside, and allow the student to choose five pennies. Points are *doubled* on these final two questions. For example, a bonus question in round three would multiply each point on that turn by six!

2. A student may choose to stop at any time during his or her turn. For instance, a player may have drawn a capture card with a four, then captured a flag on the first penny. She may choose to stop at that point, rather than risk a bomb and loss of the points.

3. Rather than following suggestion #2, you may decide to require each student to complete his or her turn. The decision is yours, but you need to announce it before the game begins.

4. You may decide to announce point totals after each turn, but we have found it more fun and suspenseful to record the score without announcing it until the end of the game.

PIRATE TREASURE

Treasure! Pirates! Gold! Diamonds! Pearls! These words all bring exciting images to the mind of a child, and *Pirate Treasure* delivers the adventure and excitement! Get ready to sail the seven seas in a thrilling search for buried treasure! Thirty-nine pennies, one transparency, twelve treasure cards and a crowd of eager students are all you need to have a rollicking good time.

The student answering the Bible question correctly comes to the projector and chooses one of thirty-nine pennies. His choice may reveal a gold coin for 100 points, a pearl necklace for 200 points, a diamond for 300 points, or a treasure chest for 500 points! The student may choose as many pennies as he desires, but if his choice reveals a scorpion in the sand, his turn ends and he loses all his points.

The student who stops before finding a scorpion then selects one of twelve treasure cards in an attempt to get his treasure safely back to the ship. A ship card means that the treasure is now safely aboard the ship, and the points are recorded on the score sheet. A treasure chest card also secures the points, but with a 500 point bonus! A pirate card signifies the loss of the treasure and points.

Get ready to sail the seven seas in a thrilling search for buried treasure!

Making the Game

Using one of the three *Pirate Treasure* game masters on pages 97, 98, or 99, make a transparency on your copier or thermofax machine. Mount the transparency to a cardboard frame.

Copy the twelve treasure cards (page 100) onto bright paper, then cut the cards apart. Cut 12 2½" x 3" cards from white poster board, then paste the treasure cards to the poster board with a glue stick. (The cards will adhere best to the porous side of the poster board, rather than the slick side.) Or simply copy the treasure cards directly to colored card stock.

Make sure that you have your thirty-nine pennies, and you are ready to enjoy *Pirate Treasure* with your students!

Playing the Game

Place the *Pirate Treasure* game in position on your projector, then make sure that all the jewels and scorpions are covered with pennies before you turn your projector on. Spread the twelve treasure cards face down on a nearby table or chair, select your game starter and spotter, then explain the rules.

"Have you ever dreamed of taking a cruise in the South Seas, landing on a secluded island, and discovering buried treasure? I have, and I'm sure that most of you have, too! Imagine walking on the beach and finding gold coins, diamonds, and pearls lying in the sand! Today, we're going to do just that! Our new Bible game is called *Pirate Treasure!* Listen carefully to the rules of the game.

"Each student who answers a Bible question may come to the projector to search for buried treasure. Remember not to stand before you hear the horn after each question. When you come to the projector, I will have you choose a penny, then I will remove it for you. If you find a gold coin, you score 100 points for your team! If you find a pearl necklace, you score 200 points! A diamond gives you 300 points, and a treasure chest earns you 500 points!

"Here's the fun part — when you are at the projector, you may choose as many pennies as you want! But a word of warning — if you find a scorpion, your turn ends, and you lose all the points from your turn! Be careful not to grab a scorpion!

"Even when you stop choosing pennies, your treasure is still not safe. You have to try to get it back to the ship! You do that by selecting a treasure card. If you find a ship card, your treasure is safely aboard the ship, and your team gets the points. If you find a treasure chest card, your points are safe, and you receive a 500 point bonus! But if you find a pirate card, the pirate steals your treasure, and you lose the points from your turn. Ready? Let's dig for *Pirate Treasure!*"

Suggestions and Variations

1. At the conclusion of *Pirate Treasure*, have a bonus question for each team and double the points. (You may even want to remove any remaining pirate cards at this point.)

2. As each penny is removed from the projector stage, add the student's points in your head, and announce his total.

3. Do not announce team totals until the conclusion of the game.

4. On occasion, or when playing *Pirate Treasure* with younger classes, remove the pirate cards before the game begins.

5. You may choose to give the students the option of whether or not they even choose a treasure card. The treasure chest card would give them a 1,000 point bonus if you play the game this way, while a pirate card would still forfeit all their points. With a ship card, their points would remain the same.

SMILES AND LADDERS

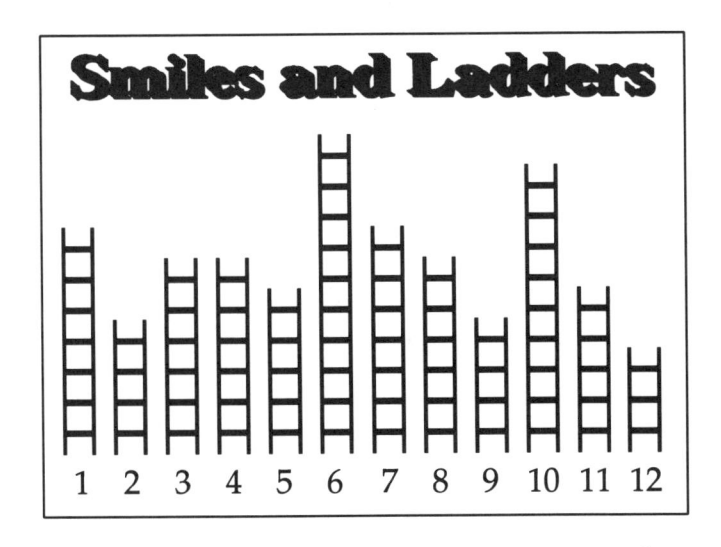

This game was designed for the Primary students, but it can be used successfully with Beginners, or even with Juniors. I used it recently in a kids' crusade, and the crowd of kids really enjoyed it. The next evening after the service, a photographer was shooting pictures of the game for me, and his fourth-grade son walked in and saw the *Smiles and Ladders* on the screen. *"Smiles and Ladders!"* he exclaimed. "That's my favorite game!"

Twelve ladders reach skyward on the screen, varying in length from three to ten rungs. The student answering the Bible question comes forward and chooses a ladder card, which assigns him a particular ladder to climb. He places a smiley face (red for girls, blue for boys) on the bottom rung of his ladder, then chooses a climb card. This card tells him how many rungs to climb, ranging from two rungs to ten. Any smiley face reaching the top of a ladder scores 1,000 points for that team.

If a smiley does not reach the top of the ladder, a teammate may help him on a later turn, or an opponent may try to "bump" him. The students will quickly discover that there are risks involved in bumping!

The team with the most smileys to reach the top is the winner!

"Smiles and Ladders! *That's my favorite game!"*

Making the Game

Select one of the three *Smiles and Ladders* game masters from the book (pages 101, 102, or 103) and make a clear transparency from it. (It is best not to use a colored transparency for this game, as this would make it more difficult to distinguish between the red and blue smiley faces.) Mount the transparency to a frame.

Make a blue transparency from the smiley face master, (page 104), and a red transparency of the same. Cut out seven smiley faces of each color, retaining the extras for spares. Place the smiley faces in a small Ziploc bag, as they are easily lost. Tape the Ziploc bag to the game folder.

Duplicate the twelve ladder cards (page 105) onto brightly colored paper, cut them apart, then mount them on 2½" x 3" cards made from white poster board, or copy them directly to card stock.

Next, duplicate the twelve climb cards (page 106) onto bright paper stock, mounting them on 2½" x 3" cards. (Make these of a different color than the ladder cards.) *Smiles and Ladders* is ready to play!

Playing the Game

Place the game transparency on your projector with the red and blue smiley faces to one side. Place the ladder cards face down on a nearby table or chair, with the climb cards in another spread beside them. Choose your game spotter and starter, then introduce the game.

"Class, we are going to play a brand-new Bible game for our review today! It's called *Smiles and Ladders!* We're going to find out which team is the fastest at climbing ladders! Boys against the girls — which team will climb the most? Listen carefully as I explain the rules.

"The first boy or girl to stand after Keisha rings the bell will have the chance to answer the Bible question. If you answer correctly, I will have you come up here and choose a ladder card. This card will tell you which ladder to climb, and you will put a smiley face at the bottom of your ladder. Red is for the girls, blue is for the boys.

"Then you will choose a climb card. This card will tell you how many rungs to climb on your ladder. If your smiley makes it all the way to the top, he scores 1,000 for your team! If the smiley does *not* make it all the way to the top, he stays where he is, and someone else from your team can try to get him to the top later.

"If there are smileys partway up the ladder when it is your turn, you may choose one of those ladders instead of choosing a ladder card. You may choose a climb card to help one of your team's smileys the rest of the way up the ladder, or you may place a new smiley at the bottom of a ladder that has the other team's smiley partway up it. If you can pass that smiley when you choose your climb card, you have 'bumped' him from the game, and I will take him from the ladder.

"But — watch out! If you don't pass the other smiley and he makes it to the top of his ladder, your smiley is 'frozen'! He can't climb anymore, even on another turn!

"Once your smiley is at the top of the ladder, he is safe. No one else can bump him! Ready? Let's play *Smiles and Ladders!*"

Suggestions and Variations

1. When a smiley reaches the top of a ladder, leave it there. At the conclusion of the game, simply count the smileys that have scored.

2. Smileys do *not* have to reach the top of the ladder by exact count. (For example, an eight-rung climb card would send a smiley to the top of a six-rung ladder to score.)

3. The climb cards are for one ladder only. (In the example of the eight-rung climb card, the two "leftover" rungs could not be used to help another smiley or start another ladder climb.)

4. At the conclusion of the game, have a *double* question for each team. The student chooses a ladder card, then chooses two climb cards. Suggestion #3 does not apply to this final turn. The two climb cards may be combined to send one smiley all the way to the top, split to send two smileys up, or even used to help existing smileys to the top. The student at the projector chooses the best way to make every rung count.

5. On occasion, don't even use the ladder cards. Cut twelve strips from dark poster board, ¾" x 5". Before turning the projector on, cover the ladders with these overlays. The student chooses his own ladder, not knowing if the ladder

chosen is long or short, then chooses a climb card.

6. On rare occasions, with an older group you may want to add a "bump rule" on the final two questions. The smileys that have reached the top are not safe on these last two questions, and may be bumped. The students will, of course, bump the smileys on the shortest ladders. This could allow one team to suddenly come from behind to win the game.

AIR BATTLE

It's an aerial dogfight, with the red air force against the blue! Four planes from each team are visible on the screen, with two of each team's planes hidden in the clouds. To win, one team must shoot down all six of the other team's aircraft before their own planes are shot down. In this game, it is very easy to shoot down your own planes by mistake! *Air Battle* may be used successfully with either Primaries or Juniors.

Air Battle *may be used successfully with either Primaries or Juniors.*

Making the Game

Select one of the three *Air Battle* game masters (pages 107, 108, or 109) and make a transparency. This game is most effective when made with two separate transparencies combined into one, as described in *Making and Storing Bible Games* (page 19). Make all the eastbound planes on one transparency: blue image on clear. The westbound planes should all be on the other transparency: red image on clear. If you do not have access to a thermofax machine to make the colored transparencies, make one transparency (black on clear) and color the planes with permanent overhead marker pens. Mount the transparency on a frame.

Using the *Air Battle* cloud patterns on page 110, cut six

clouds from dark poster board. (White poster board or paper is opaque on the screen, but the student looking at the overhead stage will see the planes through the clouds when the projector is on.)

Duplicate four sets of *Air Battle* cards (page 111) on brightly colored paper for a total of sixteen cards. Mount these on poster board cards cut to 3" x 3¾".

Make a transparency of the twelve *Air Battle* boom cards on page 112, black on clear. Then cut out the squares. This will give you twelve small boom transparency overlays. Your *Air Battle* game is ready for action!

Playing the Game

Place the *Air Battle* game in position on your overhead, being sure to put the clouds in place before turning the projector on. Two planes of each color should be covered by clouds, as well as the two empty spaces. (The illustration at the beginning of this chapter shows only four clouds in place, but you will start the game with six.)

Select your game spotter and starter, then introduce the *Air Battle* game to your class.

"We have a new Bible game today! It's called..." (Pause and turn the projector on at this point.) "*Air Battle!* The blue air force is battling the red air force — boys against the girls! Which team will win today's game?

"Each team has six planes. Two of your team's planes are hidden in the clouds, and two enemy planes are hidden in the clouds. To win the game, you must shoot down all six enemy planes, including the two in the clouds. But be careful! You may find yourself shooting down your own plane!

"Here are the rules. Any student answering a game question correctly will come up front and choose a game card. If your card says 'blue plane,' you have shot down a boys' plane."(Demonstrate by placing one of the boom overlays over one of the planes, blotting out the plane. Remember to remove it before the game begins.) "If your card says 'red plane,' you have downed a girls' plane. If you get a cloud card, you choose one of the clouds, and the plane behind it is shot down. A choose card allows you to shoot down a plane or a cloud. Remember, you must shoot down all six planes to win the game. Let's play *Air Battle!*"

Suggestions and Variations

1. The student selecting the card *must* do what it indicates, even when it means shooting down his own team's plane.

2. At the conclusion of the game, give a *double* question to each team. The students choose two cards on each of these turns.

APPLE PICKING

Here's a Bible game designed by my wife, Janice, for the little guys and gals. Juniors would be bored with it, but your Beginners (four- and five-year-olds) will love it!

The boy or girl answering the Bible question comes to the projector and selects one of fifteen juicy red apples hanging on a tree. The apple is picked from the tree and placed in one of two baskets on either side of the game. The team with the most apples in its basket wins!

Your Beginners will love Apple Picking!

Making the Game

Make a game transparency from the *Apple Picking* game master on page 113. (The best choice is a green image on clear, second choice is black on clear.) Mount the transparency.

Make one transparency of the sheet of apples on page 114, with a black image on red film. Carefully cut the apples out. (You only need twelve to fifteen apples, but save the extras as spares.) Store the tiny apples in a small Ziploc bag. You are now ready for some *Apple Picking* with your class of wigglers!

Playing the Game

Position the game on the overhead. Place twelve to fifteen apples on the tree, and turn the projector on.

"Today, boys and girls, we are going to play a Bible game! It's called *Apple Picking!* Listen carefully while I explain the rules.

"I will ask a Bible question, then I will choose one of you to answer it. If you answer the question correctly, you may come to the projector and choose an apple. I will pick the apple off the tree for you, and you may place it in one of the apple baskets.

"The girls will put their apples in this basket, and the boys will put their apples in this one. At the end of the game, the team with the most apples in its basket wins the game! Ready, boys and girls? Let's play *Apple Picking!*"

Suggestions and Variations

1. If you have a small enough group to allow every child to answer at least one question, do not use the horn or bell. Simply have the children take turns answering your questions. The teacher or a worker chooses the child to answer, making certain that each child has answered at least one question before any child gets a second chance.

2. If you have too large a class to allow every child to answer a question, use the horn or bell. At the conclusion of the game, explain to the children that you will be playing another game next week, and others will have an opportunity to play that game. The next class period, do your best to select children who didn't get to participate. You might even have an assistant make pencil marks in the roll book.

3. With a class of very young children, do not attempt to have teams. They will not understand team competition, and none is needed. These children will enjoy simply picking the apples and selecting the basket into which they will be placed.

BIBLE FOOTBALL

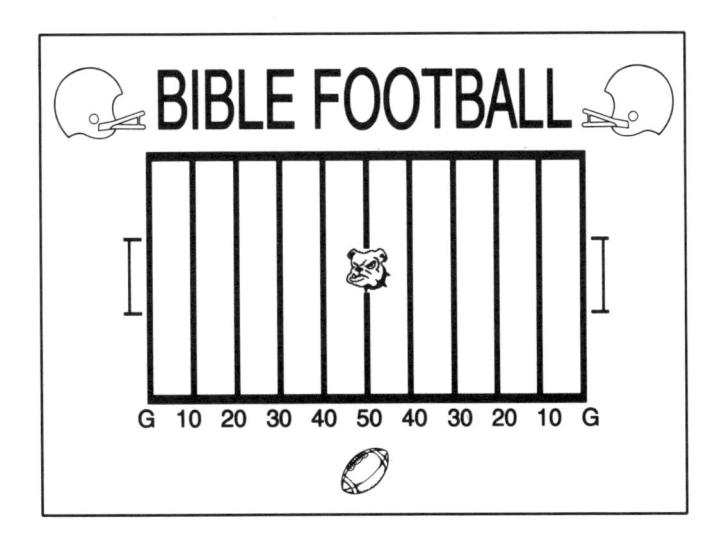

You might think that this is a Bible game just for the boys in your class, but believe me, it's not! The girls will enter into the competition just as fiercely as the boys. We recently played *Bible Football* in a kid's crusade. When I turned the projector on and the game flashed on the screen, one of the girls on the second row responded with, "Awesome!"

The game begins with the ball on the fifty-yard line. A student answering the Bible question correctly comes forward and chooses a yardage card. When the card is turned over, the ball is moved the appropriate number of yards (ranging from ten to fifty) toward that team's goal. When a touchdown is scored, the game resumes with the ball on the scoring team's thirty-yard line. Simple, but almost as exciting as the Super Bowl!

Bible Football *is almost as exciting as the Super Bowl!*

Making the Game

Using the *Bible Football* game master on page 115 of the book, make a transparency, using green film if possible. (3M makes a reverse transparency film which gives you a gold image on a green background. When the back of the image is scrubbed with rubbing alcohol, the gold is removed, leaving a white image. My game has a gold football, helmets, and headline, and a white gridiron and yardage numbers. It looks sharp on the screen!)

Copy three sets of the *Bible Football* yardage cards (page 116) on bright paper for a total of eighteen cards. Discard one each of the ten-yard, twenty-yard, and ten-yard penalty cards, leaving you with fifteen. Paste them onto 3" x 3¾" poster board cards.

Make a black-on-clear transparency of the little footballs on page 117. Cut five or six of them out, saving the others for spares. You're ready for the starting kickoff!

Playing the Game

Place the gridiron transparency on the overhead, with one of the footballs in position on the fifty-yard line. Arrange the yardage cards face down on a nearby table or chair, turn the projector on, and explain the rules.

"It's football season! Today we're playing *Bible Football!* Boys against the girls — who's going to win the pennant?

"Listen as I explain the BFL rules of the game. BFL? That's *Bible Football* League! Brandon will be our game starter, and Mrs. Underwood will be the referee — oops, game spotter. If you are the first to stand after the horn sounds, you are the quarterback for the next play.

"You will choose one of these yardage cards, which will tell you how far to advance the ball toward your goal. The cards range from ten yards to fifty, with an occasional ten-yard penalty. You might score a touchdown on the first question!

"The ball moves back and forth on the playing field until it crosses the goal line, scoring a touchdown and six points for that team. After each touchdown, the ball is placed on that team's thirty-yard line, giving the other team a slight advantage on the next question.

"Ready? It's time for the kickoff!"

Suggestions and Variations

1. As with the other Bible games, at the conclusion of *Bible Football,* have a final question specifically for each team. These final questions are *double*, with the students choosing two cards each. It's possible to score two touchdowns on one turn!

2. Keep score right on the game. When a touchdown is scored, leave the ball at the end of the playing field. Place another ball on the other thirty-yard line. At the end of the game, simply count the footballs for the final score.

3. Each time a touchdown is scored, allow the student to try for the extra point by flipping a coin. Heads: attempt is good and extra point is scored, tails: attempt for extra point fails.

SEA BATTLE

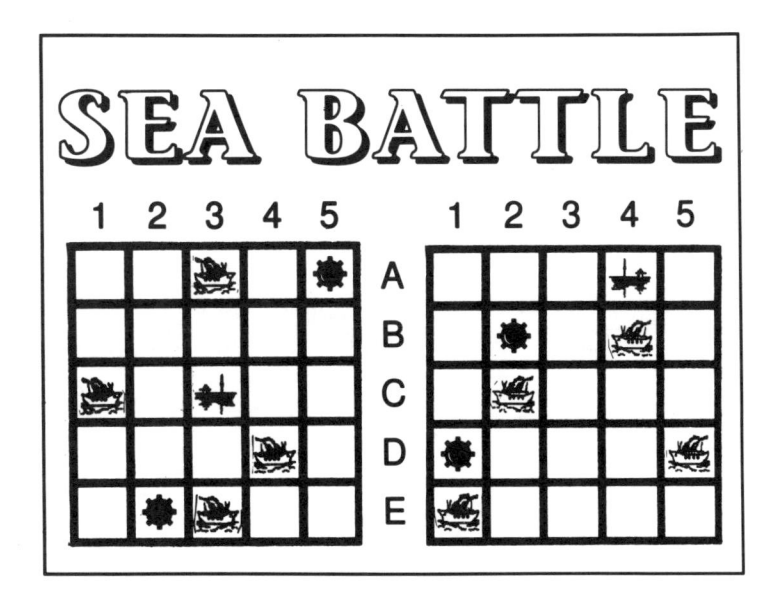

The boys' navy has challenged the girls' navy to a battle, and the torpedoes and missiles are sure to be flying! It's time for *Sea Battle!*

Fifty pennies on two grids hide eight destroyers, two submarines, and four mines. When a student answers a Bible question correctly, he or she comes forward and chooses one of twelve fleet commander cards, authorizing the firing of one, two, three, or four rounds. The student chooses the appropriate number of squares on the opponents' grid, sinking any vessel that is revealed when the pennies are removed. When a sub is sunk, the student automatically receives authorization to fire an extra round, revealing another square. But if a mine is revealed on any turn, the student must fire one round at his own grid, revealing one square and possibly sinking one of his own ships!

Making the Game

Select a *Sea Battle* game master (pages 118 and 119). You'll notice that one game master has the battle grid with the ships, subs, and mines printed on it. This master may be used to make the entire game on a single transparency, but the location of the vessels and mines is fixed.

> *The boys' navy has challenged the girls' navy to a battle, and the torpedoes and missiles are sure to be flying! It's time for* Sea Battle!

The other master has the battle grid only, with the ships, subs, and mines on two separate masters. This battle grid master may be made into a game transparency, which is then mounted on a transparency frame. The two pages of ships, subs, and mines on pages 120 and 121 may be made into separate transparencies, one of which is to be taped temporarily to the game frame, being careful to center the vessels within the squares. To change the location of the ships, subs, and mines, simply remove the tape, flip the transparency over, and retape it to the frame. These two masters of the ships, subs, and mines will give you four different setups for the *Sea Battle* game!

Make two copies of the fleet commander cards (page 122) on bright paper, cut them out, and paste them to 12 3" x 3½" poster board cards. *Sea Battle* is ready for action!

Playing the Game

Place the *Sea Battle* game transparency on your projector with the ships in place. Cover each of the fifty squares on the two grids with pennies. Spread the fleet commander cards face down on a nearby table or chair, select a game spotter and starter, and turn the projector on as you introduce the game to your eager students.

"Today, class, we are playing *Sea Battle*! The boys' fleet, consisting of four destroyers and one submarine, is concealed somewhere on this grid to the left. The girls' fleet of four destroyers and one sub is concealed on this grid to the right. The object of the game is to sink the enemy's fleet before they sink yours! Listen carefully as I explain the game.

"The first student to stand after the horn sounds will answer the Bible question. If your answer is correct, you will be given the opportunity to come forward and choose a fleet commander card. The card will authorize the firing of one, two, three, or four rounds, meaning that you may uncover that many squares on the enemy grid to search for the enemy ships and sub. Simply call the location of the squares you wish to uncover — B-3, C-5, A-4, etc. I will move the pennies for you. If you discover an enemy vessel, that vessel is sunk.

"If the enemy vessel is a submarine, you are authorized to fire an extra round and uncover an extra square. But, if you uncover a mine, you must uncover one of your own team's squares! Ready? Battle stations!"

Suggestions and Variations

1. At the game's conclusion, give a *double* question to each team. Two fleet commander cards are chosen instead of one.

2. Two or three times during the game, you may announce a bonus question. On a bonus question, one more round is fired than the fleet commander card authorizes.

3. Occasionally, let the sinking of a sub yield two or even three extra rounds. Announce this before the game begins.

BIBLE TIC-TAC-TOE

Here's an old game — with a new twist! *Bible Tic-Tac-Toe* is played in much the same way as the old recess favorite, *Tic-Tac-Toe*. Three Xs or three Os in a row wins the game. But in this version of the game, the student answering the Bible question draws a game card, which instructs him where to play his X or O!

Making the Game

Using the *Bible Tic-Tac-Toe* game master on page 123, make a clear transparency. (It is best not to use a colored transparency for this game, as the game pieces will be red and blue.) Mount the game transparency to a frame.

Make a red transparency of the Xs and butterflies, and a blue transparency of the Os and beetles. (They may all be found on page 124.) Cut the game pieces apart, putting them into a small Ziploc bag for safekeeping.

Using bright paper, make two copies of the game cards on page 125, for a total of eighteen cards. Cut them apart and paste them to 18 2½" x 3" cards of poster board. You and your class are ready to play *Bible Tic-Tac-Toe!*

Here's an old game — with a new twist!

Playing the Game

Place the *Bible Tic-Tac-Toe* game on your overhead, with the game cards face down on a nearby table or chair. Choose your game spotter and starter, then introduce the game.

"Today we are playing a Bible review game! As you can see, it's *Bible Tic-Tac-Toe*! The girls are Xs, the boys are Os. Three in a row wins — which team will it be?

"This game may be just a little different from the game you are used to. Listen carefully as I explain. The person answering the Bible question correctly will come to the front and choose a game card. If her card says 'top row,' she may only place her X in one of the empty spaces in the top row. Her card may say 'center row' or 'bottom row.' Again, she may only place her X in one of the boxes on the horizontal row named on the card.

"A boy may get a card that says 'left column,' or 'center column,' or 'right column.' He may only place his O somewhere in the vertical column named on the card.

"If a student receives a card which says 'your choice,' he or she may place the X or O anywhere there is an empty square. Ready? Let's play *Bible Tic-Tac-Toe!*"

Suggestions and Variations

1. If there are no empty squares in the row or column indicated by the game card, the player forfeits his turn.

2. If all nine squares are filled and it is a "cat's game," continue to play until one teams wins. The students continue to draw cards as before, but now they may replace a game piece from the other team with one of their own. As before, they must follow the instructions on the game card.

3. For variety, use beetles for the boys and butterflies for the girls instead of Xs and Os.

4. On occasion, play *Mystery Tic-Tac-Toe*. The student draws a game piece from a grab bag, not knowing whether he will be playing an O for the boys or an X for the girls! *Mystery Tic-Tac-Toe* may be played with or without the cards.

5. On occasion, play *Bible Tic-Tac-Toe* the way the regular game is played, without cards. The student places his game piece anywhere he finds an empty square.

OPERATION SPY TRAP

Here's an intriguing game that will keep your students in suspense! Like *Surprise Ending!*, *Operation Spy Trap* keeps everyone guessing until the last split second of the game.

Your mission is to identify secret agents who have infiltrated our country. Twenty-five suspects are displayed on the screen, but sixteen of them are innocent. The nine true spies must be identified and apprehended.

The student who answers the Bible question correctly comes forward and selects a mission card. The mission card authorizes an attempt to identify one, two, or three spies. The students make their selections by placing colored squares of acetate on the game board. At the conclusion of the game, a "super secret spy identifier" overlay is placed on the board, correctly identifying the nine enemy agents. The team making the most correct identifications is the winner!

> *Here's an intriguing game that will keep your students in suspense!*

Making the Game

Using the *Operation Spy Trap* game master on page 126 of the book, make a black-on-clear game transparency. Mount the transparency to a frame.

Cut 15 1" squares from a piece of red transparency film, and 15 1" squares from a piece of blue film. (If the film is unavailable, use colored acetate report folders, available at almost any school supply retailer.)

Photocopy the twelve mission cards on page 127 onto bright paper, cut apart, and paste to cards or poster board.

Make a photocopy of the super secret identifier overlay on page 128. Cut out the large square, then carefully cut out the center of the nine smaller squares indicated, using a razor blade or X-Acto knife. For durability, make the overlay from poster board, using the paper photocopy as a template.

Operation Spy Trap is finished, and your class is authorized to accept its first mission!

Playing the Game

Place the *Operation Spy Trap* game on your overhead, with the thirty colored film squares and the super secret spy identifier nearby. The twelve mission cards should be placed face down on a nearby table or chair. Switch the projector on and introduce the game to your class of secret agents.

"Have you ever thought that it would be exciting to be an F.B.I. agent? To be assigned to a top-secret case, and perhaps to capture enemy agents? Today's Bible game will give you that chance! We're playing *Operation Spy Trap!*

"Mission Control has been alerted that enemy agents have been infiltrating our country, stealing top secret information regarding America's supply of jaw breakers and bubble gum. The enemy agents must be stopped and the top secret information retrieved. It's up to you!

"Here's how the game works. When I ask a Bible question, do not stand until Ashley rings the starter bell. Mr. Jarvis is the game spotter today. He will choose the first person to stand after the bell, and he will allow you to answer the question. If your answer is correct, you may come forward to play *Operation Spy Trap*.

"These twenty-five suspects have been placed under surveillance, but only nine of them are actually spies. The other sixteen are innocent. Your job is to correctly identify the nine enemy agents. You will select a mission card, which will authorize you to try to identify one, two, or three enemy agents.

"Let's say that your mission card says '3.' I will give you three colored squares — blue if you are a boy, red if you are a girl — and you may lay them down over the three suspects that you believe are spies. We will continue asking questions and guessing until nearly all the squares are covered.

"At the very end of the game, we will find out who the nine spies really are. The team that has correctly identified the most spies wins the game. Here's how we will find out who the nine spies are. I will place the super secret spy identifier on the projector, like this." (Place the identifier over the game grid, but upside down and backwards.) "The faces you see in the windows are the nine spies! As I said, the team that correctly identifies the most spies wins the game!

"Ready? Let's play *Operation Spy Trap!*"

Suggestions and Variations

1. If the game ends in a tie, carefully lift the super secret spy identifier from the game grid and rotate it ninety degrees in either direction. Place it over the grid again, and a whole new set of faces will appear in the windows! The tie should be broken. If by chance there is still a tie, simply rotate it again.

2. On occasion, play *Operation Spy Trap* with a mastermind spy and two ambassadors. The mastermind spy is worth triple points when captured, but the two ambassadors each subtract one point if arrested by mistake!

Type "mastermind," "ambassador," "ambassador" on a sheet of paper, then use this as a master to make a clear transparency. Cut out 3 1¼" squares, leaving the words on a diagonal across each square. Tape these to the super secret spy identifier overlay, with the words showing in the windows.

3. At the conclusion of the game, plan a *double* question for each team. Allow the students to choose two mission cards on this turn.

4. The double questions could be done in this alternate way. On the last turn for each team, write "double" on the colored squares as you give them to the student. Use a non-permanent transparency marker pen. If these squares are used to correctly identify any spies, those points are doubled.

5. Be careful not to leave the super secret spy identifier in plain view beside the projector where a player may study it to figure out where the spies are.

RATTLESNAKE!

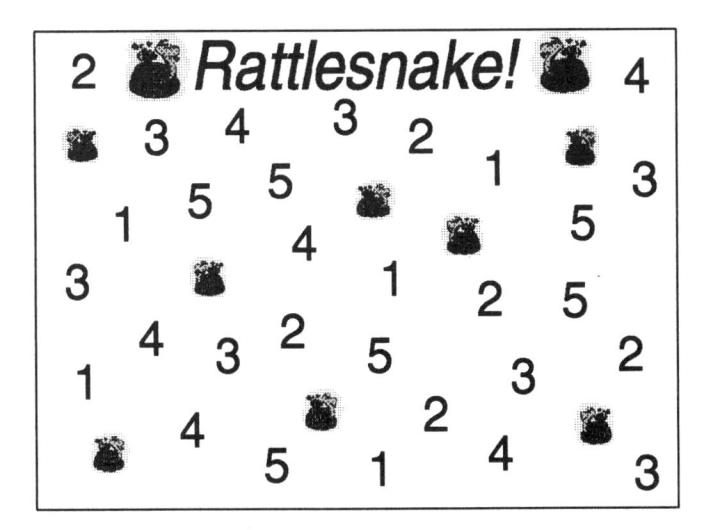

```
2  🐍 Rattlesnake! 🐍  4
🐍  3  4   3   2      3
      5  5      1   5
   1           🐍
 3    🐍   4   🐍   5
            1     2  5
   4     2            2
 1    3     5    3
         🐍    2     🐍
   🐍  4           4   3
         5   1
```

Rattlesnake! is the newest of all the Bible games. It has already been a lot of fun. We played it recently in our own church at a Junior overnight, and the kids responded with enthusiasm. As we finished the service and prepared for an activity time, one of the boys blurted, "Can't we just play *Rattlesnake!* again?"

Briefly, here's how the game is played. The student answering the Bible question correctly comes forward and chooses one of fourteen game cards, which assigns him a "game number" between three and twelve. He then chooses a penny from the stage of the overhead projector, revealing a number between one and five. The number found beneath the penny is then multiplied by the student's game number, scoring that many points for his team. The student may select as many pennies from the game as he desires, each time multiplying by his game number and adding to his score. But — if he finds a rattlesnake, his turn comes to an abrupt end, and he loses all the points for his turn. Bonus cards yield big points, which are safe from rattlesnake attack.

"Can't we just play Rattlesnake! *again?*"

Preparing the Game

Remove one of the three *Rattlesnake!* game masters from the book (pages 129, 130, or 131) and make a game transparency as described earlier. Mount the transparency to a frame for durability.

Duplicate the *Rattlesnake!* game cards (page 132) onto bright paper, making two each of the bonus cards for a total of fourteen cards. Paste these to 2½" x 3" poster board cards.

Obtain thirty-eight pennies to use as cover tabs, and your *Rattlesnake!* Bible game is ready to play.

Playing the Game

Place the game transparency on the stage of the overhead projector. Cover the rattlesnakes and numbers with pennies before you turn the projector on. Spread the game cards face down on a nearby table or lectern. Choose your game starter and spotter, and introduce the game to your class.

"Today, class, we're going to play an awesome new game called *Rattlesnake!* Listen closely as I explain the rules.

"Each time I ask a question from today's lesson, try to be the first person to stand after Rebecca honks the horn. If you answer the question correctly when Mr. Moore calls on you, you may come forward and choose a game card. On the back of your card, you will find a number between three and twelve. This becomes your 'game number' for your entire turn.

"You will then choose a penny from the projector by pointing at it with the pencil pointer, and I will remove the penny for you. We will then multiply the number under the penny by your game number, and you score that many points for your team!

"Now, I have good news and bad news. First, the good news — you may choose as many pennies from the projector as your little heart desires. You stop when you choose. But here's the bad news — if you find a rattlesnake beneath one of your pennies, you have to stop immediately, and you lose all the points from your turn!

"One more bit of good news — there are a few bonus cards among the other game cards. A bonus card gives your team 50 or 100 points before your turn really even starts! And best of all, you cannot lose bonus points — even if you get a rattlesnake! After your bonus score is recorded on the score sheet, we'll have you choose another game card so that you'll have a game number for your turn.

"Ready? Let's play *Rattlesnake!*"

Suggestions and Variations

1. As the student chooses each penny, multiply the number by the student's game number, then announce the result to an adult scorekeeper, who records it on a "temporary" score pad. The scorekeeper announces the total from the student's turn after each penny, and the student decides whether to stop or continue. Once the student elects to stop, his total is then recorded on a "permanent" score pad.

2. Once a score is recorded on the permanent score pad, it is there to stay. The discovery of a rattlesnake on another turn does not affect these points.

3. When a bonus card is found, record the score immediately on the permanent score pad. A student may draw more than one bonus card on the same turn.

4. On an occasional game, let even the bonus points be subject to loss by the finding of a rattlesnake. Announce this option at the beginning of the game.

5. Plan an occasional double question. Allow the student to choose two cards on one turn.

MATCHIT!

Matchit! seems to be a game for all ages. Primaries, Juniors, and Junior Highers have responded enthusiastically to this game.

Twenty-five 1¼" poster board squares on a game grid conceal pictures of various objects. The student answering the Bible question correctly comes to the projector and selects two of the squares, which are removed by the teacher. If two pictures of the same item are revealed, a match has been made, and the student scores 1,000 points for his team. If a match is not made, the squares are replaced on the game grid and the game continues. A bonus square scores 1,000 points when revealed.

Making the Game

Select one of the *Matchit!* game masters (pages 133, 134, or 135) and make a transparency, mounting it to a transparency frame if desired.

Cut 25 1¼" squares of dark-colored poster board, and secure a small envelope to store them in. You and your class are ready to play *Matchit!*

> **Matchit!** *seems to be a game for all ages. Primaries, Juniors, and Junior Highers have responded enthusiastically to this game.*

Playing the Game

Place the *Matchit!* game transparency on your overhead. Position the twenty-five cover squares before turning the projector on. Select your game starter and adult spotter, and explain the game to your class.

"Today, young people, we are going to play a new Bible game — *Matchit!*" (Turn the projector on at this point.)

"Here are the rules for this exciting game. The student answering a Bible question correctly will come to the projector and choose two squares. I will remove the squares for her. She might find..." (Lift one square, revealing one picture) "a star, or," (Cover the first square and reveal another) "a circle, or...a triangle, or...a square." (Continue revealing and covering the squares as you speak. Show the students four or five different pictures, being careful not to reveal a bonus or two of the same item. This will get the game off to a fast start, as the students now know where several different items are found.)

"If she finds two of the same item — let's say two crosses — she has made a match worth 1,000 points for her team! If she finds two different items, we will cover those two squares again, and everyone will try to remember what was in those squares. If the student finds a bonus square, that square is worth 1,000 points by itself! If you find two bonus squares on the same turn, that match is worth 3,000 points! Ready? Let's play *Matchit!*"

Suggestions and Variations

1. When a student is at the projector, do not allow the class to call out hints, as this can lead to disorder. Simply inform the class that if a student calls out a hint, the player at the board cannot choose that square. Announce this rule before the game begins.

2. At the game's conclusion, plan a *double* question for each team. You may allow each student to choose four squares, or double the points on any match made, or both!

3. On occasion, mark "double" or "triple" on two or three squares on the transparency grid. Use a nonpermanent overhead marking pen. When the match to that square is found, the points are doubled or tripled. You're in for an excited response at that point!

SPACE RACE

In this game, your students race across a foreign solar system in search of a captive princess! Each team must obtain a space ship, a security robot, and a floppy disk for the ship's computer guidance module before they can proceed to search for the princess. The team that finds the right planet and rescues the princess wins the game.

Making the Game

Select one of the three *Space Race* game masters from the book (pages 136, 137, or 138) and make a transparency. Mount the transparency to a frame for durability.

Cut 12 pieces of dark poster board, 1" x 1⅛". Store the pieces in a small Ziploc bag. Stick six nickels in your pocket, and you are ready to play *Space Race!*

Playing the Game

Place the *Space Race* transparency on the stage of your projector. Position each nickel to cover the circle in the center of each planet, and cover the six boxes along each side with the twelve rectangular cover slips.

In this game, your students race across a foreign solar system in search of a captive princess!

Choose your game spotter and starter, then explain the rules.

"Today we are playing a Bible game called *Space Race*! The Princess Adelia is being held captive on an unknown planet in the Kroton solar system. Your mission is to find her and free her. Before your team can search the six planets of the Kroton system, you must have a space ship, a security robot, and a floppy disk to give directions to your ship's computerized guidance system.

"I will ask a Bible question, and Shawn will ring the bell. Mr. Thomas is our spotter today. If you answer the question correctly when Mr. Thomas calls on you, you may come to the projector and choose a galactic card from your side of the game. When your team has found a ship, a robot, and a computer disk, you may proceed to search the planets. The team finding the planet where the princess is held wins the game! Ready? Let's play *Space Race!*"

Suggestions and Variations

1. Occasionally prepare a *double* question. The student answering the question uncovers two galactic cards, or reveals two planets.

2. At the conclusion of the game, plan a *double* question for each team.

3. If a team has an extra ship when they uncover the "lose your ship" square, they lose only one ship.

4. If neither team has all three necessary components, but both teams have an extra that the other team needs, offer to let the teams swap. For instance, the boys have two computer disks and the security robot, while the girls have two ships and the security robot. The computer disk could be traded for a ship, and both teams would be ready to search the planets. Let the students vote as to whether or not they want to swap. It's interesting to see their responses.

THE BERMUDA TRIANGLE

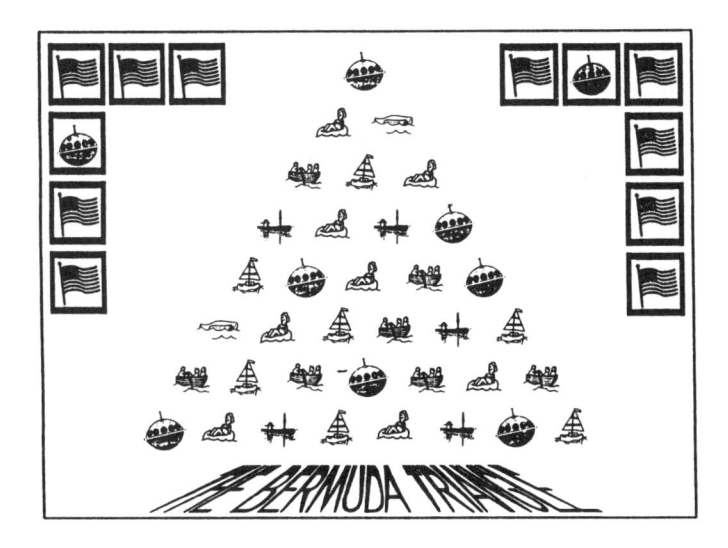

Here's another rescue game that your students will enjoy. The action takes place in *The Bermuda Triangle*, that mysterious region of the Caribbean where ships, aircraft, and people seem to vanish into thin air!

Students answering the Bible questions remove pennies from the game to "rescue" people from rubber rafts, rowboats, sailboats, and even submarines in the Triangle. Notes in bottles yield bonus points, but UFOs threaten disaster for both the rescuers and the rescued. Are you brave enough to enter *The Bermuda Triangle*?

Here's another rescue game that your students will enjoy.

Making the Game

Select one of the three *Bermuda Triangle* game masters (pages 139, 140, or 141) and make a transparency. Mount it to a transparency frame. Obtain twelve nickels and thirty-six pennies, and you are ready for action!

Playing the Game

Place the *Bermuda Triangle* game on the overhead projector. Cover the thirty-six items in the triangle with pennies and the twelve bases in the upper corners with nickels before turning on the projector. Select a game spotter and starter, and introduce the game to your class.

"Today we are playing a Bible game called *The Bermuda Triangle!* As you probably know, there is an area just off the coast of Florida where many ships and planes have disappeared through the years, along with all the people aboard! This area is known as the 'Bermuda Triangle,' and many people are afraid to sail or fly through that region.

"An invasion of UFOs has entered the Triangle. Your mission: to pilot an Air Force chopper into the danger zone and rescue as many people as possible before they are zapped by the invaders. Each person you rescue scores one point for your team.

"Here's how our game is played. When Brad honks the horn at the end of each Bible question, try to be the first to stand. Mrs. Adams will choose you if you are first, and you may answer the question.

"When you answer correctly, you may come to the projector and choose a penny. If you uncover a rubber raft, you have rescued one person, and you score one point for your team. A rowboat contains three people, a sailboat, eight people, and a submarine, twelve! You may choose as many pennies and rescue as many people as you want. But, if you uncover a UFO, you get zapped out of the solar system, and you lose your people and your points.

"Once you choose to stop, you must fly your survivors safely back to the Air Force base before your team scores the points. You will choose a nickel from one of the six bases on your side of the game. If you find an American flag, you have landed safely back at the air base. If you make a navigational error and uncover a UFO, you and your cargo of people are zapped, and you lose all the points from your turn.

"If you find a bottle with a message inside, your team immediately receives a twenty point bonus! You receive the bonus points even if you don't make it back safely to base.

"Ready? Let's play *The Bermuda Triangle!*"

Suggestions and Variations

1. The six bases in the upper right-hand corner of the game are the girls' bases; those in the left-hand corner are for the boys.

2. When the player lands safely back at the base, his points are recorded by the scorekeeper, and the points are permanent. A UFO later in the game does not erase these points. Once a player lands at the base, his turn is over.

3. When a bottle is discovered, the twenty point bonus is recorded immediately. The discovery of a UFO — even in the same turn — does not affect the bonus points.

4. At the conclusion of the game, plan a *double* question for each team. Points are doubled on these two final questions, including the bonus points for the discovery of a bottle.

5. On occasion, change the results of finding the bottles. The discovery of a bottle concludes that student's turn and gives his points to the other team! Announce this variation before starting the game.

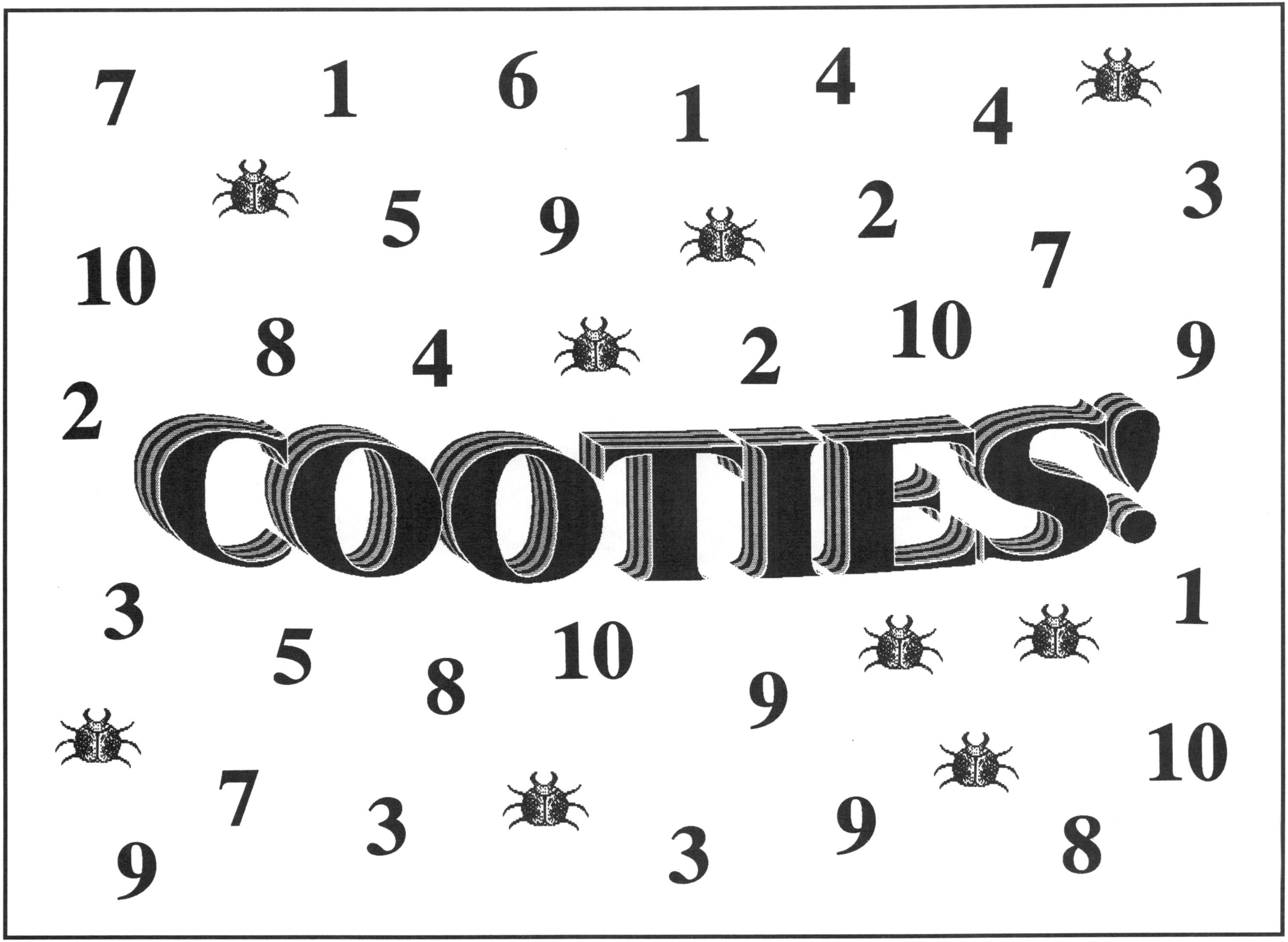
COOTIES!

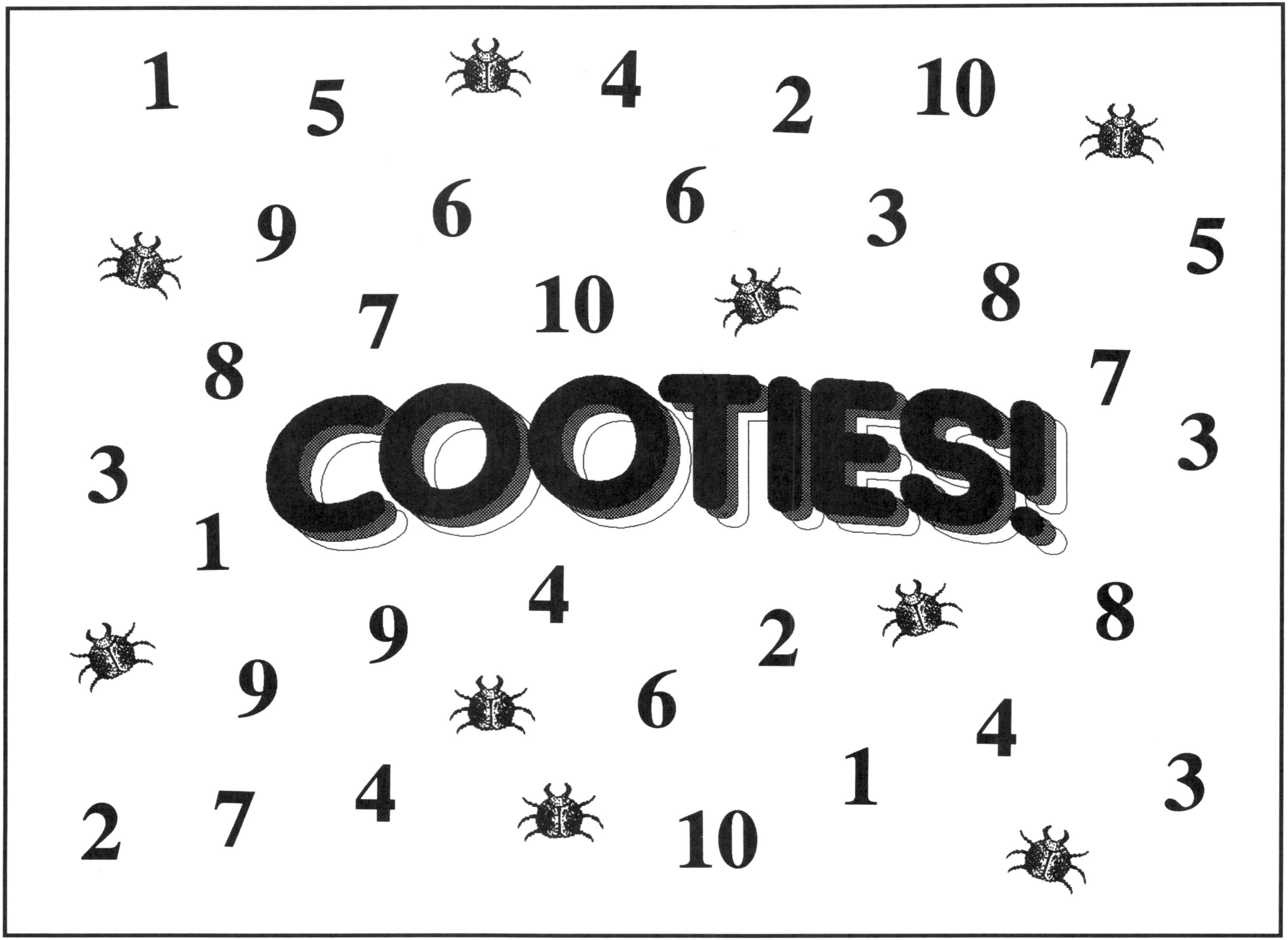
COOTIES!
1 5 4 2 10
9 6 6 3 5
7 10 8
8 7
3 3
1
4 8
9 2
9 6
4
2 7 4 1 3
10

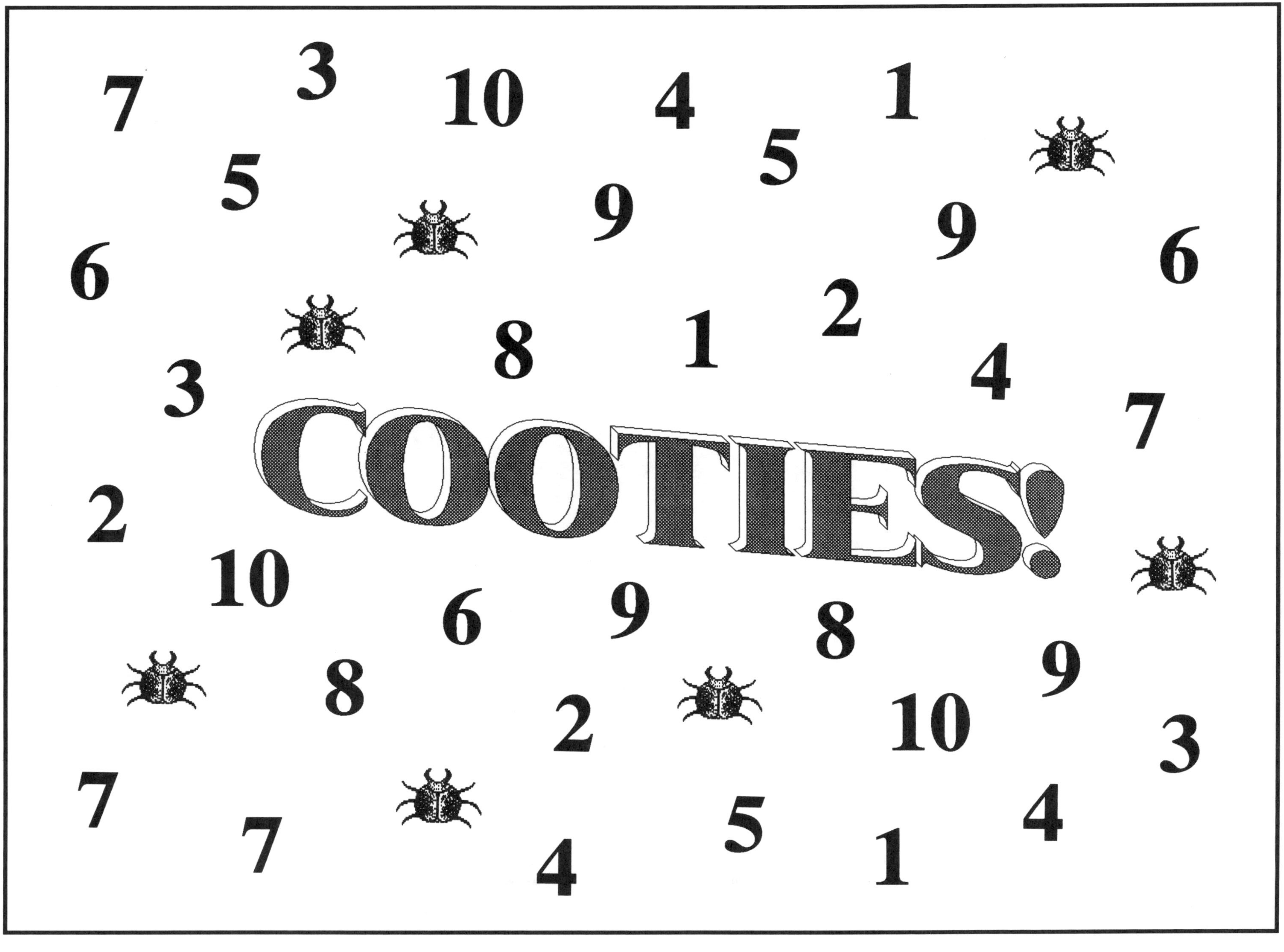
COOTIES!

SURPRISE ENDING!

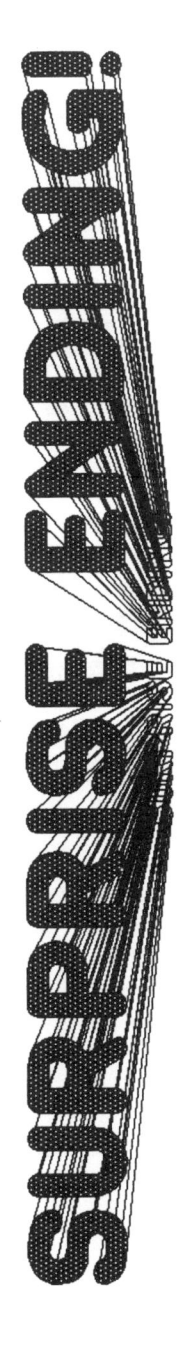

SURPRISE ENDING!

	Cut Out Center		Cut Out Center	
		Cut Out Center		Cut Out Center
				Cut Out Center
Cut Out Center		Cut Out Center		
	Cut Out Center			Cut Out Center

Cut out large square, then carefully cut out center of marked small squares to form Surprise Ending overlay.

↑

JONKENPON

JONKENPON

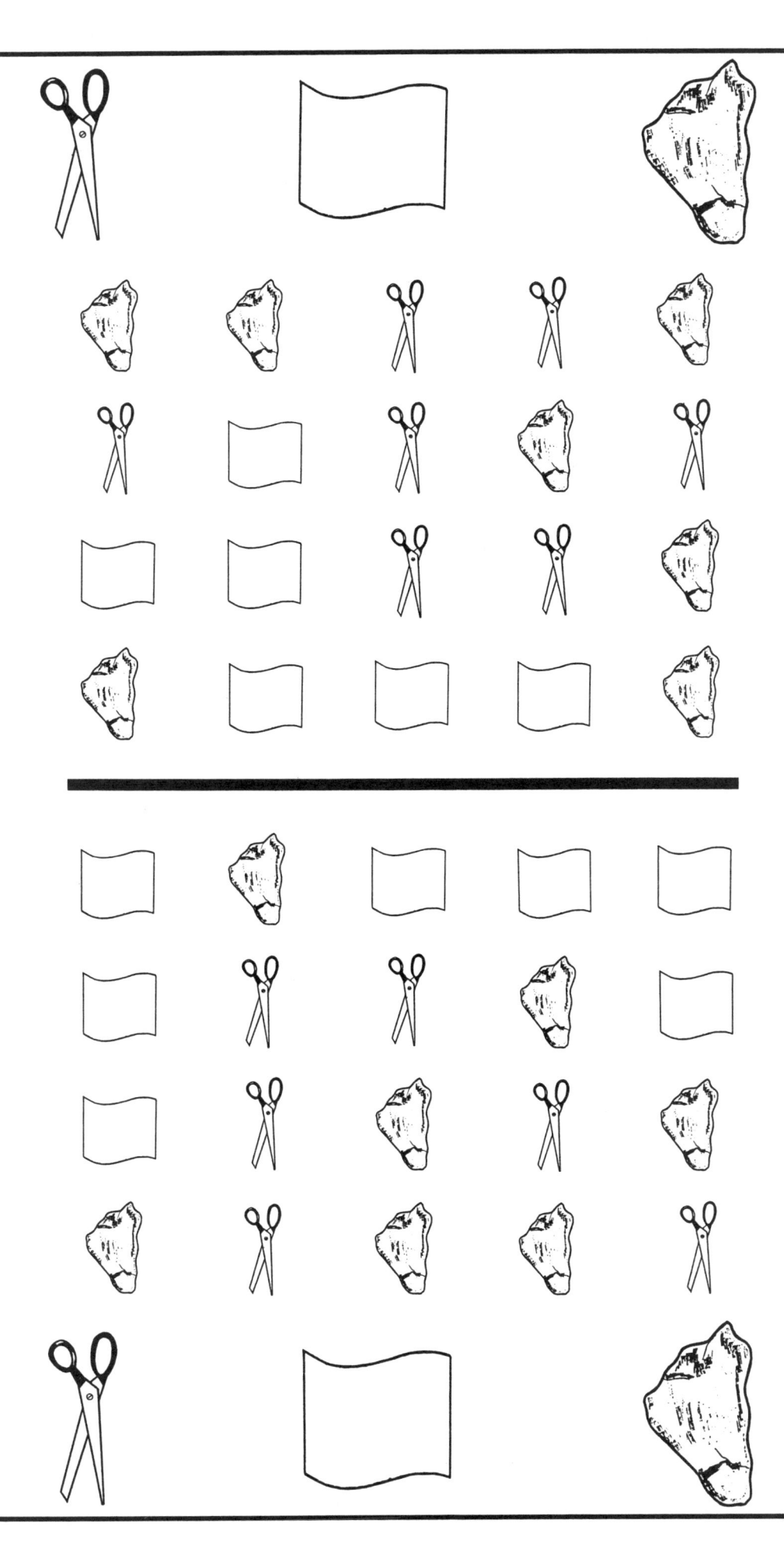

JONKENPON

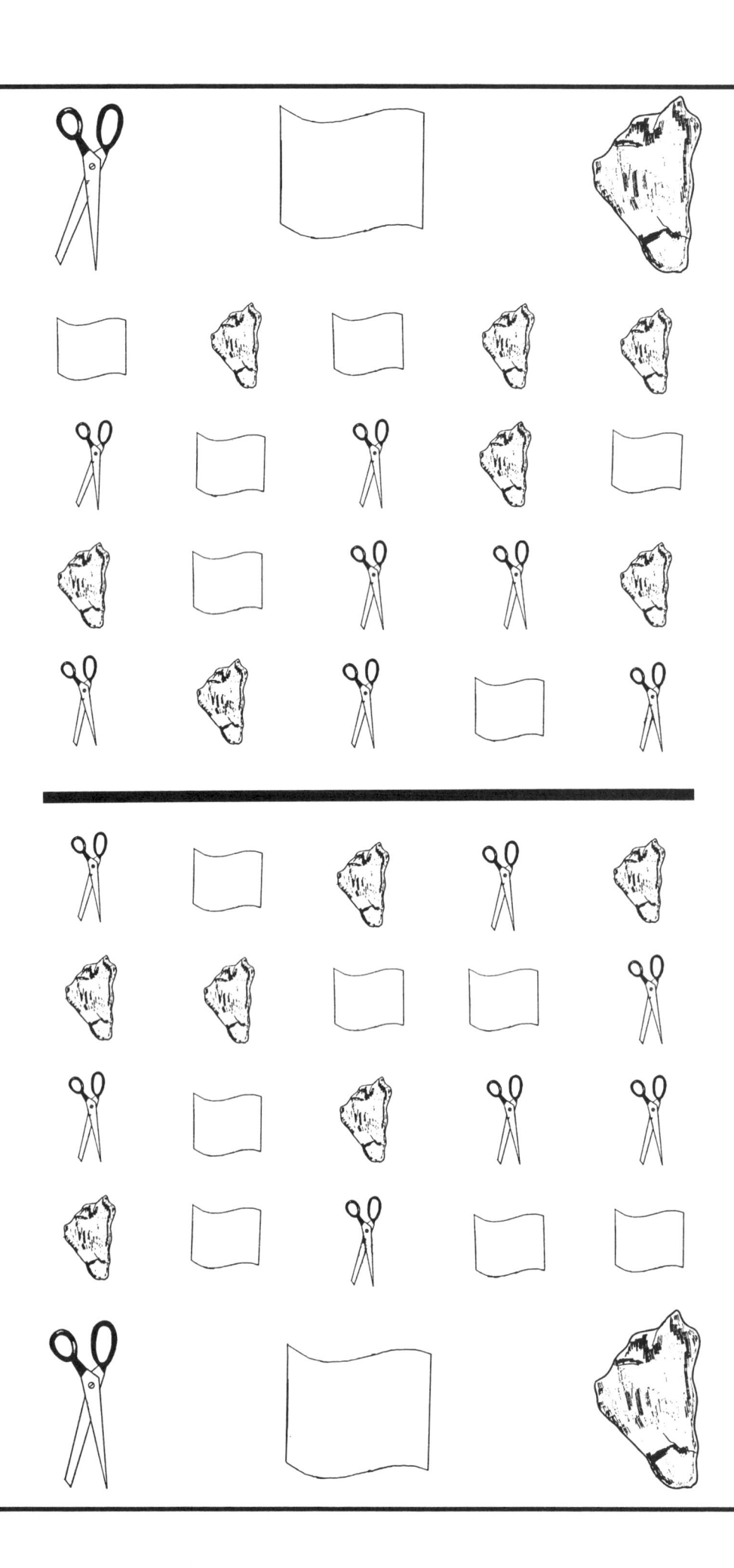

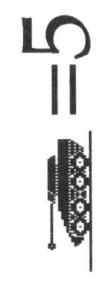

CAPTURE the FLAG!

Round 1
Single

Round 2
Double

Round 3
Triple

CAPTURE the FLAG!

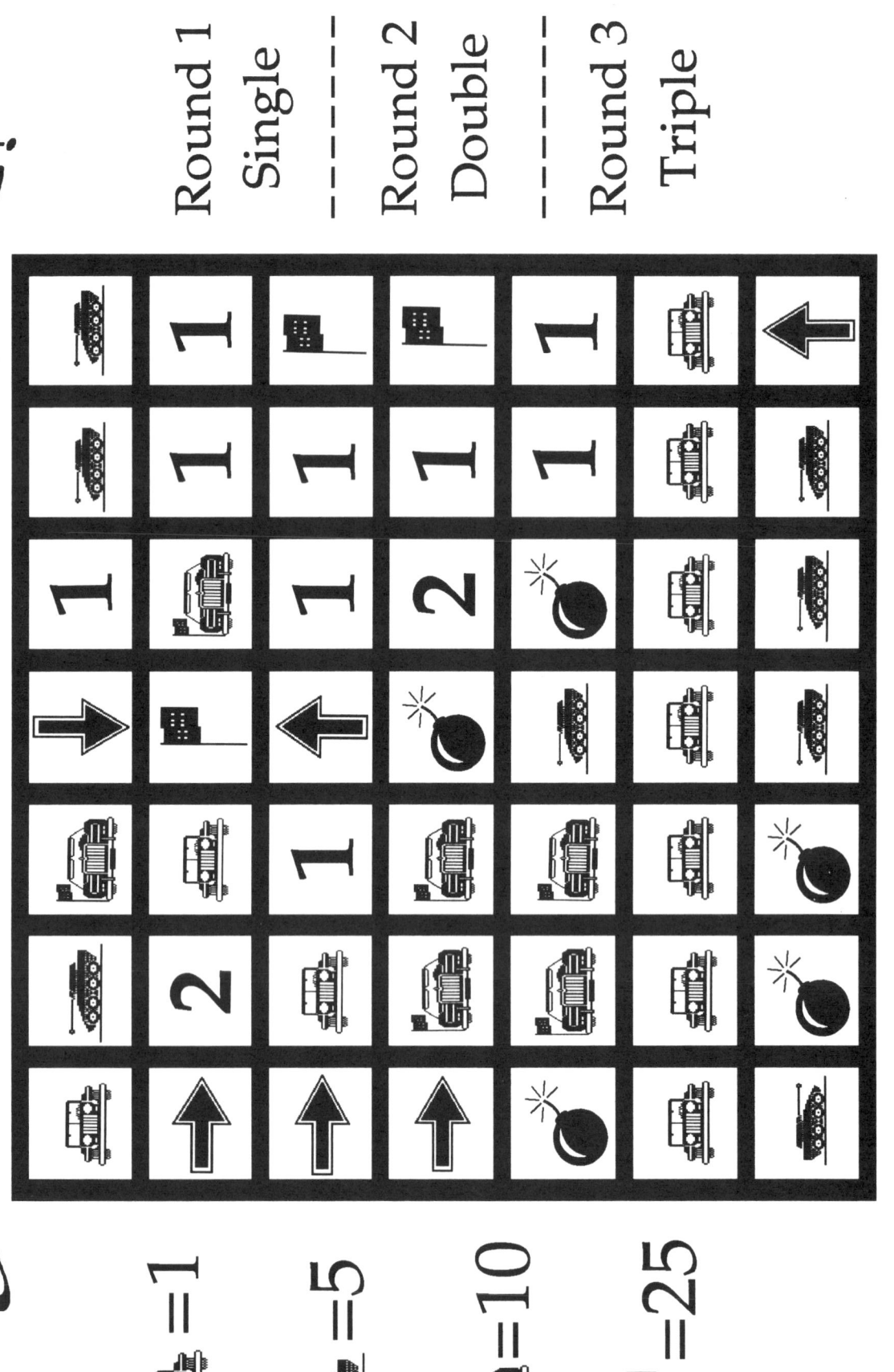

Round 1
Single

Round 2
Double

Round 3
Triple

= 1
= 5
= 10
= 25

CAPTURE the FLAG!

Round 1 — Single

Round 2 — Double

Round 3 — Triple

🚚 = 1
🚢 = 5
🚛 = 10
⚑ = 25

Capture the Flag!

(When preparing this game for a large class, enlarge these game cards on a copier for greater visibility.)

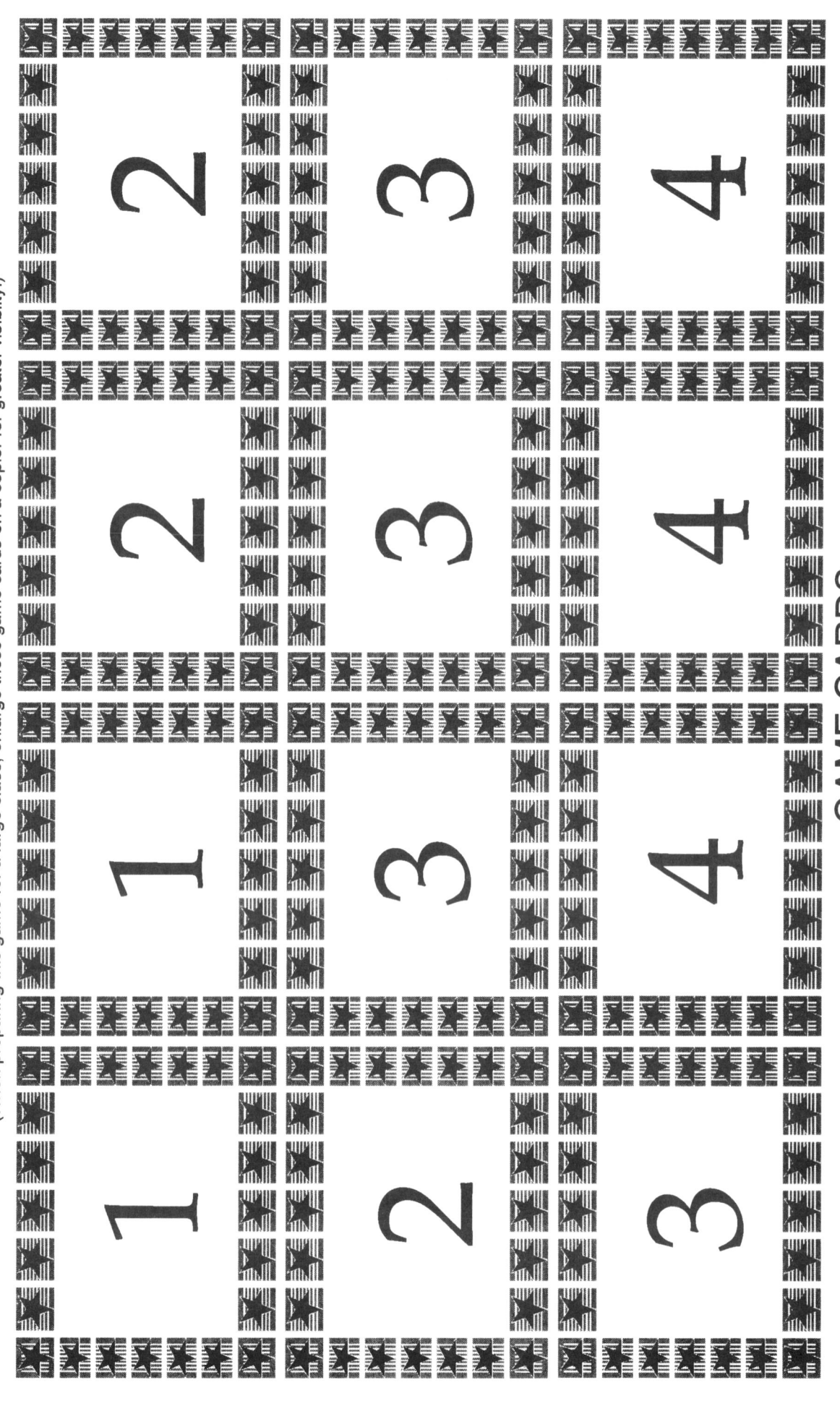

1	1	2
2	3	3
3	4	4

GAME CARDS

Pirate Treasure

Pirate Treasure

Pirate Treasure

Pirate Treasure

(When preparing this game for a large class, enlarge these game cards on a photocopier for greater visibility.)

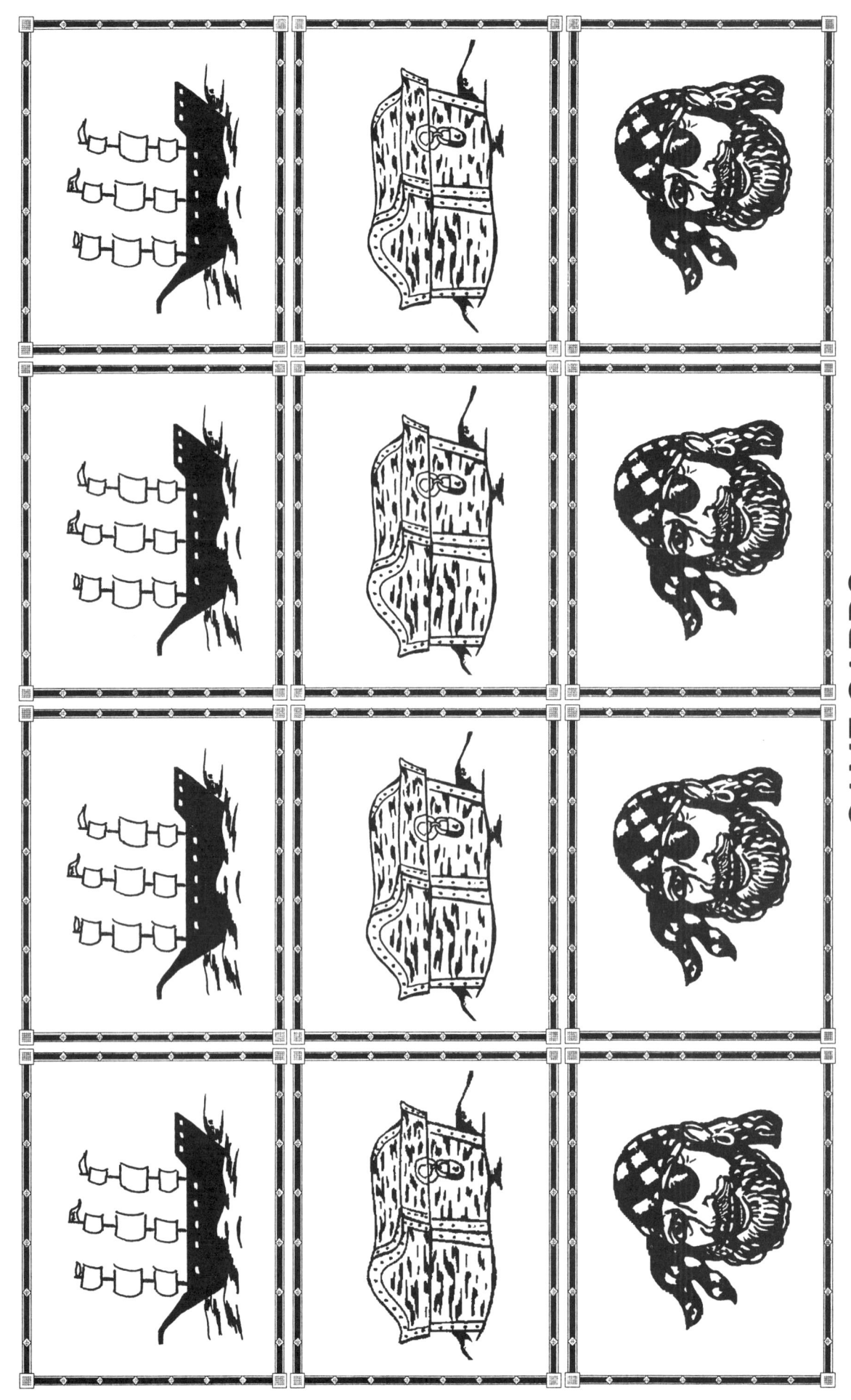

GAME CARDS

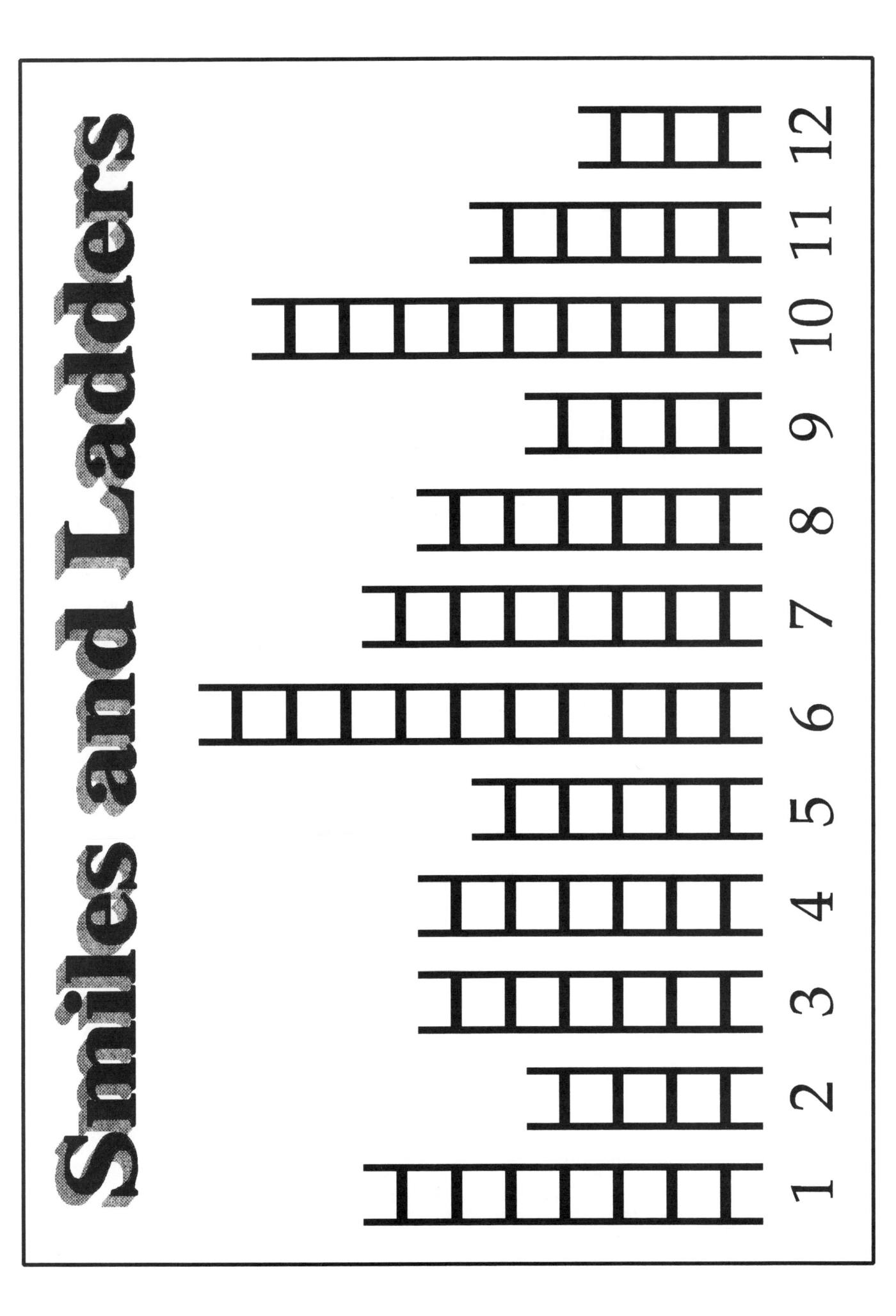

Smiles and Ladders

1 2 3 4 5 6 7 8 9 10 11 12

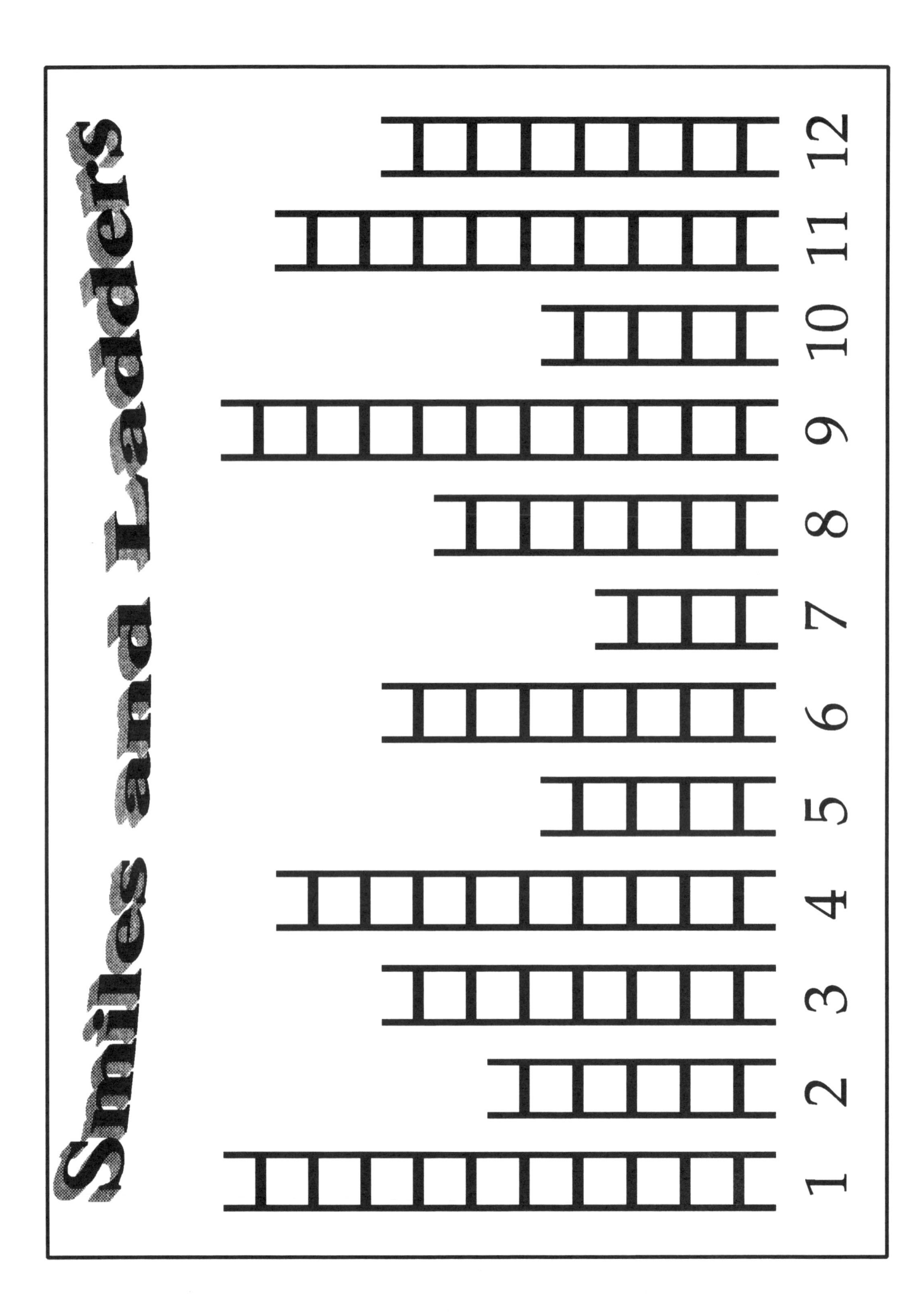

Smiles and Ladders

1 2 3 4 5 6 7 8 9 10 11 12

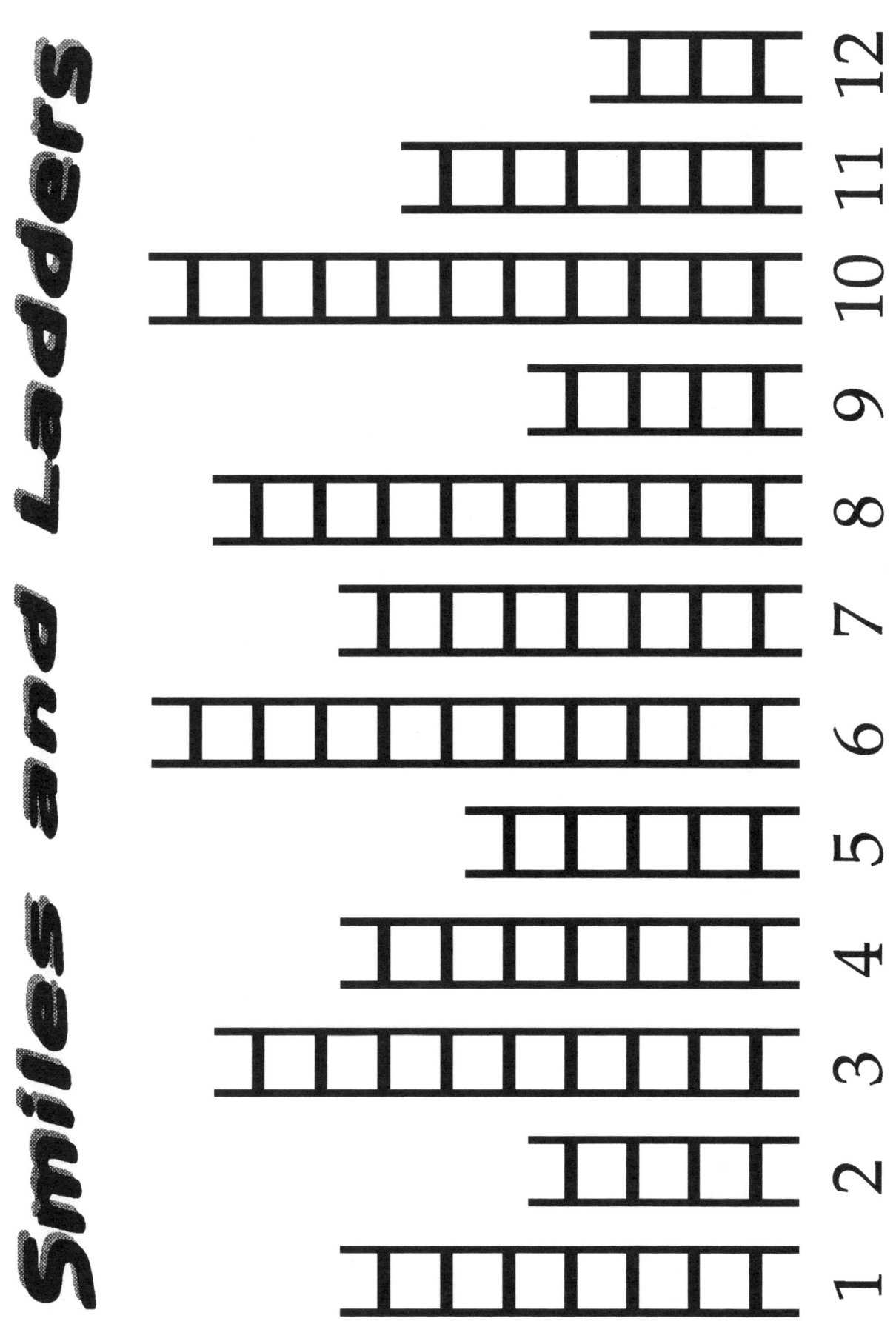

Smiles and Ladders

1 2 3 4 5 6 7 8 9 10 11 12

Smiles and Ladders
GAME PIECES

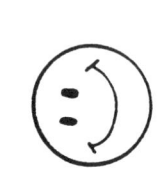

Smiles and Ladders

(When preparing this game for a large class, enlarge these game cards on a copier for greater visibility.)

Ladder #9	Ladder #10	Ladder #11	Ladder #12
Ladder #5	Ladder #6	Ladder #7	Ladder #8
Ladder #1	Ladder #2	Ladder #3	Ladder #4

GAME CARDS

Smiles and Ladders

(When preparing this game for a large class, enlarge these game cards on a copier for greater visibility.)

Climb 2	Climb 3	Climb 3	Climb 4
Climb 4	Climb 5	Climb 5	Climb 5
Climb 6	Climb 6	Climb 8	Climb 10

GAME CARDS

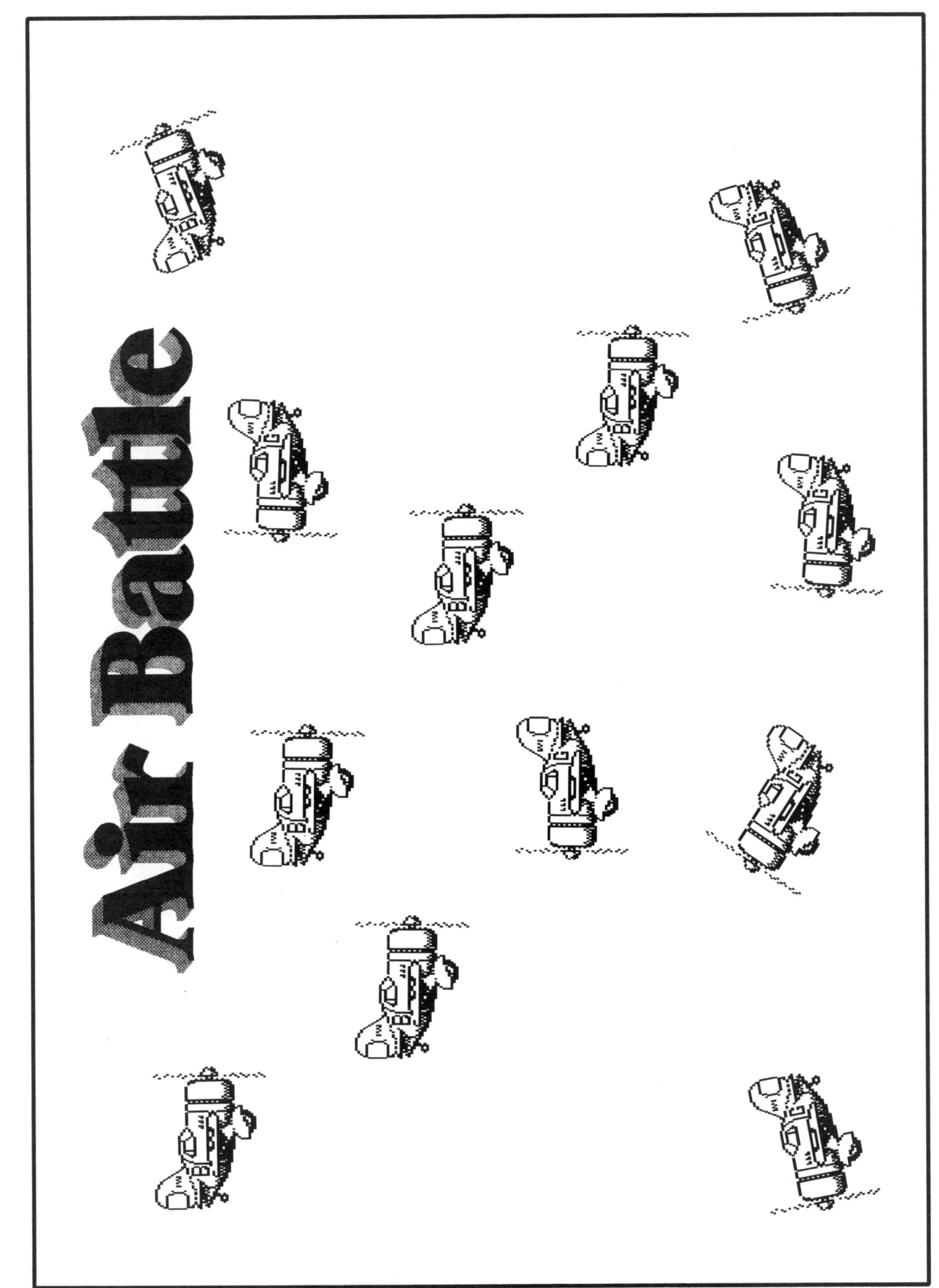

Air Battle

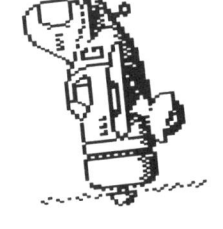

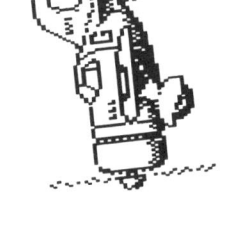

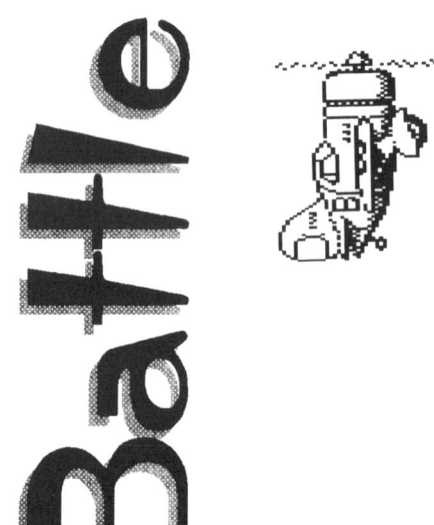

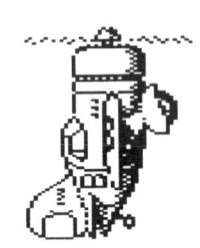

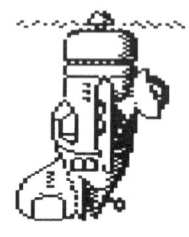

Air Battle

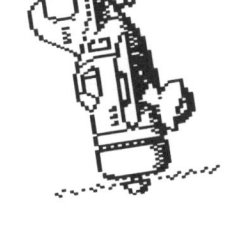

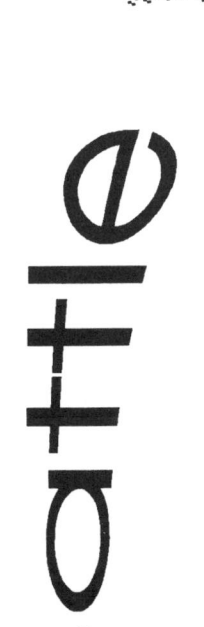

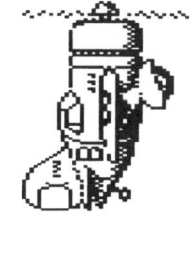

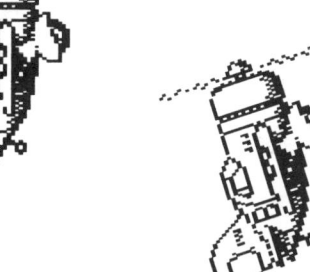

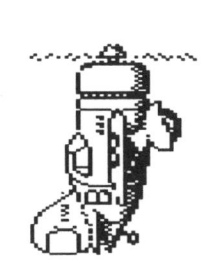

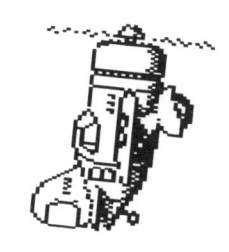

Air Battle

Air Battle
CLOUD PATTERNS

Air Battle

(When preparing this game for a large class, enlarge these game cards on a copier for greater visibility.)

Blue Plane	Red Plane
Choose	**Cloud**

GAME CARDS

Air Battle

GAME PIECES

Apple Picking

Apple Picking
GAME PIECES

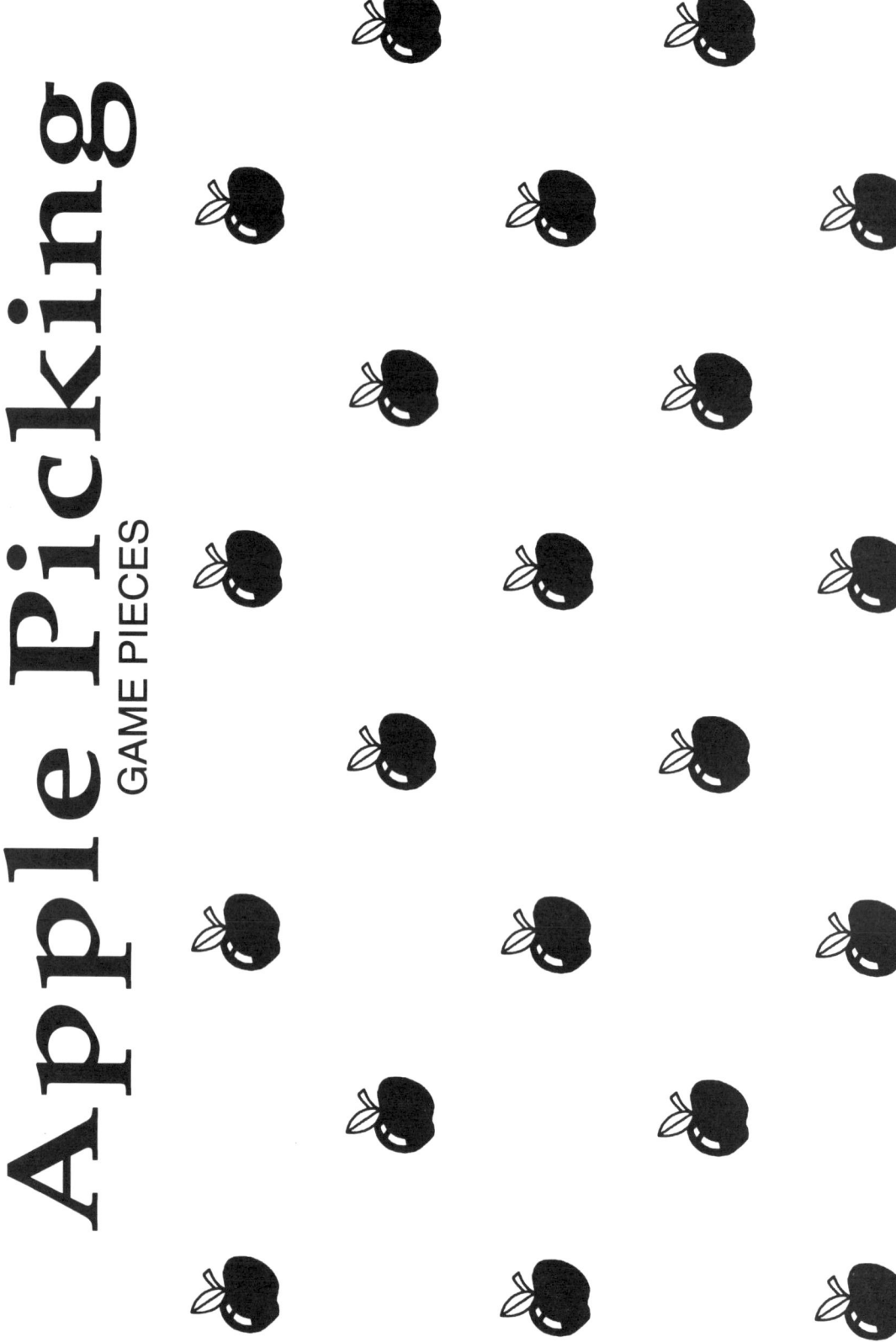

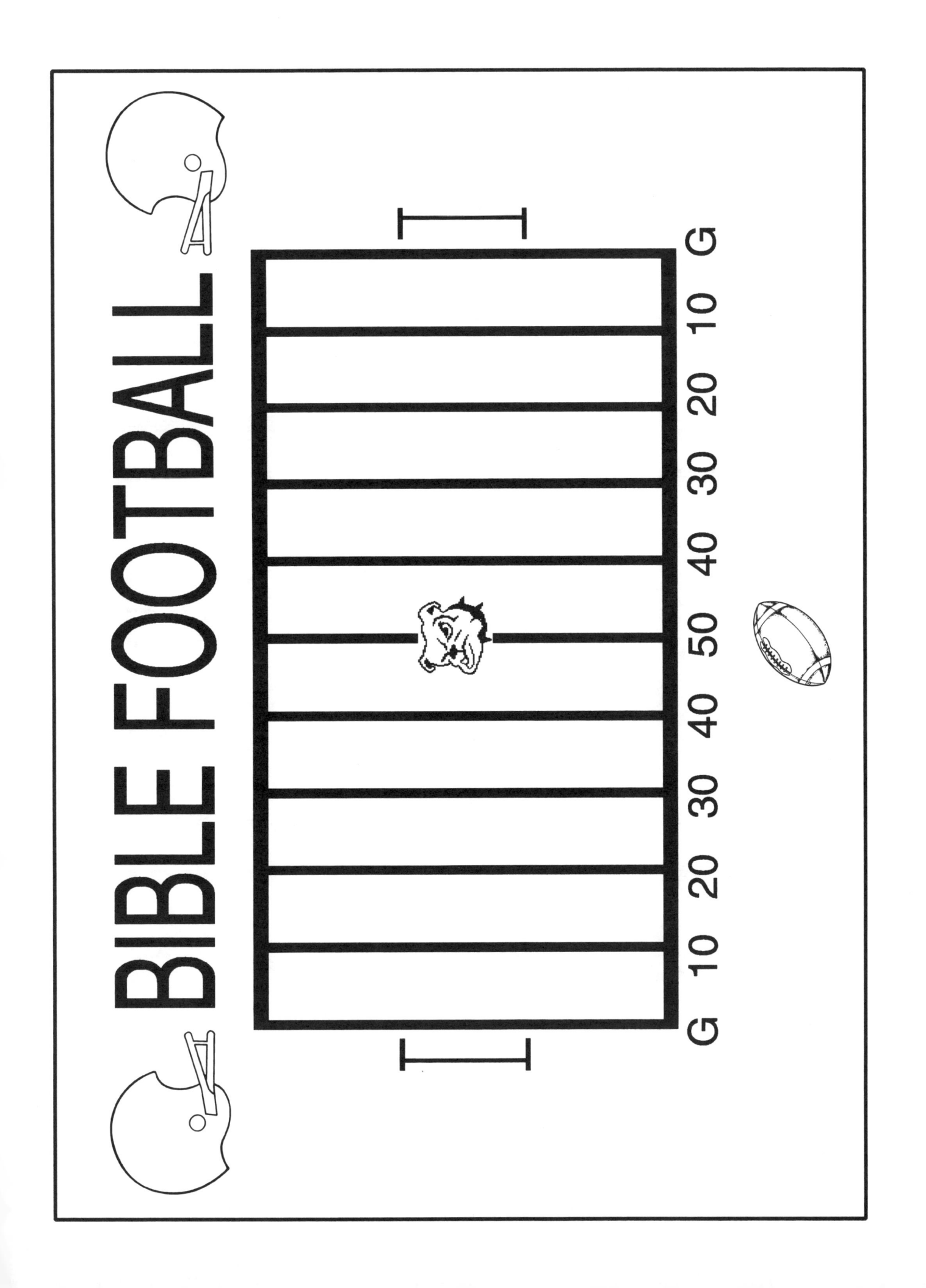

BIBLE FOOTBALL

G 10 20 30 40 50 40 30 20 10 G
G 10 20 30 40 50 40 30 20 10 G

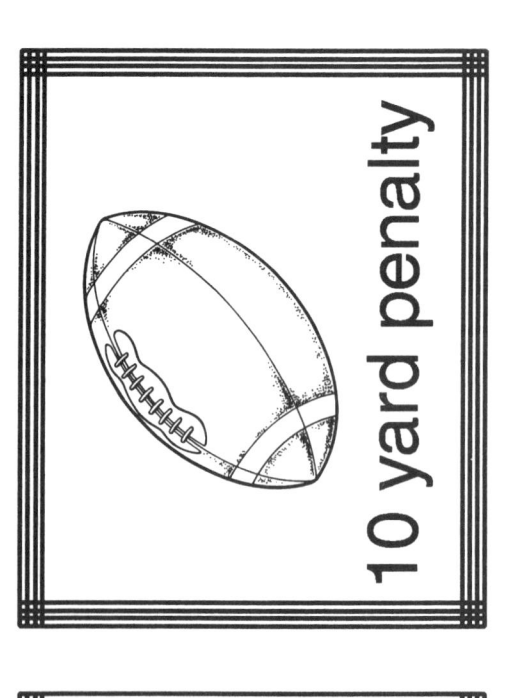

Bible Football

(When preparing this game for a large class, enlarge these game cards on a copier for greater visibility.)

10 yards	20 yards	30 yards
40 yards	50 yards	10 yard penalty

GAME CARDS

Bible Football
GAME PIECES

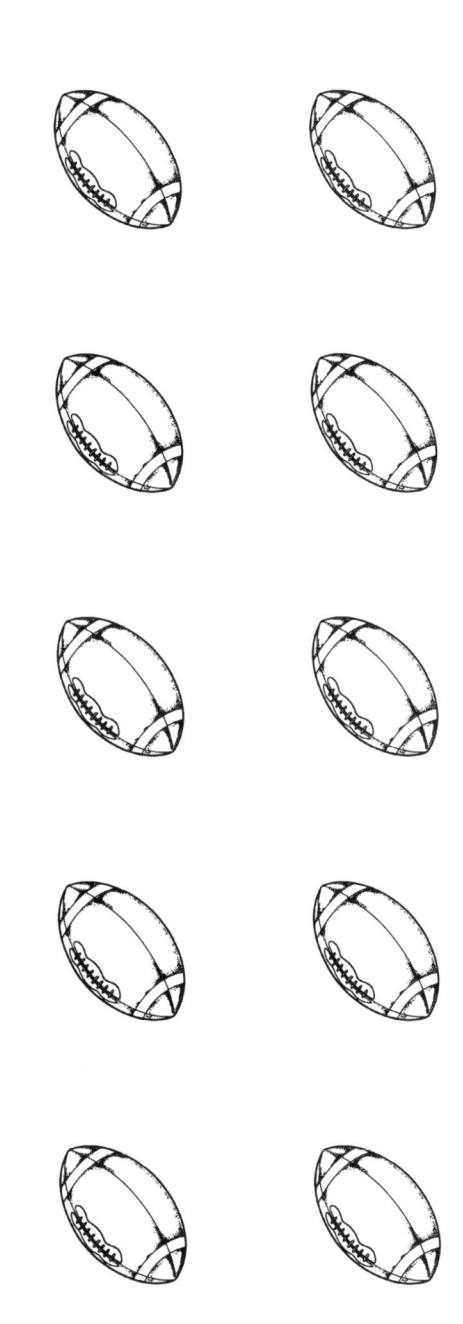

SEA BATTLE

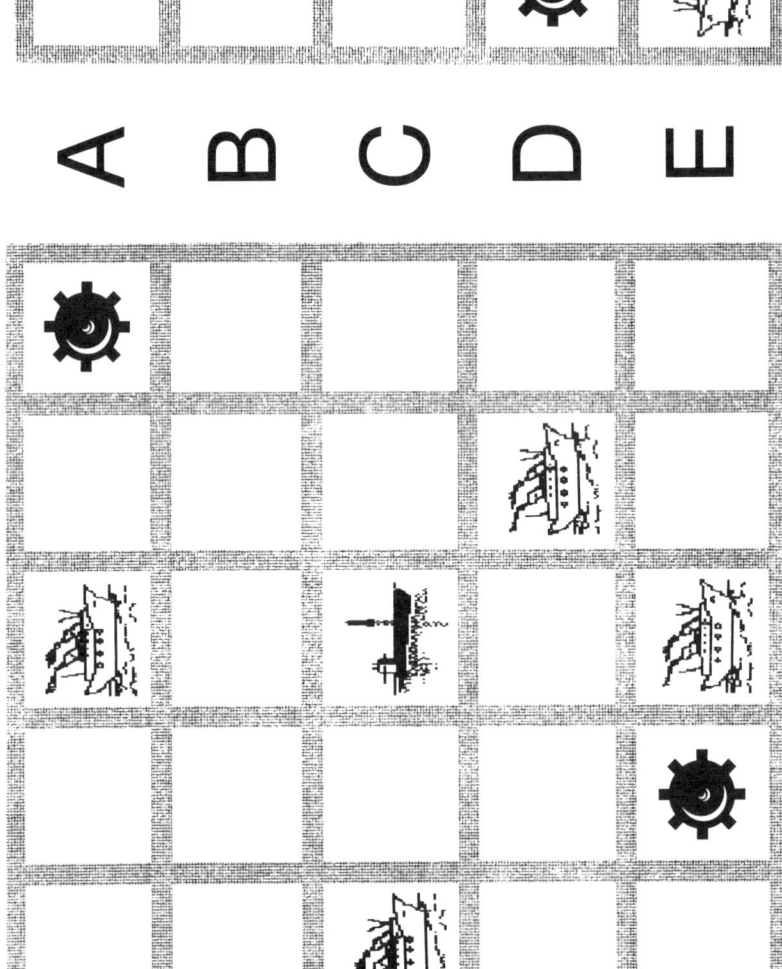

SEA BATTLE

	1	2	3	4	5
A					
B					
C					
D					
E					

	1	2	3	4	5
A					
B					
C					
D					
E					

SEA BATTLE
SHIPS, SUBS, AND MINES

SEA BATTLE
SHIPS, SUBS, AND MINES

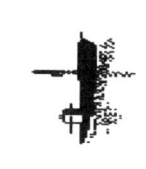

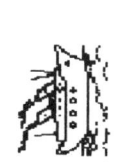

SEA BATTLE

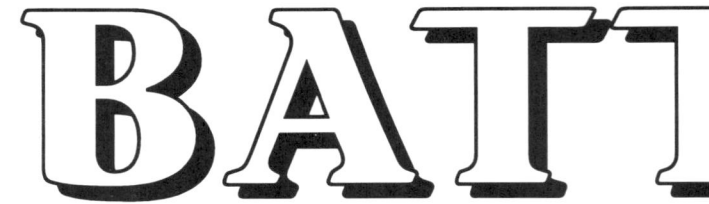

(When preparing this game for a large class, enlarge these game cards on a copier for greater visibility.)

Fire 1 Round	Fire 2 Rounds	Fire 3 Rounds
 Fire 4 Rounds	Fire 2 Rounds	Fire 3 Rounds

GAME CARDS

Bible Tic-Tac-Toe

Bible Tic-Tac-Toe

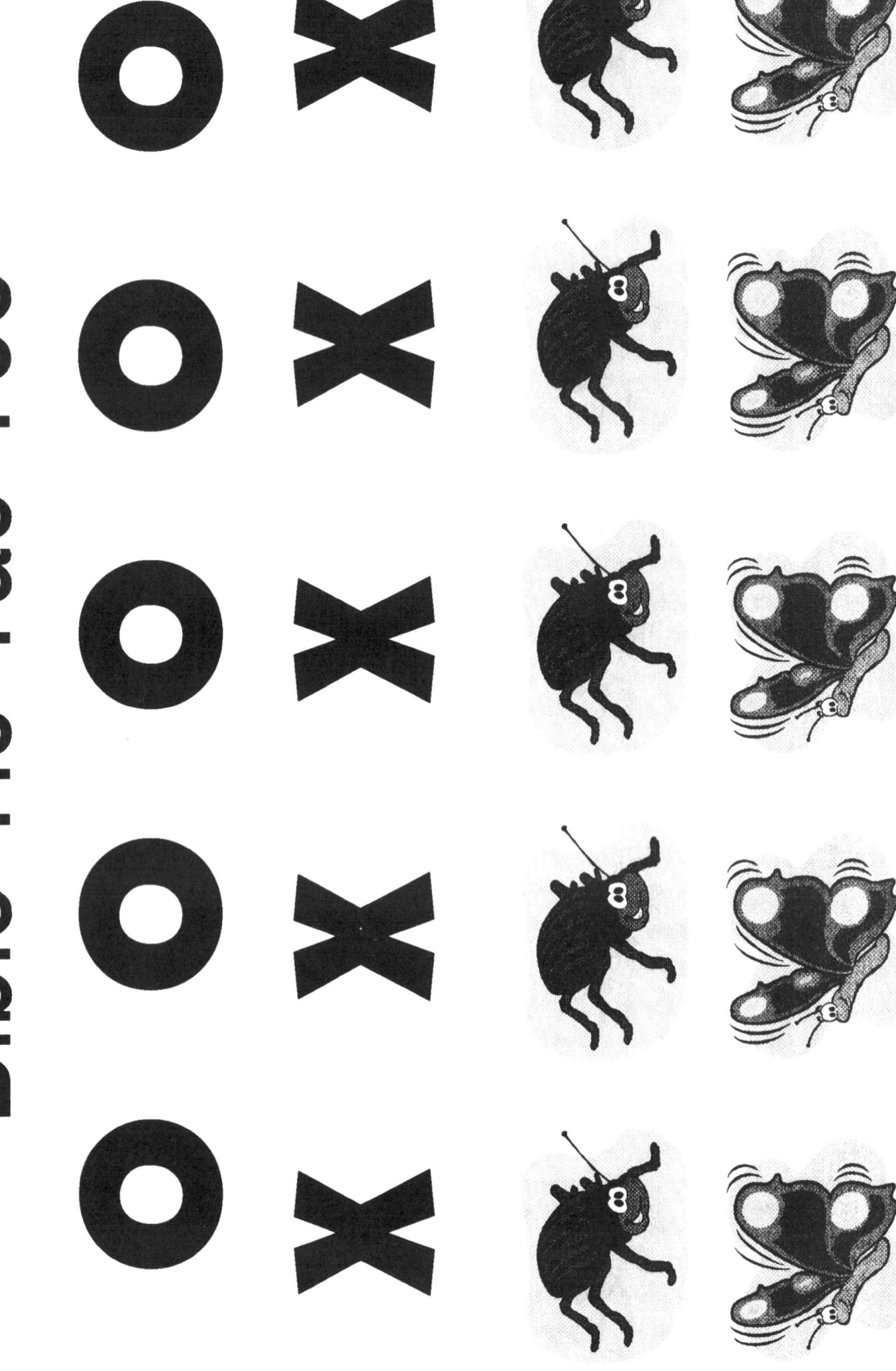

GAME PIECES

Bible Tic-Tac-Toe

(When preparing this game for a large class, enlarge these game cards on a copier for greater visibility.)

Top Row	Center Row	Bottom Row
Left Column	Center Column	Right Column
Your Choice	Your Choice	Your Choice

GAME CARDS

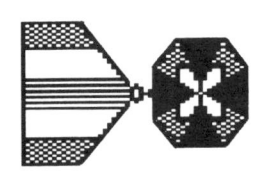

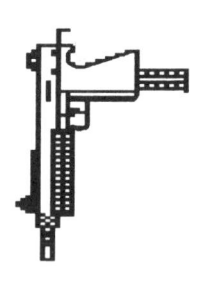

Operation Spy Trap

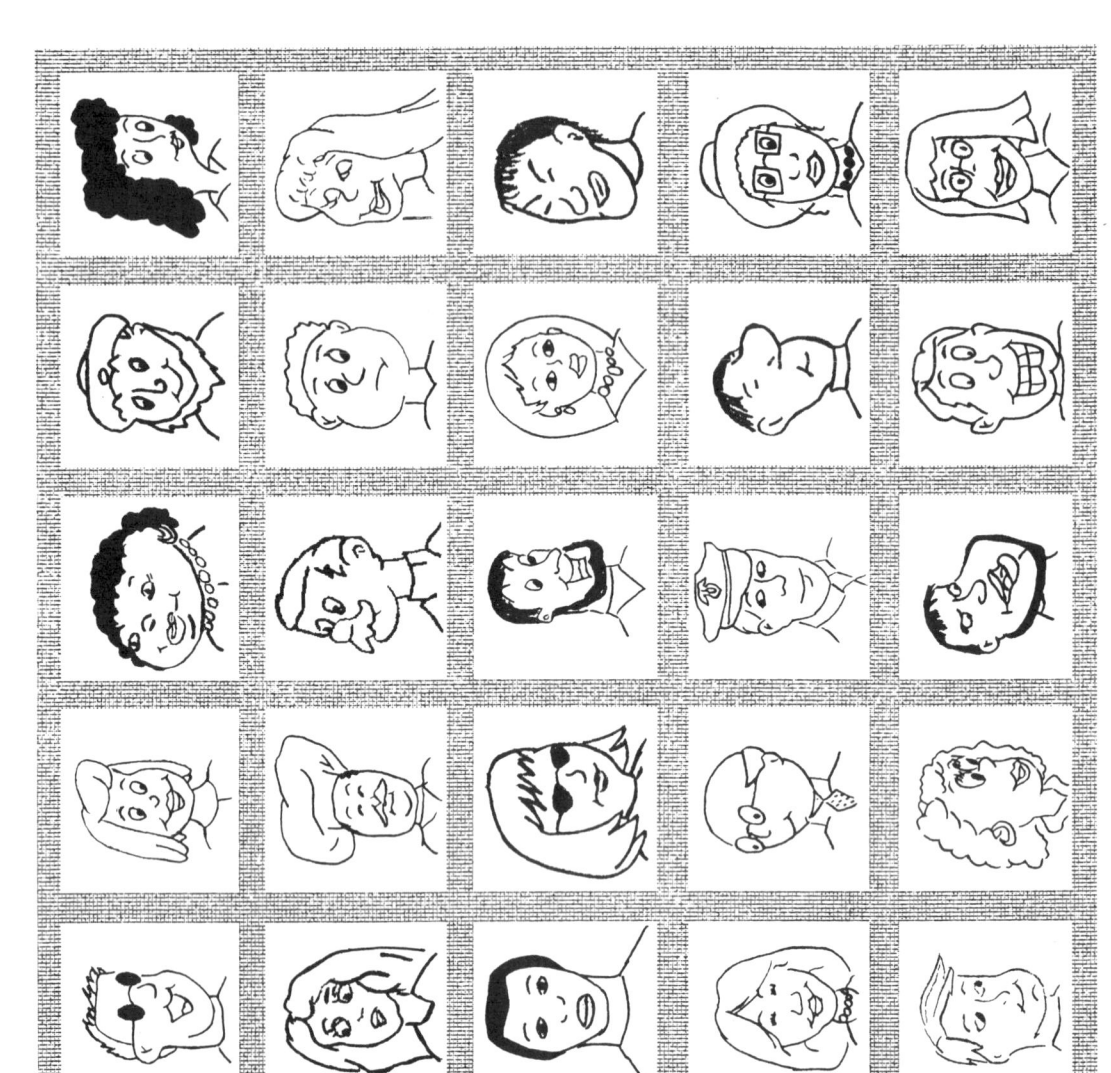

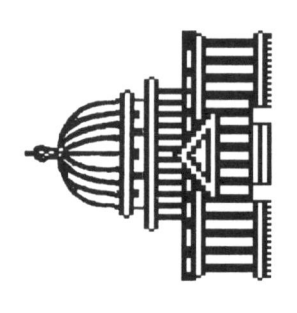

Operation Spy Trap

(When preparing this game for a large class, enlarge these game cards on a copier for greater visibility.)

1	1	1
1	2	2	2
2	3	3	3
3

GAME CARDS

Operation Spy Trap

Cut Out Center		Cut Out Center		
Cut Out Center	Cut Out Center		Cut Out Center	Cut Out Center
		Cut Out Center		
	Cut Out Center			Cut Out Center

Cut out large square, then carefully cut out center of smaller squares to form Super Secret Spy Identifier overlay.

RATTLESNAKE!

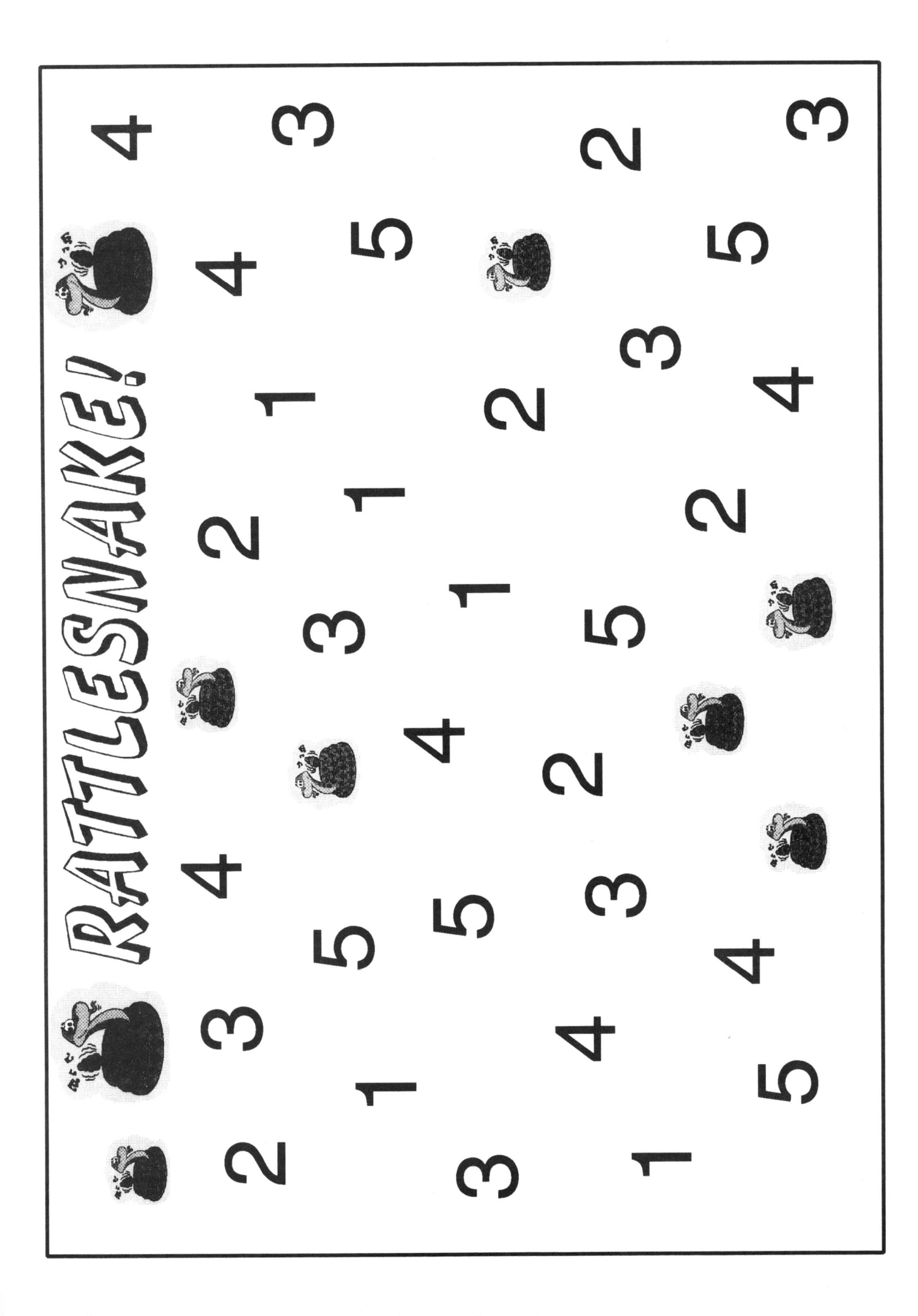

2 3 4 5 2 3 1 2 4
1 5 4 3 1 2 5 3
3 5 4 1 5 2
2 1 3 4 2 5
5 4 3 2 5
1 4 3 1

Rattlesnake!

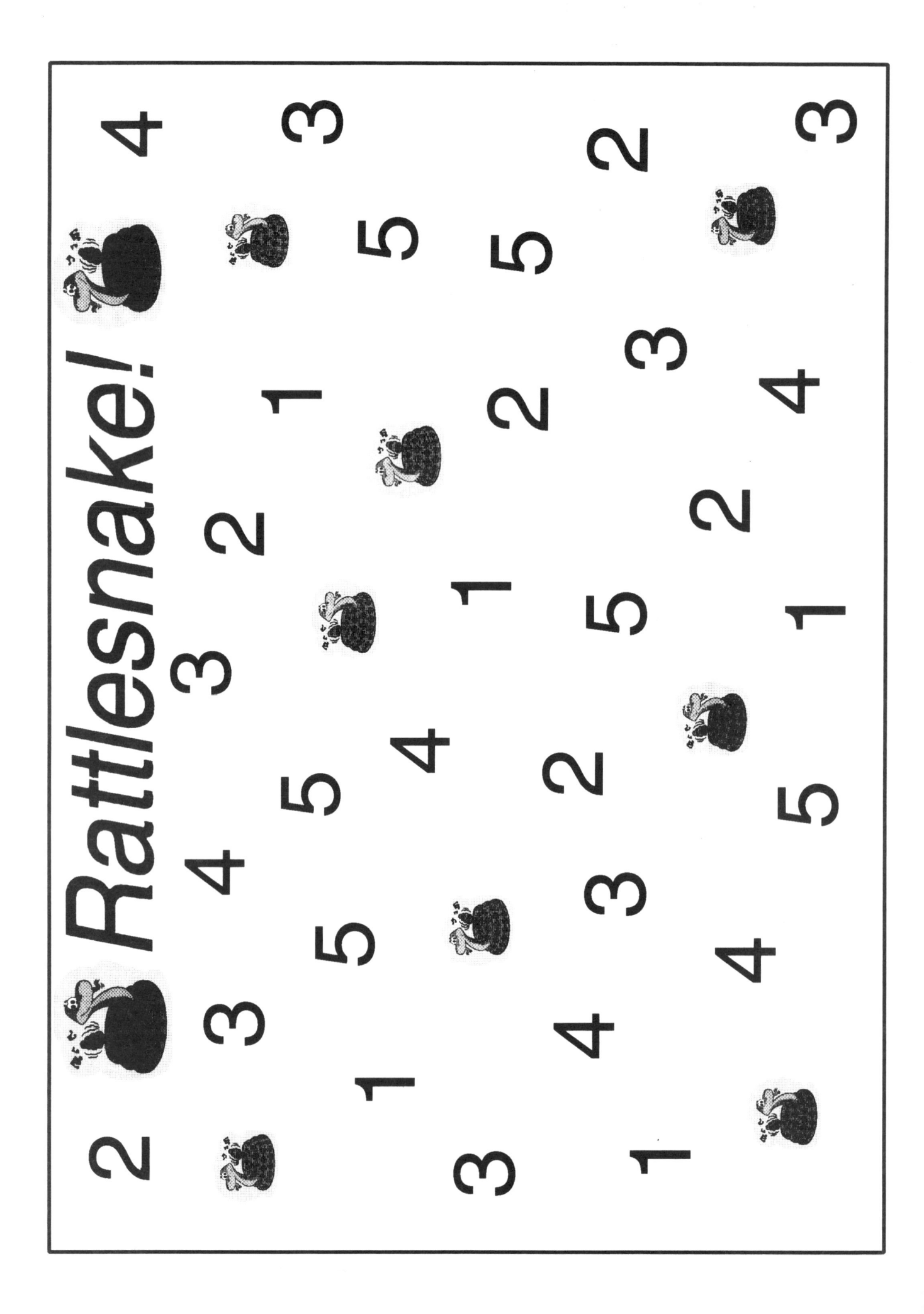

4 3 2 3
5 5 2
1 3
3 2 1 5
5 4 1 2
3 4 5 2
1 4 3 5
2 1 3 1

Rattlesnake!

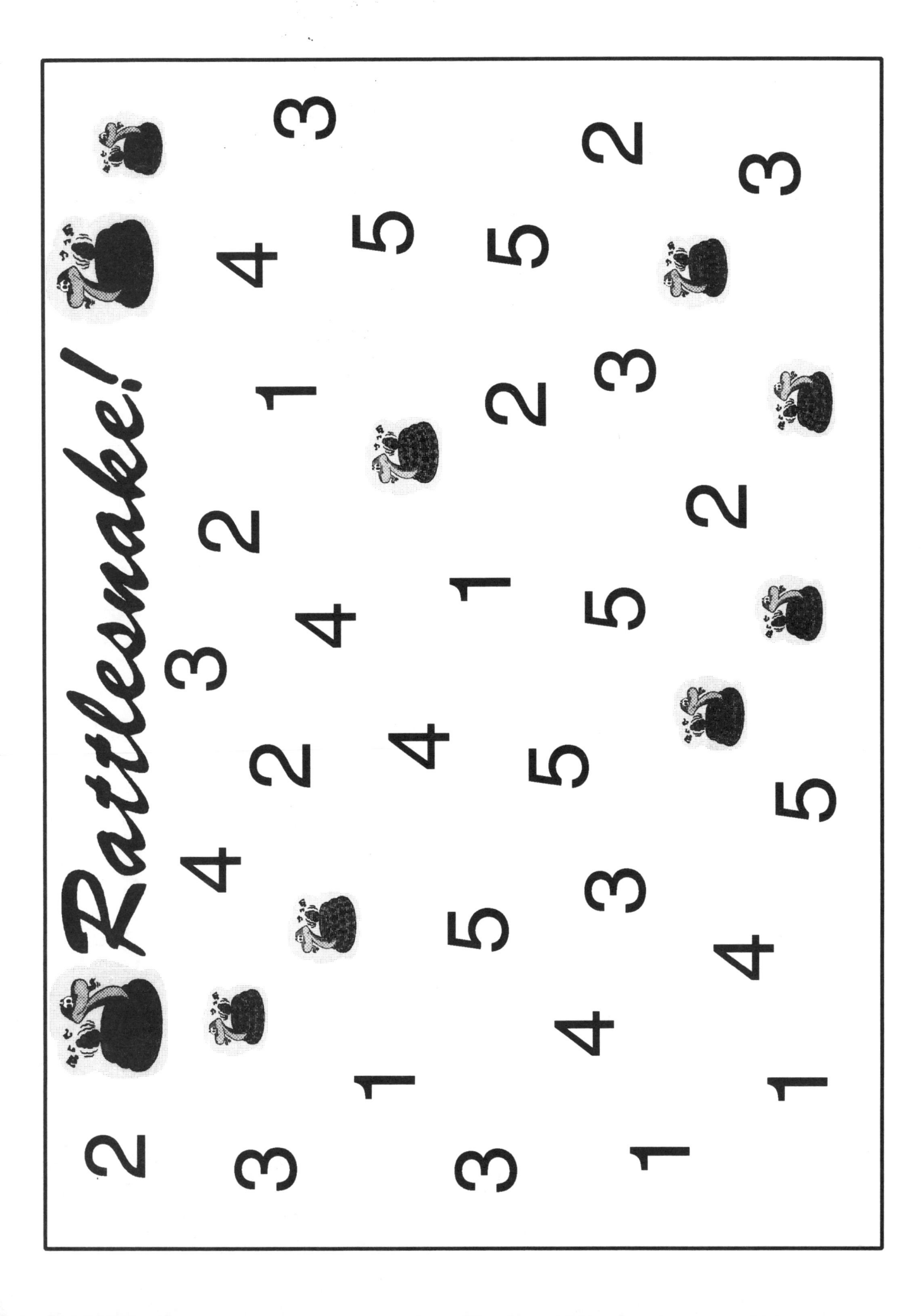

2 3 4 2 1 4 5 3
3 4 3 2 1 2 5 5 2
3 1 4 2 4 1 3 2 5 3
1 4 3 5 5 5 5 2
1 1 4 5

RATTLESNAKE!

(When preparing this game for a large class, enlarge these game cards on a copier for greater visibility.)

3	4	5	6
7	8	9	10
11	12	50 BONUS POINTS!	100 BONUS POINTS!

GAME CARDS

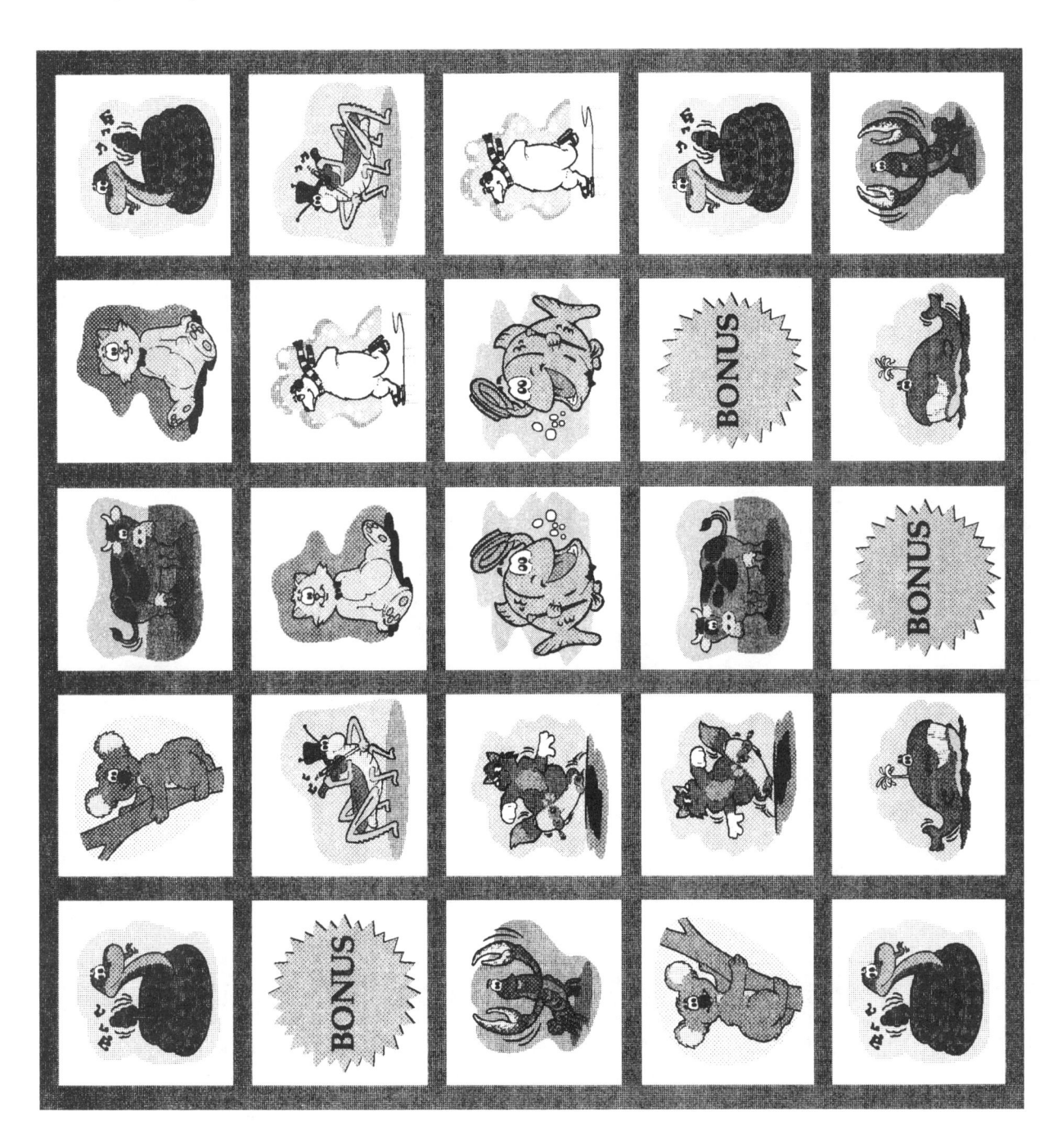

MATCH*IT!

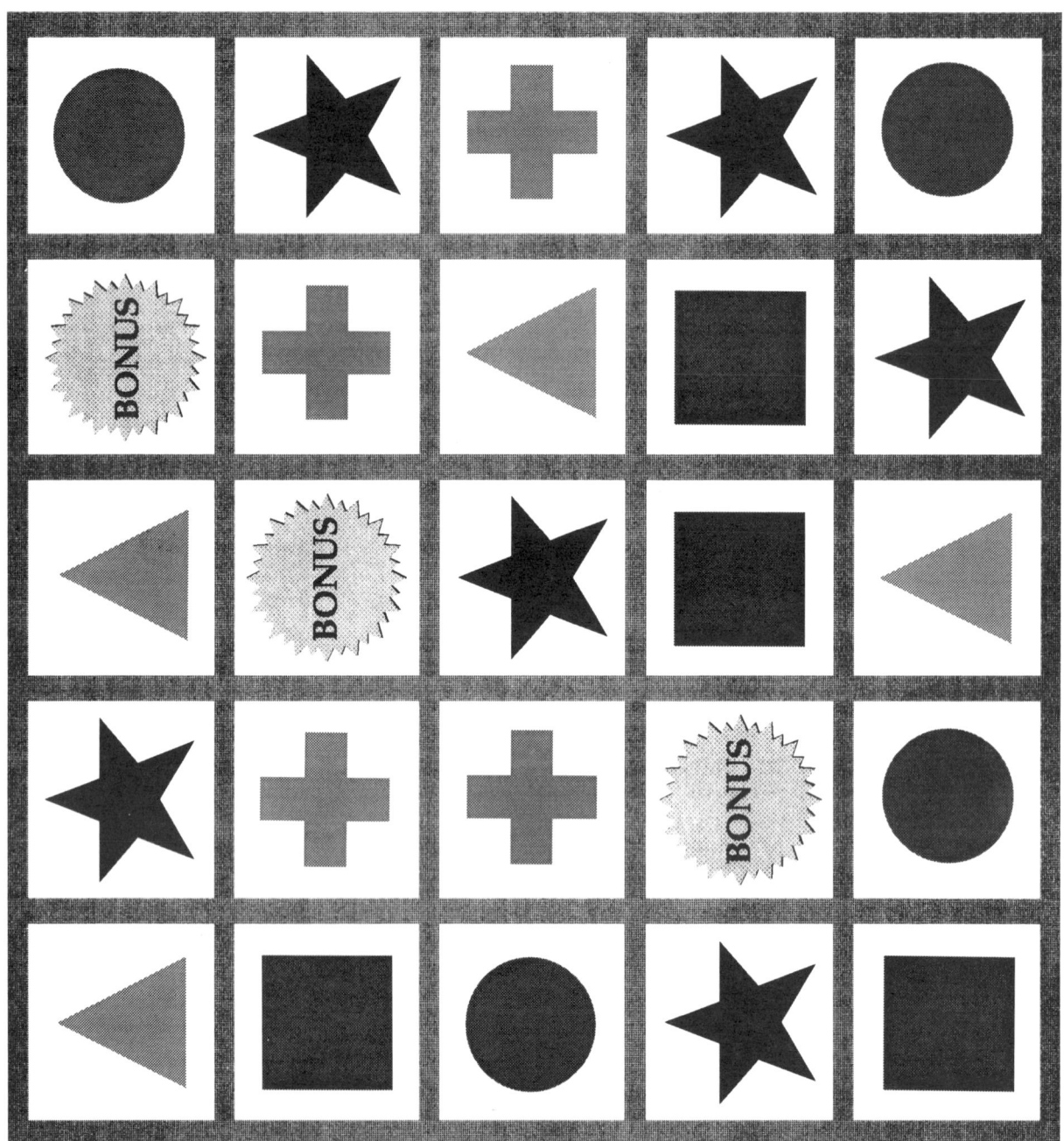

MATCH*IT!

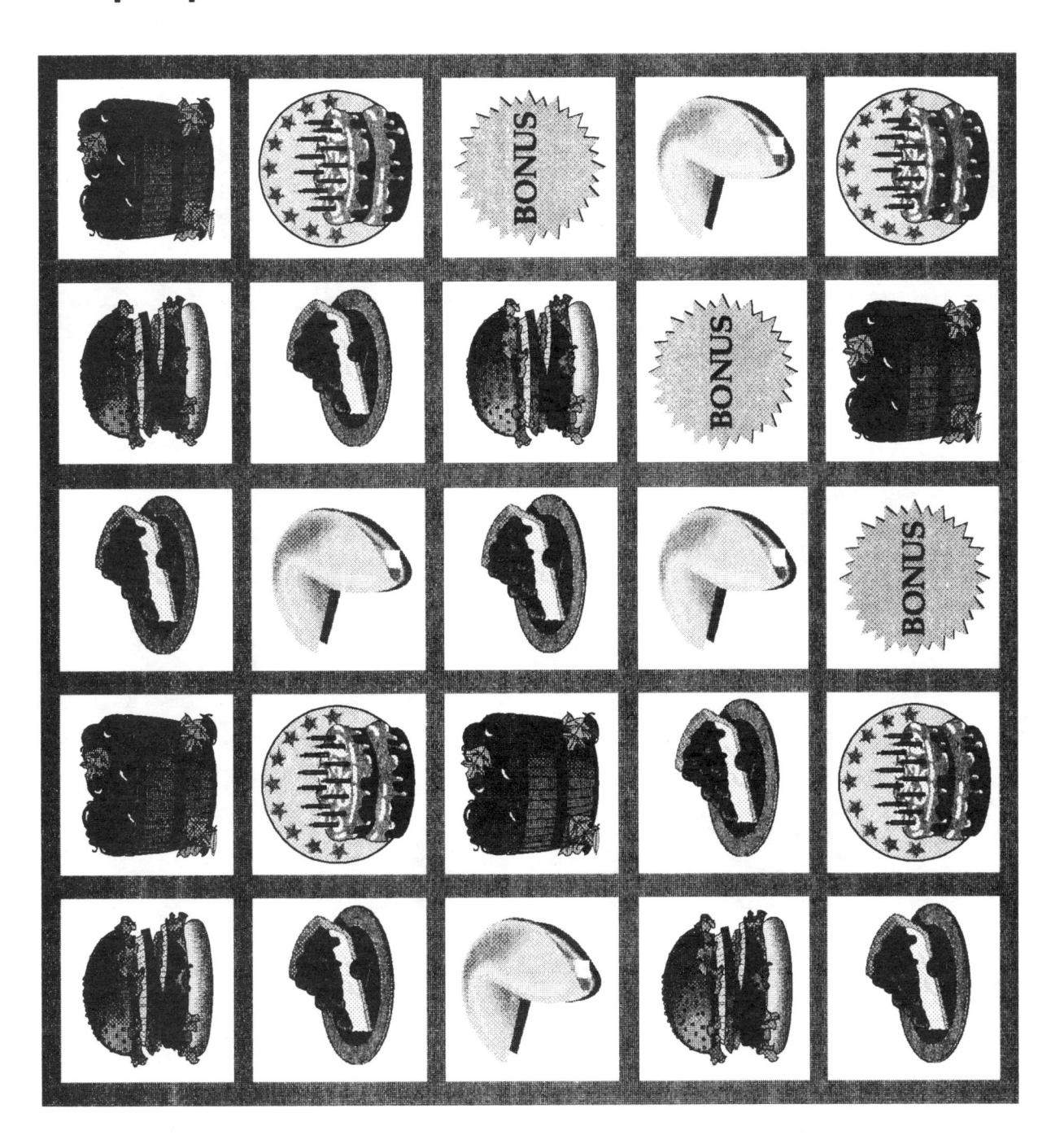

MATCH*IT

MATCH*IT

Space Race

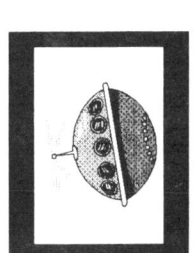

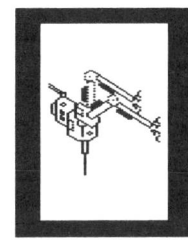

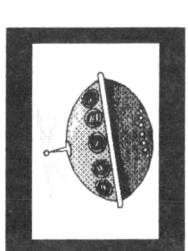

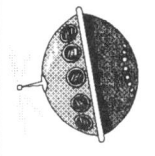

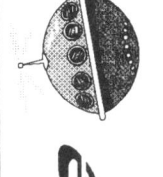

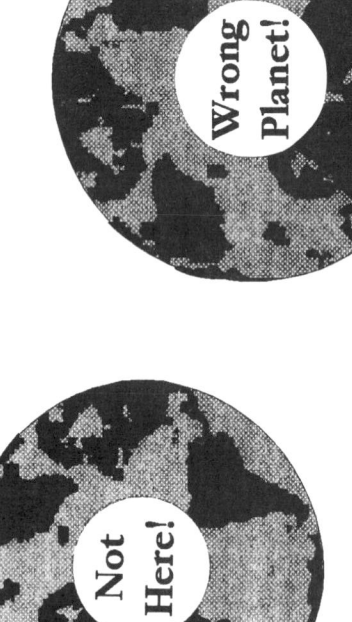

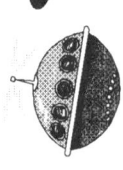

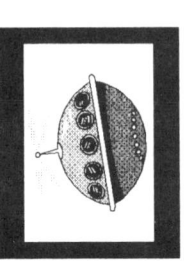

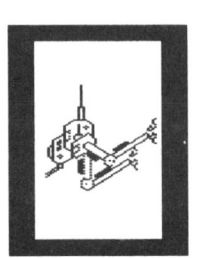

Space Race

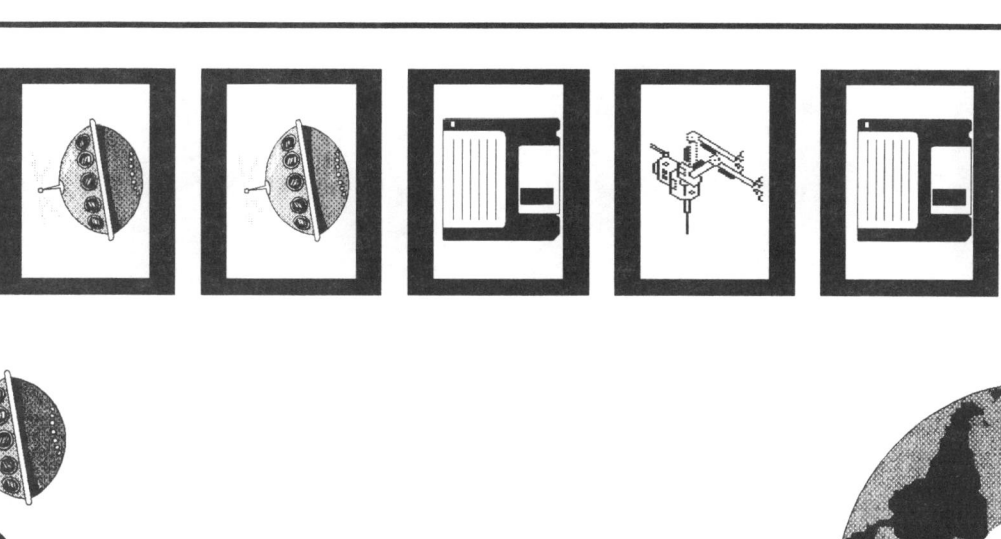

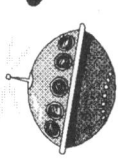

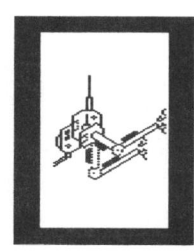

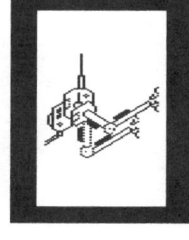

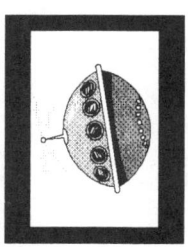

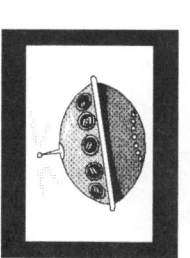

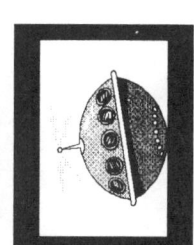

Space Race

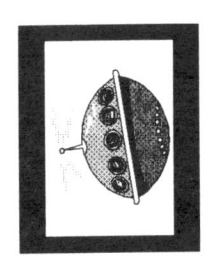

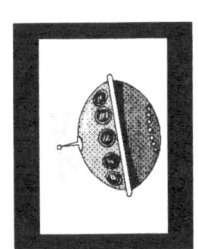

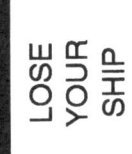

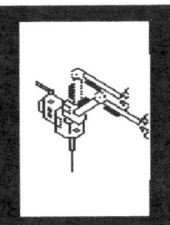

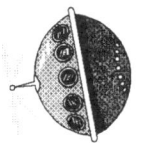

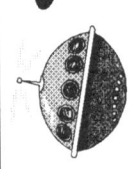

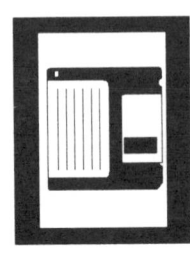

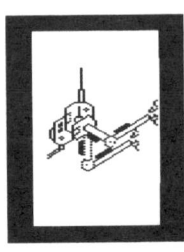

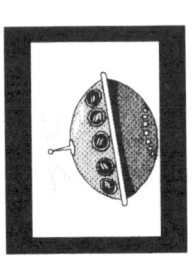

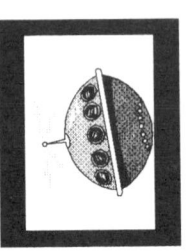

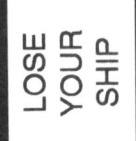

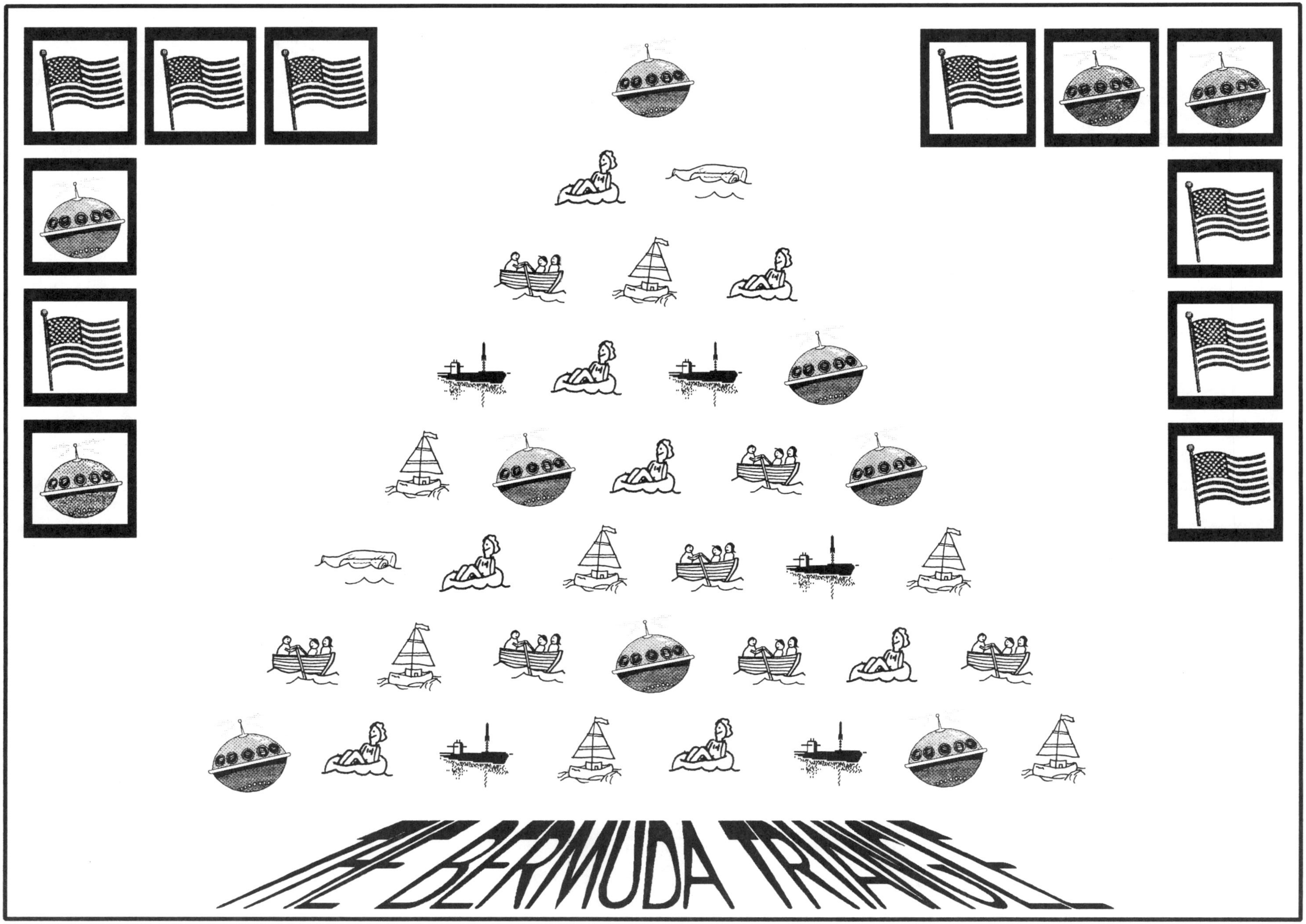
THE BERMUDA TRIANGLE

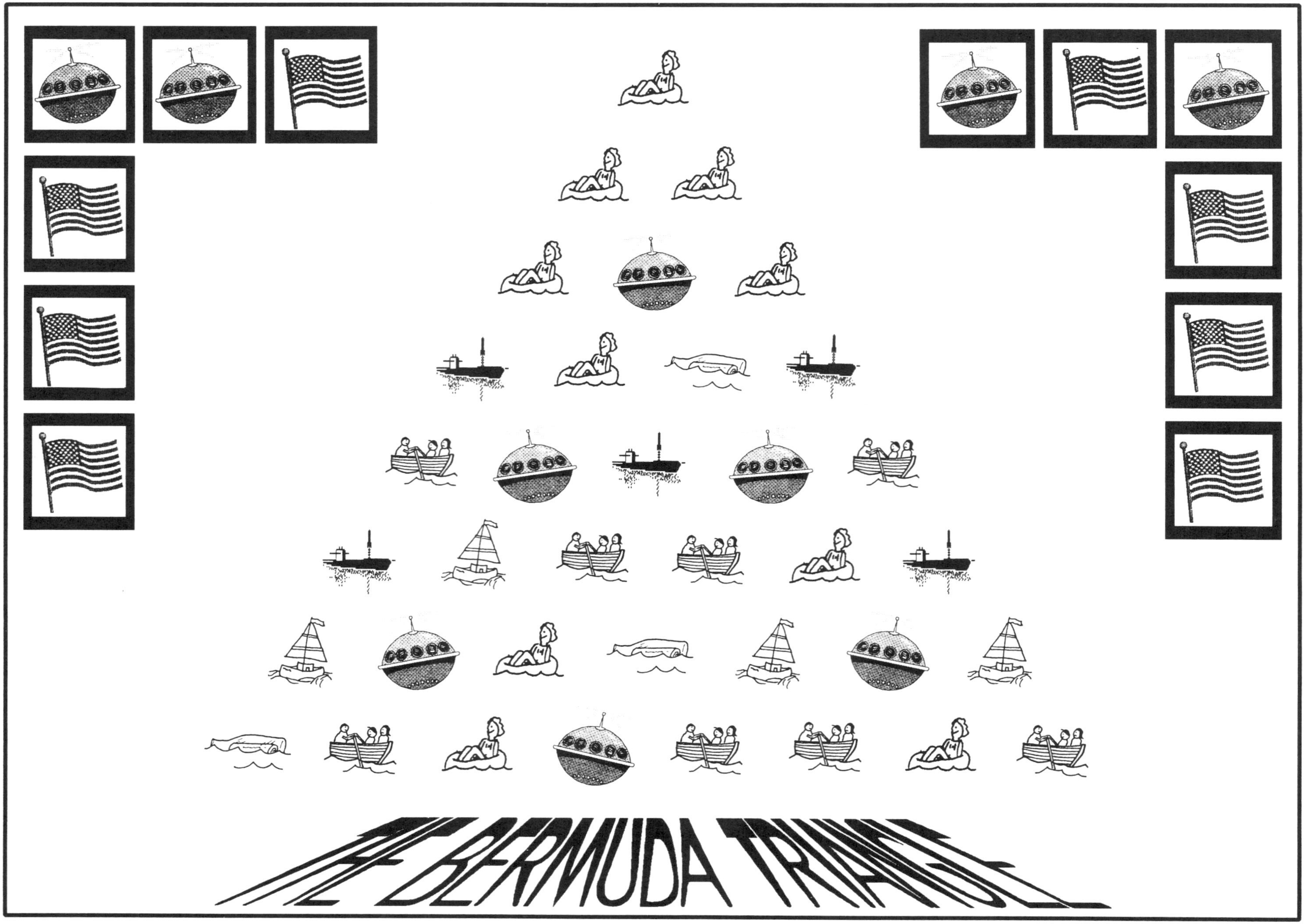
THE BERMUDA TRIANGLE

BERMUDA TRIANGLE

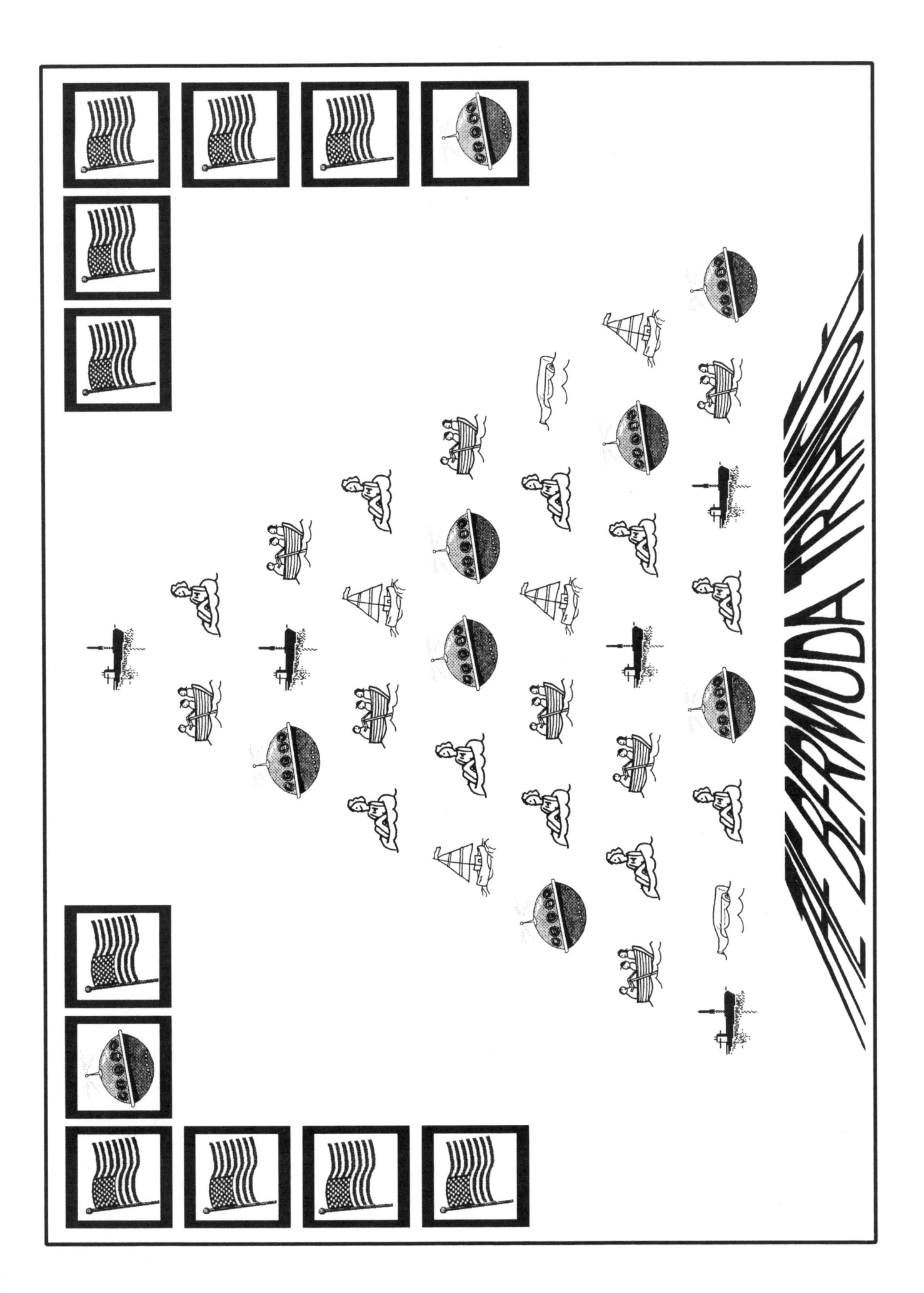

PART THREE

THIRTY-TWO SCRIPTURE PUZZLES THAT YOUR CLASS WILL LOVE

Scripture Puzzles

Looking for another new idea that will spark some enthusiasm in your class of Primaries, Juniors, or Junior Highers? This week, try a Scripture puzzle!

The Scripture puzzles take only four or five minutes of class time, but they can be used to introduce a verse or a Bible study topic in a fun, interesting way. Your students will enjoy them thoroughly. Thirty-two different puzzles are included in this book, along with eight blank puzzles that you can use to custom-make your own!

The idea for the Scripture puzzles came from the Open Air Campaigners. I watched OAC team members use the puzzles with groups of kids in housing projects in Chattanooga and New Orleans. Using colorful poster paints and large brushes, they painted their puzzles on 3' x 4' sheets of newsprint clipped to a large wooden sketch board. I couldn't help but notice how the kids responded with enthusiasm. A team member later used a puzzle in my children's church, and the response was the same.

I was sold, and began to use the puzzles in my ministry with the kids. I've used them at camps, in Christian school chapels, in Sunday school and children's church, and in backyard clubs. I've even used them in my public school assemblies!

But I found that it took too much time to prepare a Scripture puzzle on the sketch board like the Open Air Campaigners did. I'm slow and meticulous in making my visuals, and it took me nearly twenty minutes every time I painted a puzzle before class! Eventually I quit using the puzzles just because they took so much setup time.

And then the Lord showed me a faster, more effective way — do the puzzles on the overhead projector! The puzzles in this book can be made in just a few seconds on any plain paper copier or thermofax machine. File them away carefully, and there's no more setup time whatsoever! Simply lay a puzzle on the overhead, grab a nonpermanent marker pen, turn on the projector, and that's all there is to it! Try a couple of the puzzles that follow, and you and your class will soon be hooked, too.

Looking for another new idea that will spark some enthusiasm in your class of Primaries, Juniors, or Junior Highers? This week, try a Scripture puzzle!

Each puzzle has a different picture, part of which is crossed out when a child misses a letter. The students try to finish the puzzle before the picture is completely crossed out. For example, in puzzles four and twenty, the aliens "steal" a hamburger each time a letter is missed. Simply cross out a burger each time a child guesses an incorrect letter. If all the hamburgers are gone before the students solve the puzzle, you win and the students lose! In puzzles eight and eighteen, the fuse burns closer to the bomb each time a student chooses an incorrect letter. In puzzles sixteen and twenty-seven, a dinosaur becomes "extinct" for each letter missed. The students will do their best to keep you from winning!

Let's pop in on a Junior class to see how the puzzles are played. As we open the classroom door, the teacher, a friendly, middle-aged woman, has just turned on her overhead projector. She flashes us a smile as we quietly slip into seats in the back of the room, but the students haven't even noticed our arrival. All eyes are on Mrs. McCorkle, or "Mrs. Mac," as she is affectionately called by her Juniors.

"Today, class, we have another Scripture puzzle! The secret message in the puzzle is actually a Scripture verse, and we're going to discover the secret message one letter at a time! It's boys against the girls!"

Mrs. Mac's voice has a cheerful, almost musical quality to it, and her eyes sparkle with excitement as she talks. The kids lean forward in anticipation. It's easy to see why this enthusiastic woman is so popular with the Juniors of the First Church.

"If you'd like to take a guess at one of the letters in our puzzle, simply raise your hand and I will call on you. If you choose a correct letter, I will put your letter in the puzzle the number of times it appears, and I will give your team that number of points. We will alternate back and forth between the boys and the girls. When the puzzle is solved, the team with the highest score wins!

"On the screen you see a picture of a scrumptious-looking piece of blueberry cheesecake. Wouldn't you just love to have a bite or two of that?" She licks her lips and rolls her eyes, and the kids nod in agreement.

"The piece of cheesecake is yours! All yours!" Mrs. Mac spreads her expressive hands wide and her warm smile broadens even further. "But — if you give me a letter that is

The students will do their best to keep you from winning!

not in the puzzle, I'm gonna take a bite out of your cheesecake! And if I finish the cheesecake before you finish the message in the Scripture puzzle, the boys lose! And the girls lose! And guess who wins?"

"You!" the kids reply, groaning in mock dismay.

"Ready? Let's begin the puzzle. This week, the boys go first!"

Hands shoot up all over the classroom, and Mrs. Mac chooses a timid-looking boy on the second row. "Justin!"

"S!" Justin answers.

"S. Hmmm, let's see." The teacher uncaps a nonpermanent overhead pen and scans across the blanks in the puzzle. "There's one for the boys," she says as she fills in a letter S, "and two, and three!" The pen dashes in two more S's, and the boys cheer as Mrs. Mac records the score with three slashes of the pen on the "B" side of the score box in the corner of the transparency.

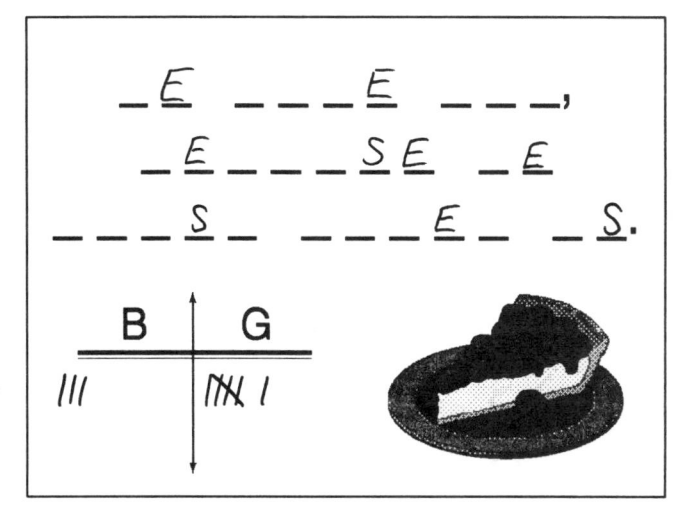

"Okay, girls! Let's have a letter, and see if you can catch up with these boys! Right now the score stands at three to nothing!"

She chooses a girl on the end of the front row who looks as though she will burst if she is not chosen. "Emily!"

Emily is so delighted at being chosen that she actually jumps out of her chair. "E!" she calls.

Mrs. Mac hides a smile as she replies, "Let's save that one for the boys' team, Emily!"

The student takes her seriously. "Mrs. Mac! That's not fair!" But the pen is already filling in the E's, and the student relaxes with a grin as she realizes that she was being teased.

"There's four, and five, and six! Six points for the girls!" The girls cheer as six quick slashes of the pen record their score.

We stay just long enough to figure out the verse for ourselves — "We love him, because he first loved us." (I John 4:19) As we slip quietly from the room, Mrs. Mac gives us a friendly wink, but the kids don't even notice. They're too engrossed in the puzzle.

After our two-minute visit to Mrs. Mac's Junior class, you're convinced that you need to start using Scripture puzzles with your own class. As we walk back down the hall, you glance over at me, your eyes sparkling with excitement. "Did you see the way the kids went for the puzzle? They were really excited!"

I shrug casually. "They always do."

"But these were Juniors! They acted like they were actually excited about being in Sunday school!"

I let just a glimmer of a smile cross my face. "They were in Mrs. Mac's class."

"I know," you reply, with a bit of a frown creasing your brow. You fall silent.

"What are you thinking about?"

You look up, as if for just a moment you had forgotten that I was even there. "Do you think that I could do it, too?"

"Do what?"

"Do you think that I could get that kind of excitement from my Juniors? Do you think I could learn to use Scripture puzzles like Mrs. Mac does?"

"I'm sure you could."

You look at me with a puzzled expression. "But how do I get started?"

"Well," I reply with a smile, "if you'll glance at the bottom of this page from where we're standing now, you'll see some suggestions for the most effective ways to use the puzzles. And the pages beyond that are filled with puzzle after puzzle that you can make yourself, in seconds, on any plain paper copier or thermofax machine."

You nod, encouraged and pleased. "If only I can show the enthusiasm and warmth that Mrs. Mac did…"

Suggestions for Using the Scripture Puzzles

1. Do not use the Scripture puzzles just as time fillers. Use them to introduce your topic of study for the day or to intro-

duce a memory verse. For instance, if you are teaching a lesson on the importance of faith, use puzzles nine or twelve. If you are teaching on love, use puzzles one or sixteen. If you cannot find an appropriate puzzle for a particular class period, use one of the blank puzzles (numbers thirty-three through forty on pages 185-192) and make your own.

2. Alternate from one team to the other throughout the entire puzzle. While you may not always do this during a Bible game, it is important that you do so during the puzzles.

3. Call only on students who are orderly, seated, and quietly (though eagerly) raising their hands.

4. Fill in the blanks with upper-case lettering. Your puzzle will look neat and uniform, and you won't have to worry about details such as forgetting to capitalize proper nouns.

5. Make your letters as large as possible, ½"-¾" high.

6. Keep score by putting large "slash marks" on the appropriate sides of the score box. Group them in fives, with the fifth mark placed diagonally across the other four.

7. The score box is labeled "B" and "G" for "boys" and "girls." If you do not have a coed class, the "B" and "G" can stand for two teams named "Best" and "Greatest," "Bears" and "Giants," or "Buffaloes" and "Giraffes."

8. If a child guesses a letter that is already in the puzzle, or has already been rejected, simply say, "We already have an R. Choose another letter." Let the same child try again.

9. If a child guesses "X" or "Z" to purposely try to throw the game, simply say, "I need a serious guess," and choose another student.

10. If a student asks if she may solve the puzzle, respond with, "No, don't solve it. Choose the letter that has the most points for your team!" If they begin to blurt out the solution to the puzzle, immediately interrupt with, "Wait! Don't solve it! Choose the letter that has..."

11. Use nonpermanent overhead markers. After class, wet a tissue and wipe the ink from the transparency, then file it for use again next year. Label the file folder with the Scripture reference and the first two or three words of the verse.

12. Do not use Scripture puzzles every week. Although they are fun, your students will tire of them if they are

overused. Once or twice a month is enough. Your class needs *variety!*

13. If you have access to a thermofax machine and color image film, make two- and three-color puzzle transparencies. Do the simple color separation described on page 20. You can use combinations of red, purple, green, blue, and black. Before making the transparency, decide what color pen you are going to use in class. Do not use that color when making the transparency.

14. If you have a small class or do not have access to an overhead projector, simply photocopy the puzzle masters in the book and use them as table top puzzles. Another option is to enlarge them on a copier and pin them to the wall or flannelboard. Twelve to fifteen kids could play the puzzle this way.

15. Puzzles thirty-three through forty (pages 185 through 192) are blank. They are designed for you to custom-make your own Scripture puzzles. If you cannot find a puzzle with the verse you want, use one of these to make your own. Here's how.

Let's say that I want a puzzle that says, "In every thing give thanks: for this is the will of God." (I Thessalonians 5:18) I glance through puzzles one through thirty-two, but I cannot find that verse. I will have to make my own puzzle.

I select puzzle number thirty-four (cheesecake), which has four lines of blanks, sixteen to a line, and make a photocopy to use as a master for my transparency. I begin by dividing the verse into four segments, each of which will fit on one line of the puzzle — "In every thing/give thanks:/for this is the/will of God."

Line 1 — "In every thing" — has fourteen letters and spaces, and there are sixteen blanks on the first line of the puzzle. By eliminating the first and sixteenth blank, I will center the first line of the puzzle. There is a space after "in" and a space after "every," so I need to eliminate the fourth and tenth blank as well. Using correction fluid, I "white out" the first, fourth, tenth, and sixteenth blanks, and the first line of my puzzle is completed.

Line 2 — "give thanks:" — takes twelve spaces counting the colon, so I white out the first two and last two blanks on the second line. I white out the seventh blank for my space between the words, then the fourteenth. With a black felt-tip pen, I place a colon in the empty space where the fourteenth blank had been.

For line three — "for this is the" — I remove blanks one, five, ten and thirteen. This line is half a blank off-center, but I realize that no one will notice. On line four — "will of God." — I eliminate blanks one, two, seven, ten, fourteen, fifteen, and sixteen. With my felt-tip marker, I place a period where blank fourteen had been.

My puzzle master is finished. It's that easy. I make a photocopy and pencil in the words to check the spacing on each line. Once I am satisfied that everything is correct, I run a transparency. My new Scripture puzzle is ready for class!

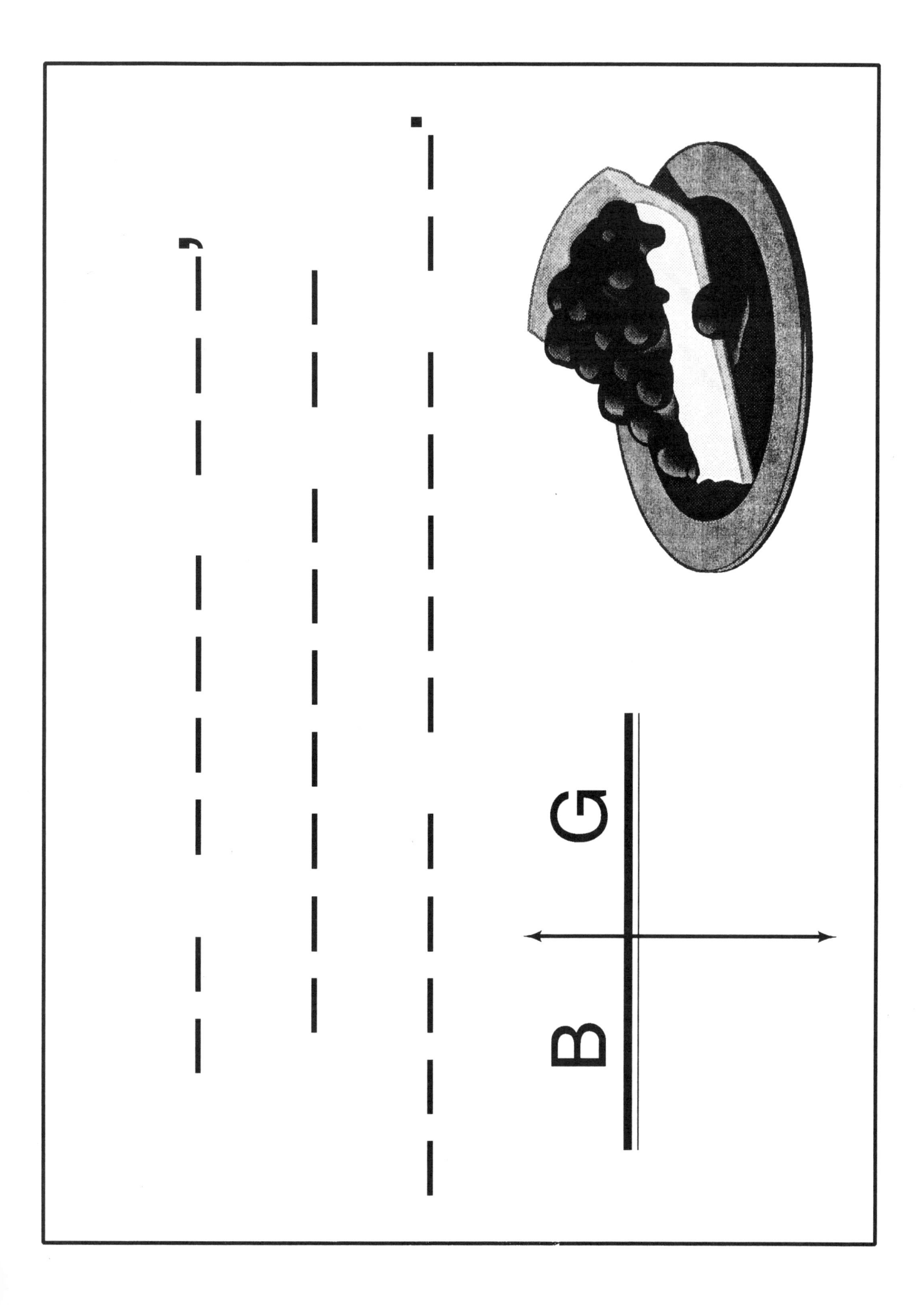

B G

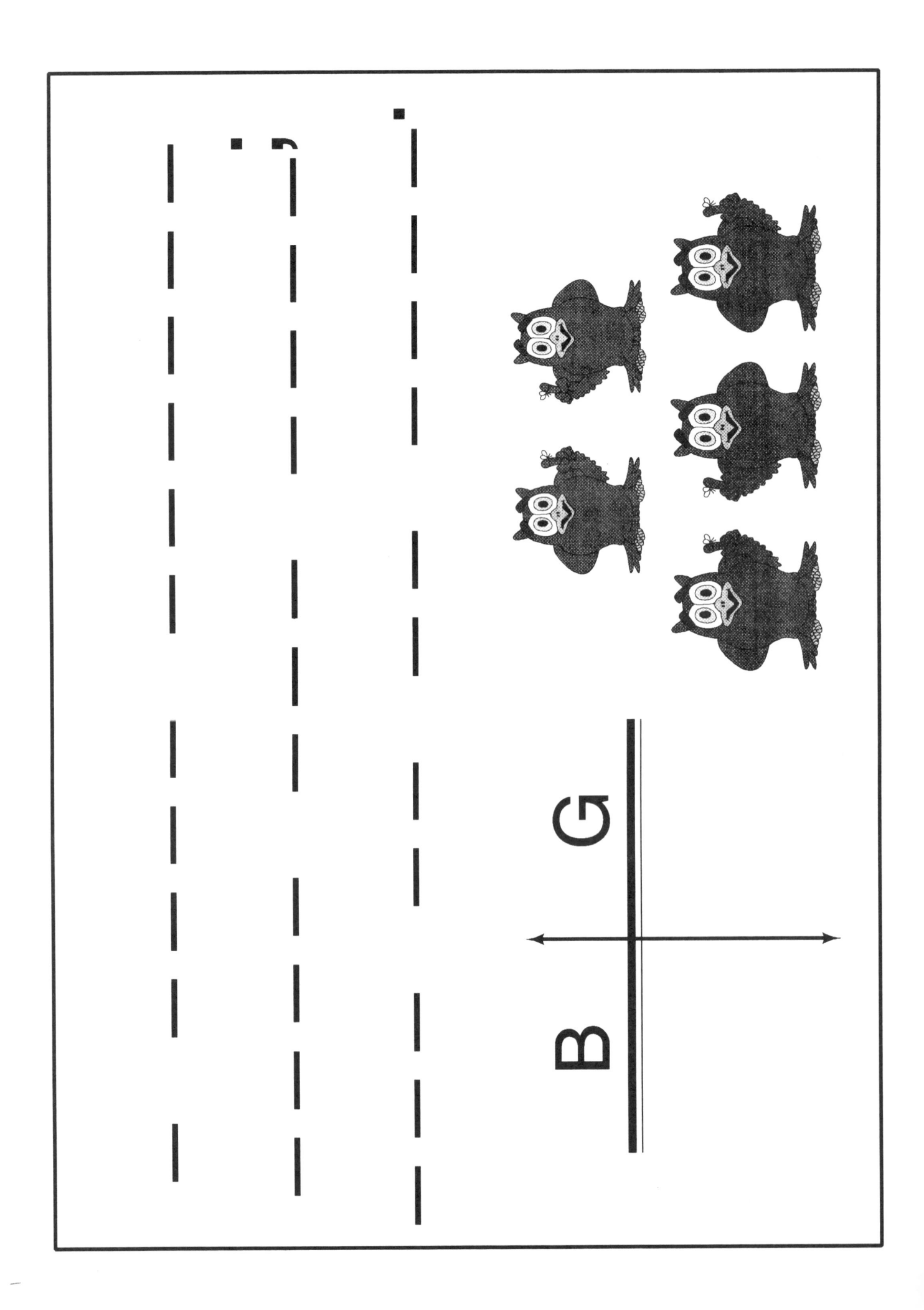

B G

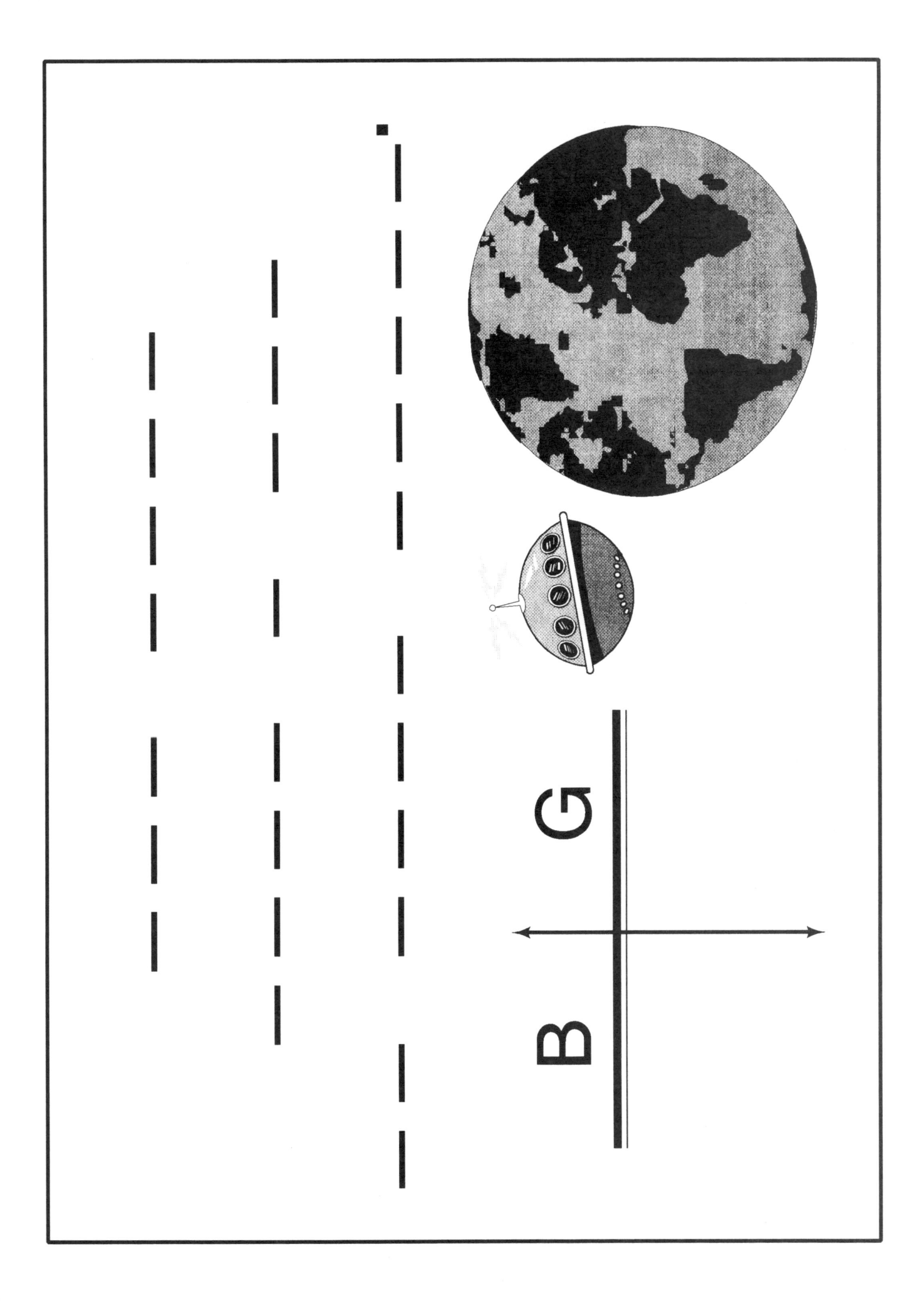

B G

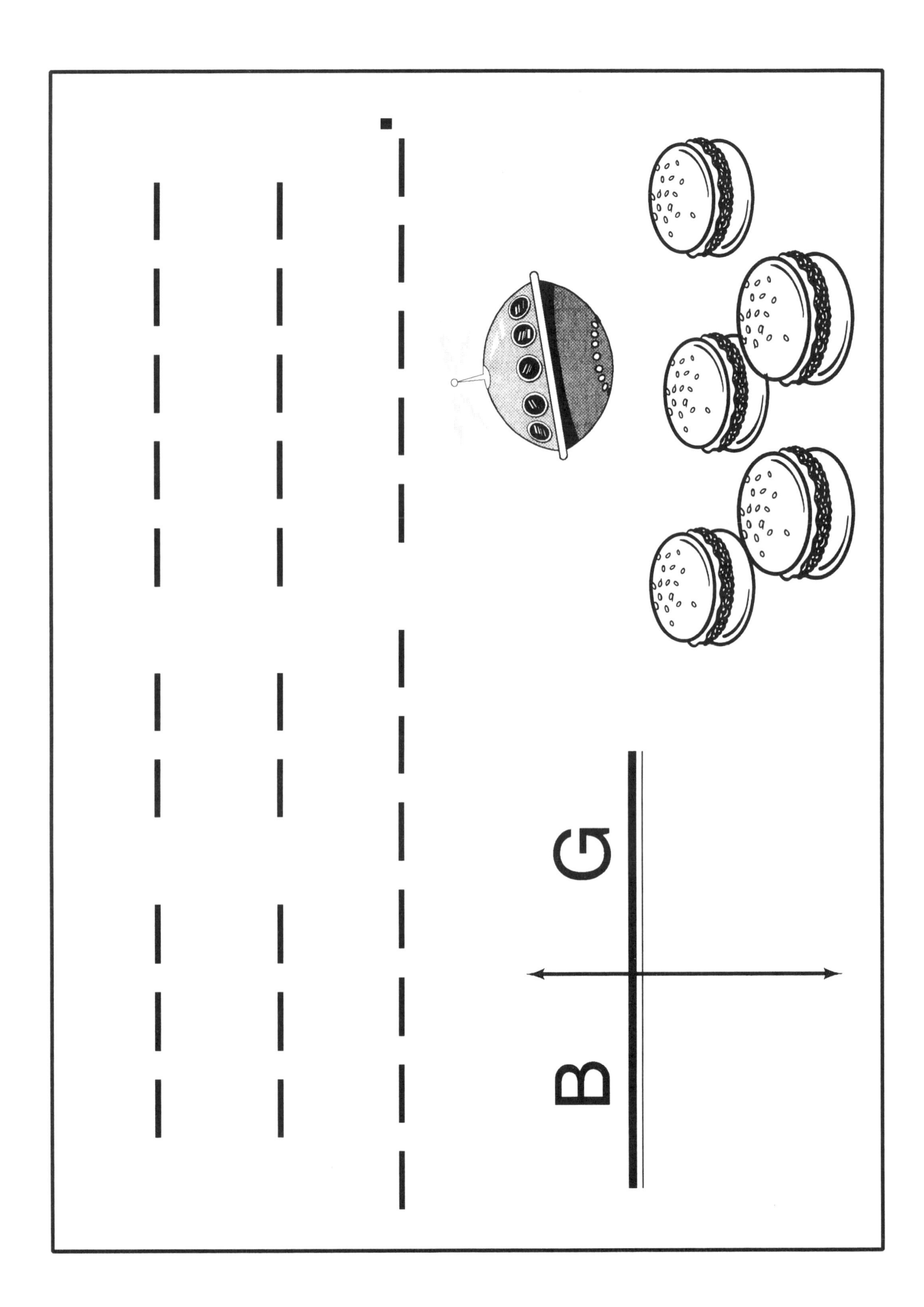

B G

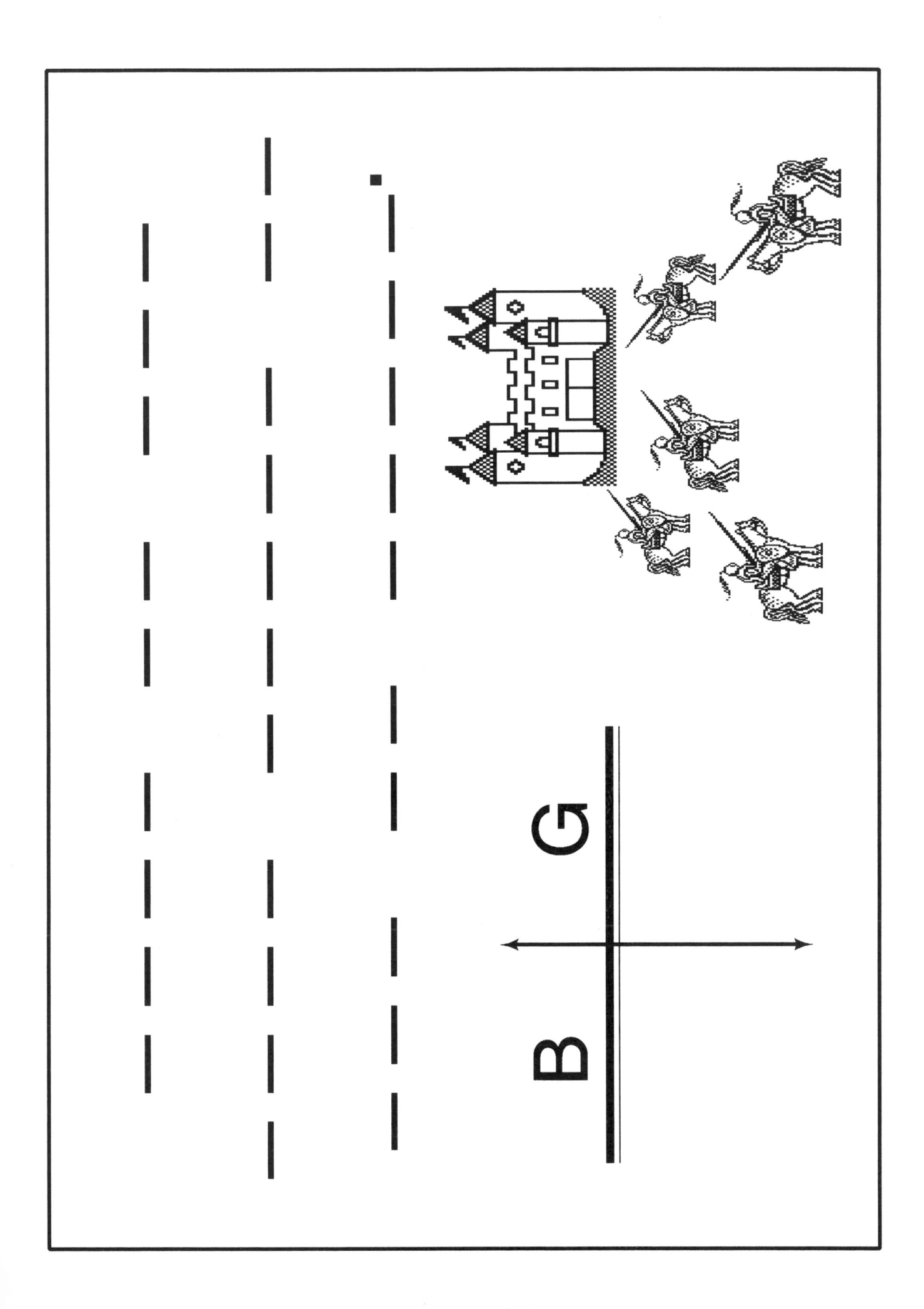

B | G

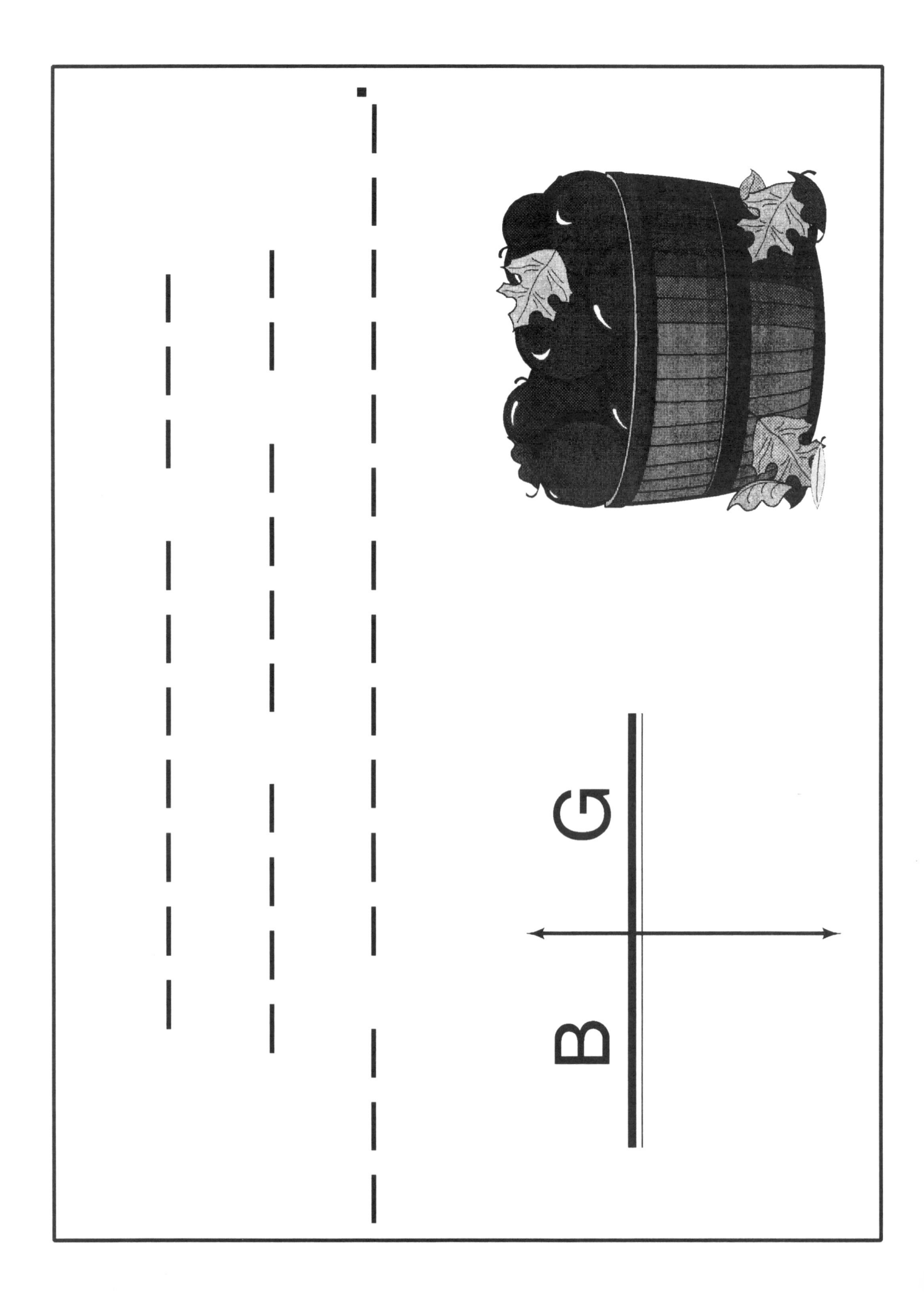

B G

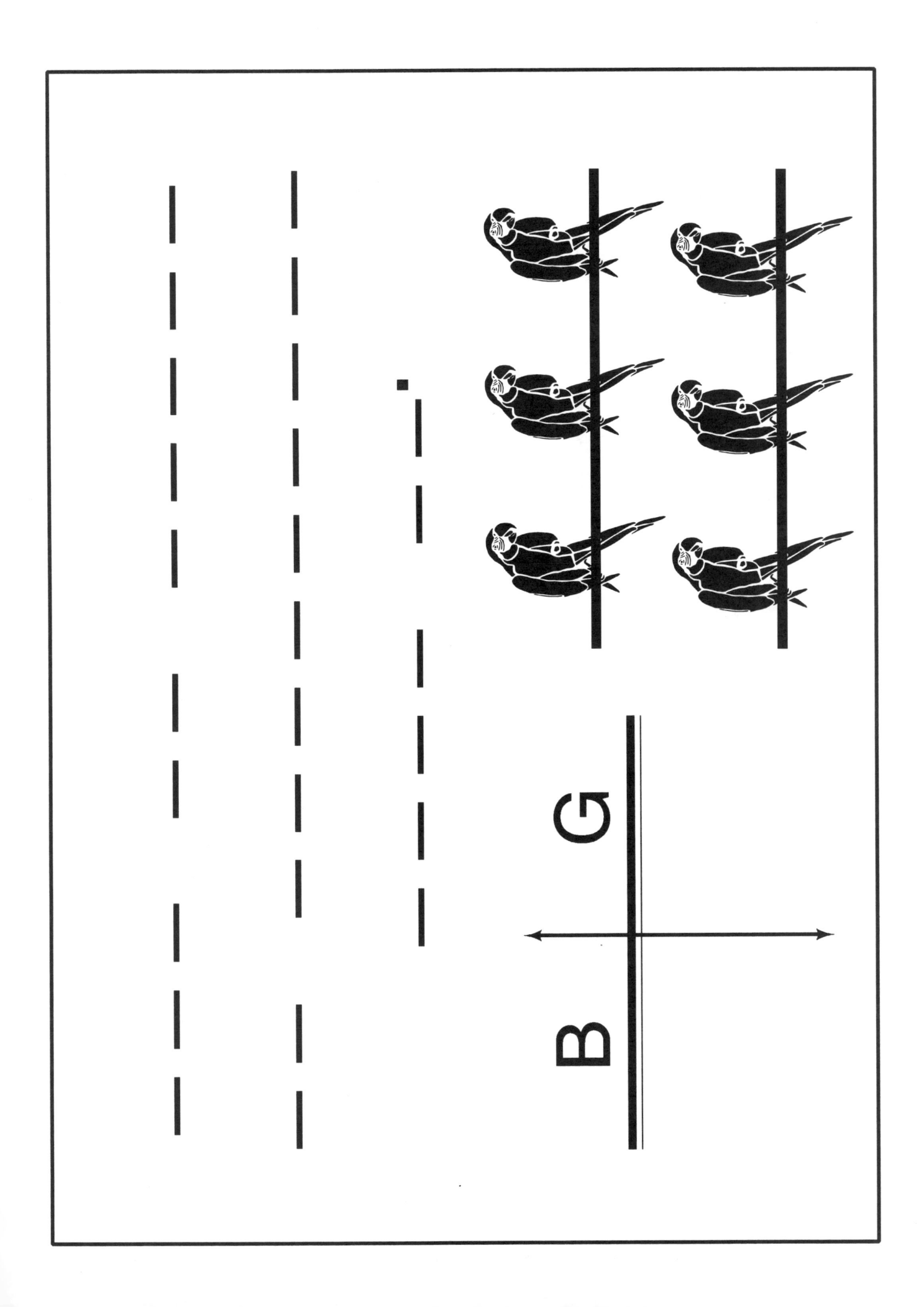

B G

_ _ _ _   _ _   _ _ _ _ _

_ _ _   _ _ _ _ _ _ _

_ _   _ _ _.

B	G

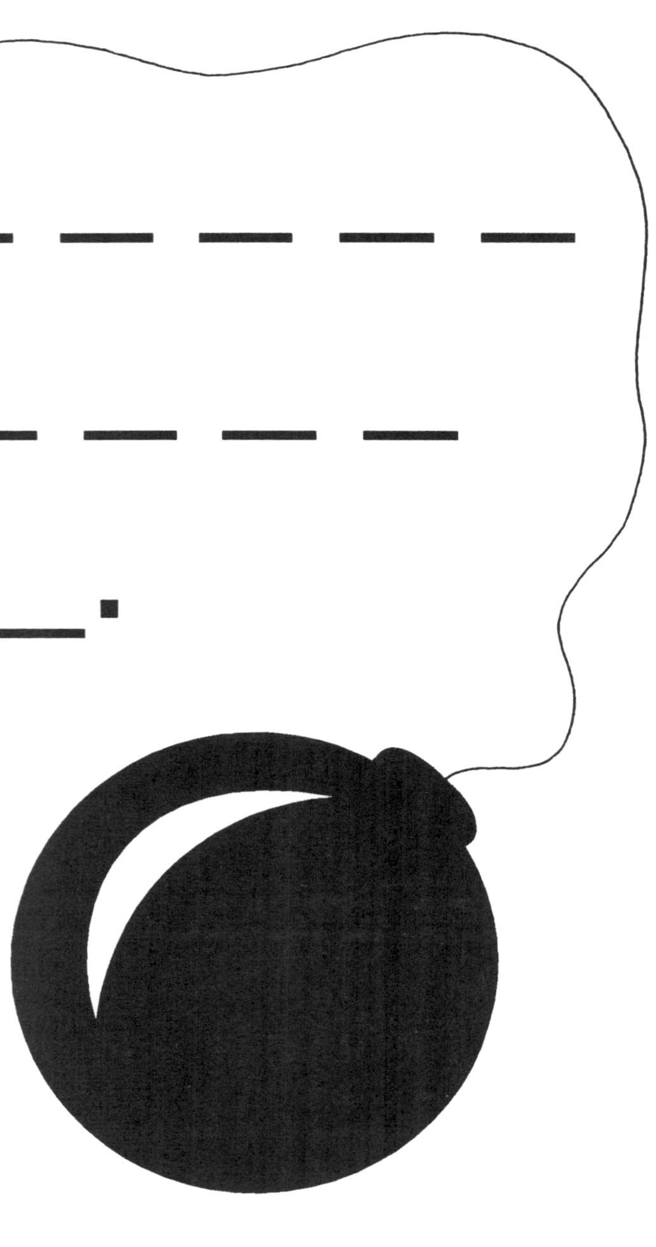

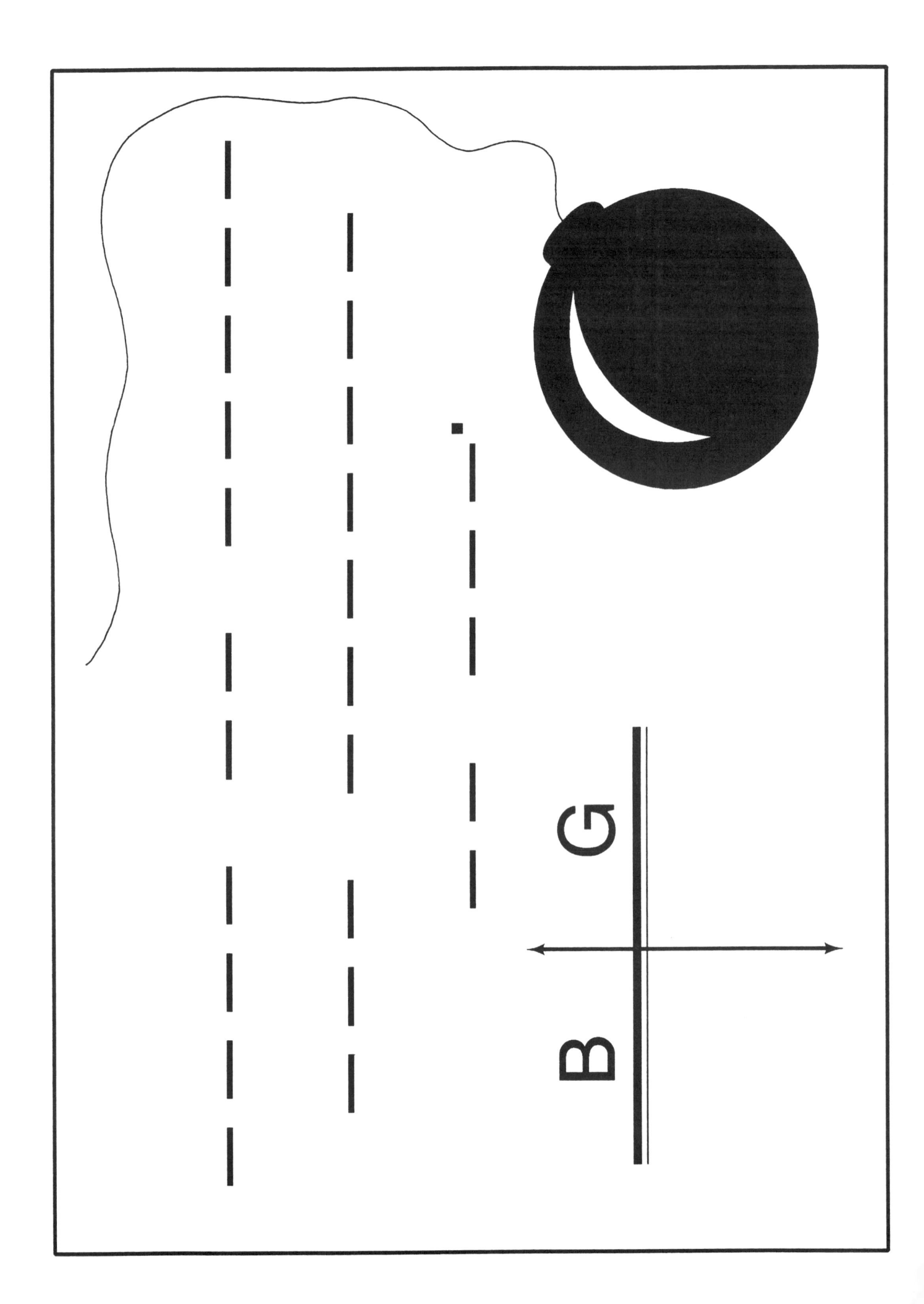

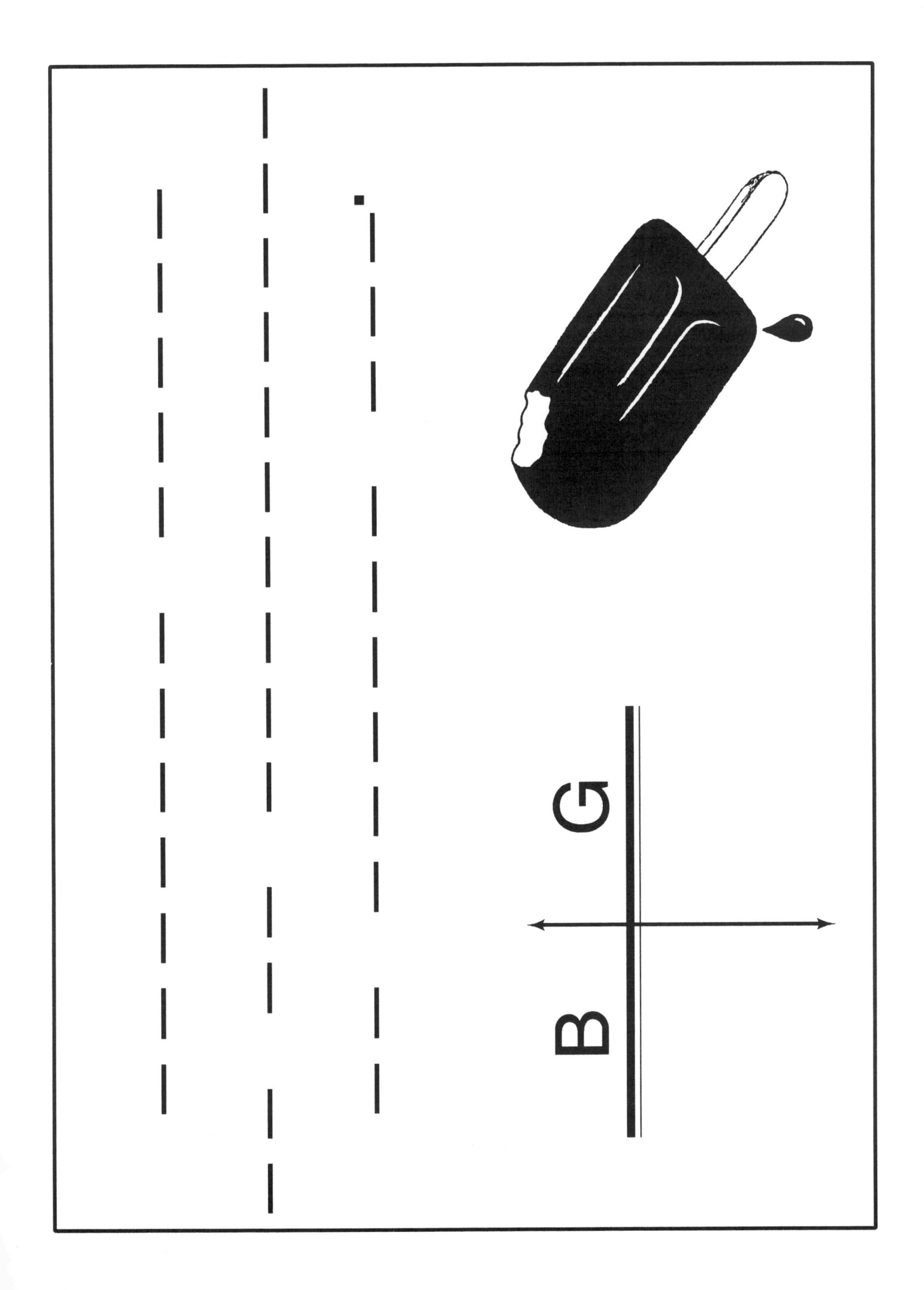

B G

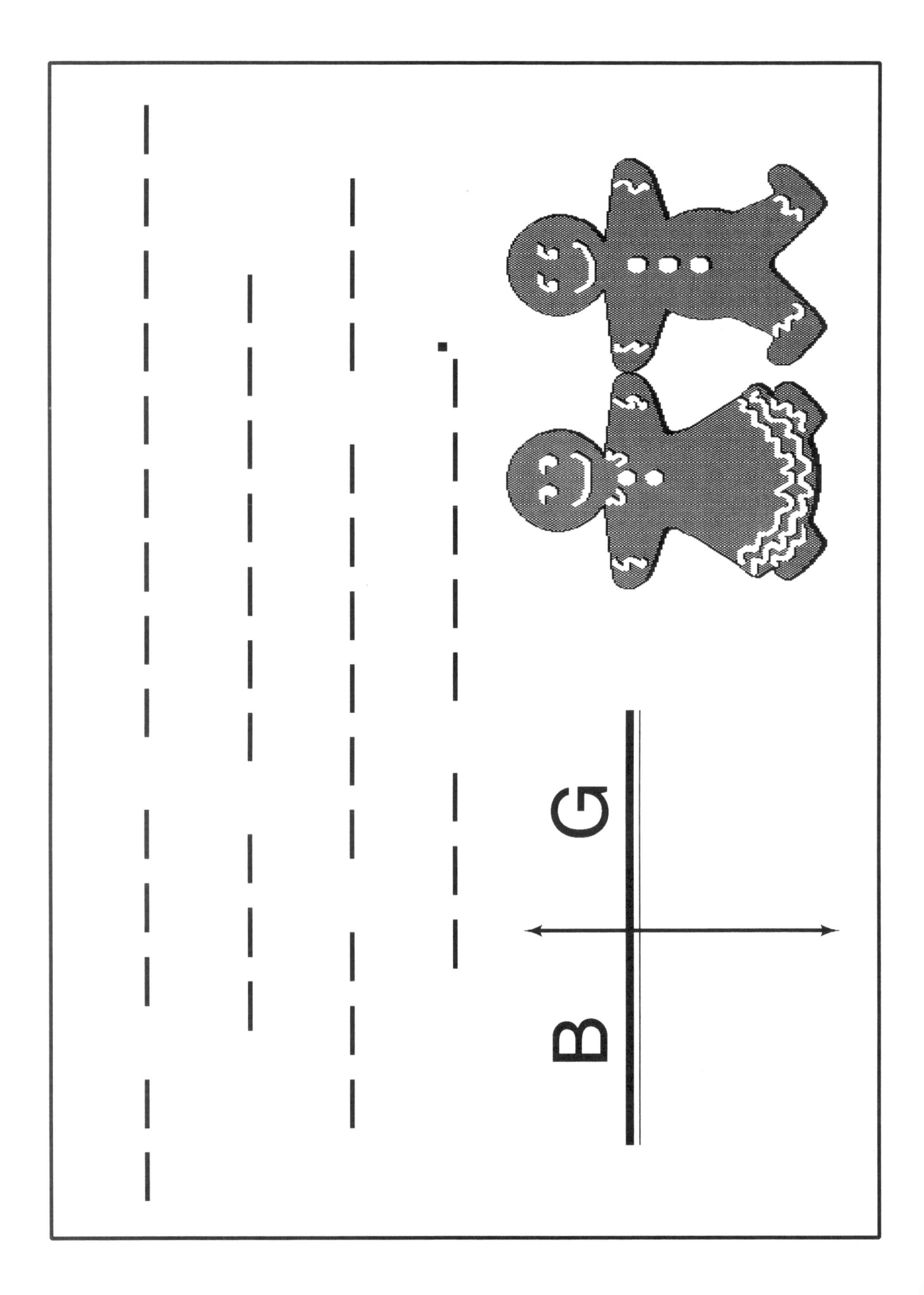

B G

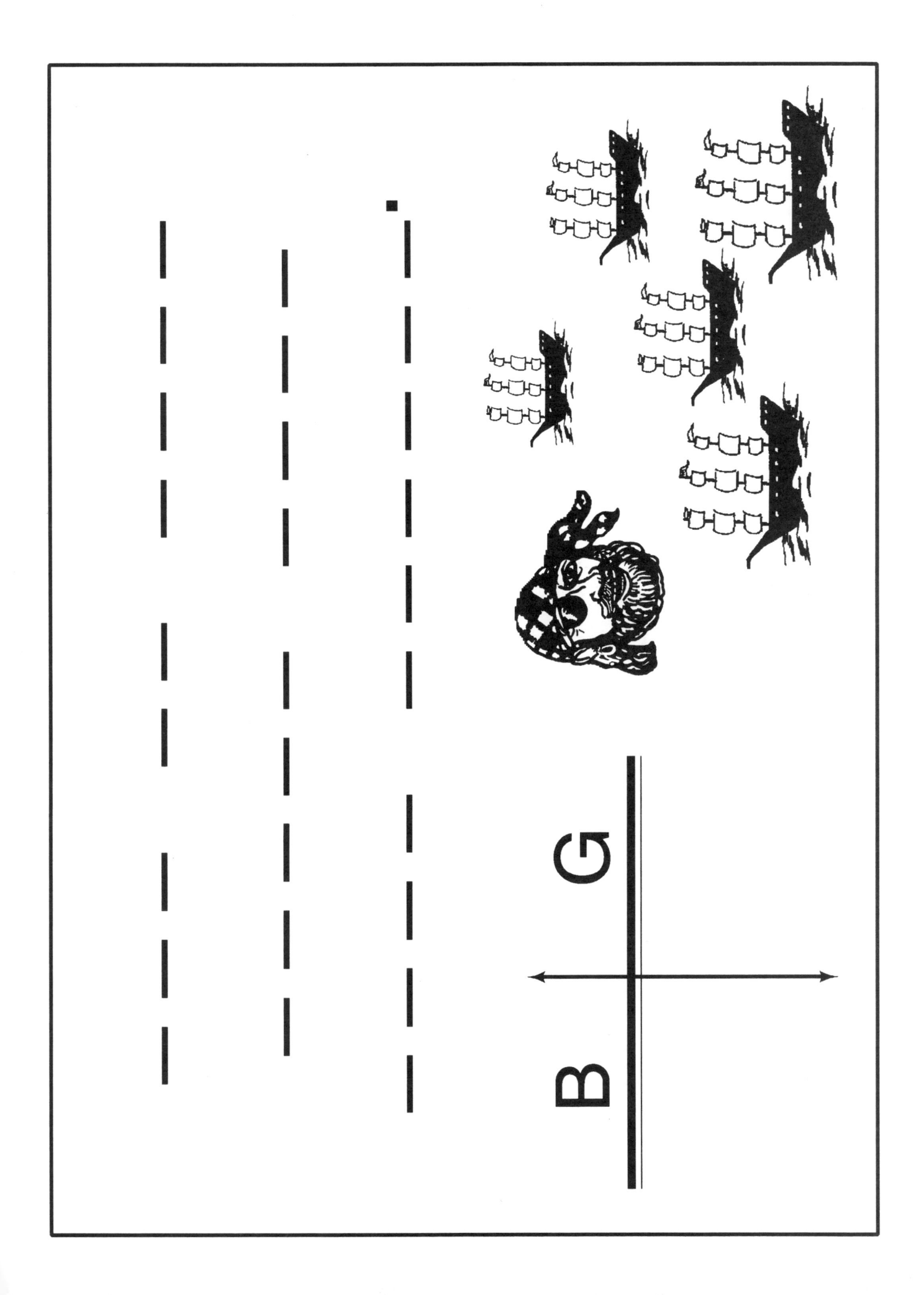

B | G

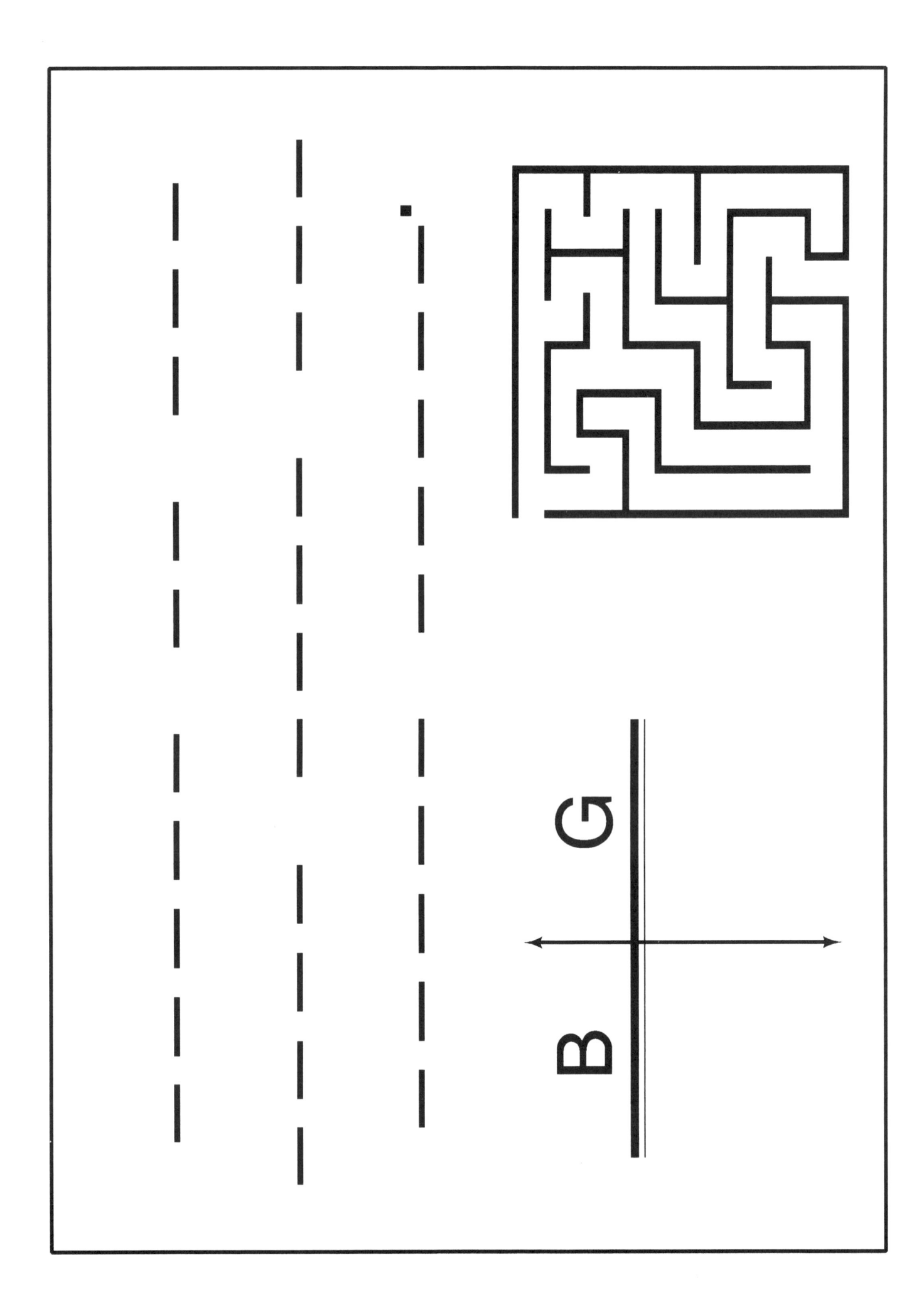

B | G

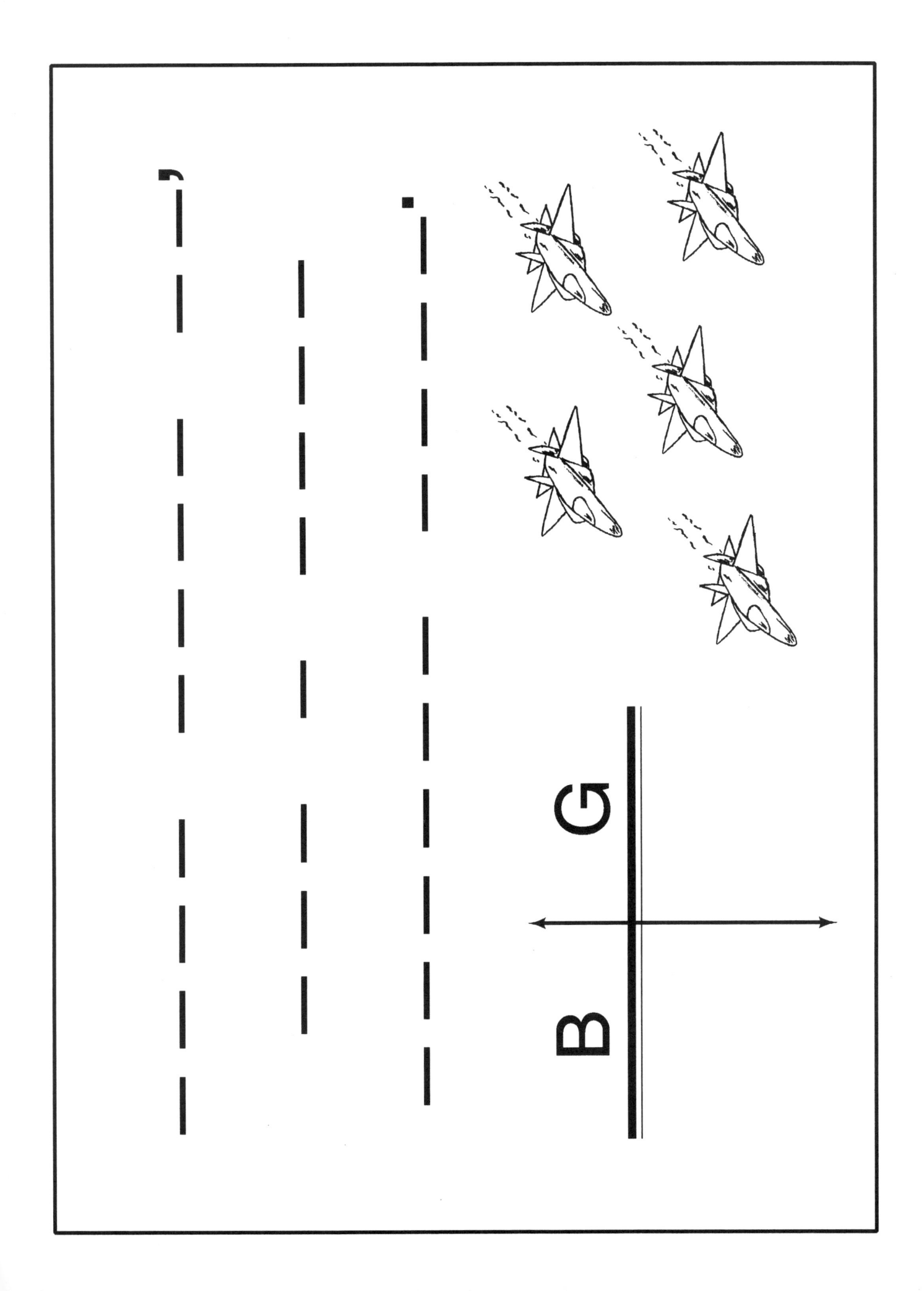

B G

_ _ _ _   _ _ _ _   _,

"

_ _ _ _   _ _   _,

"

_ _ _ _   _ _.

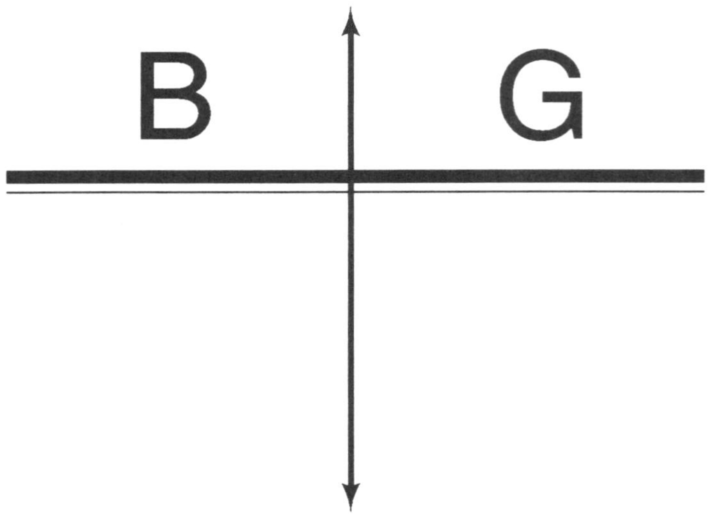
B
G

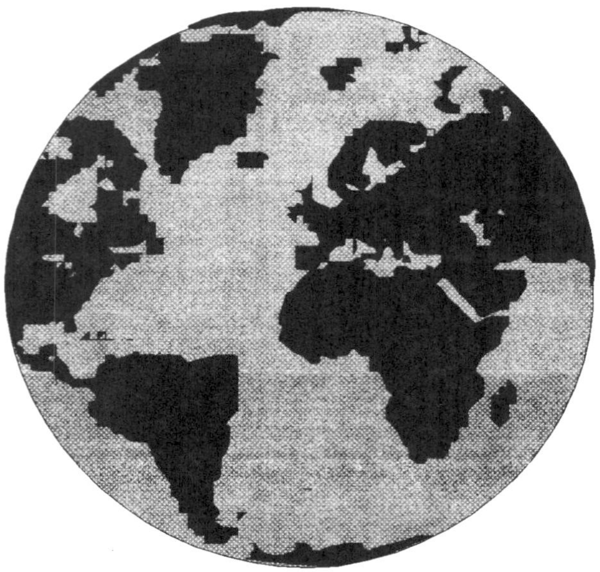

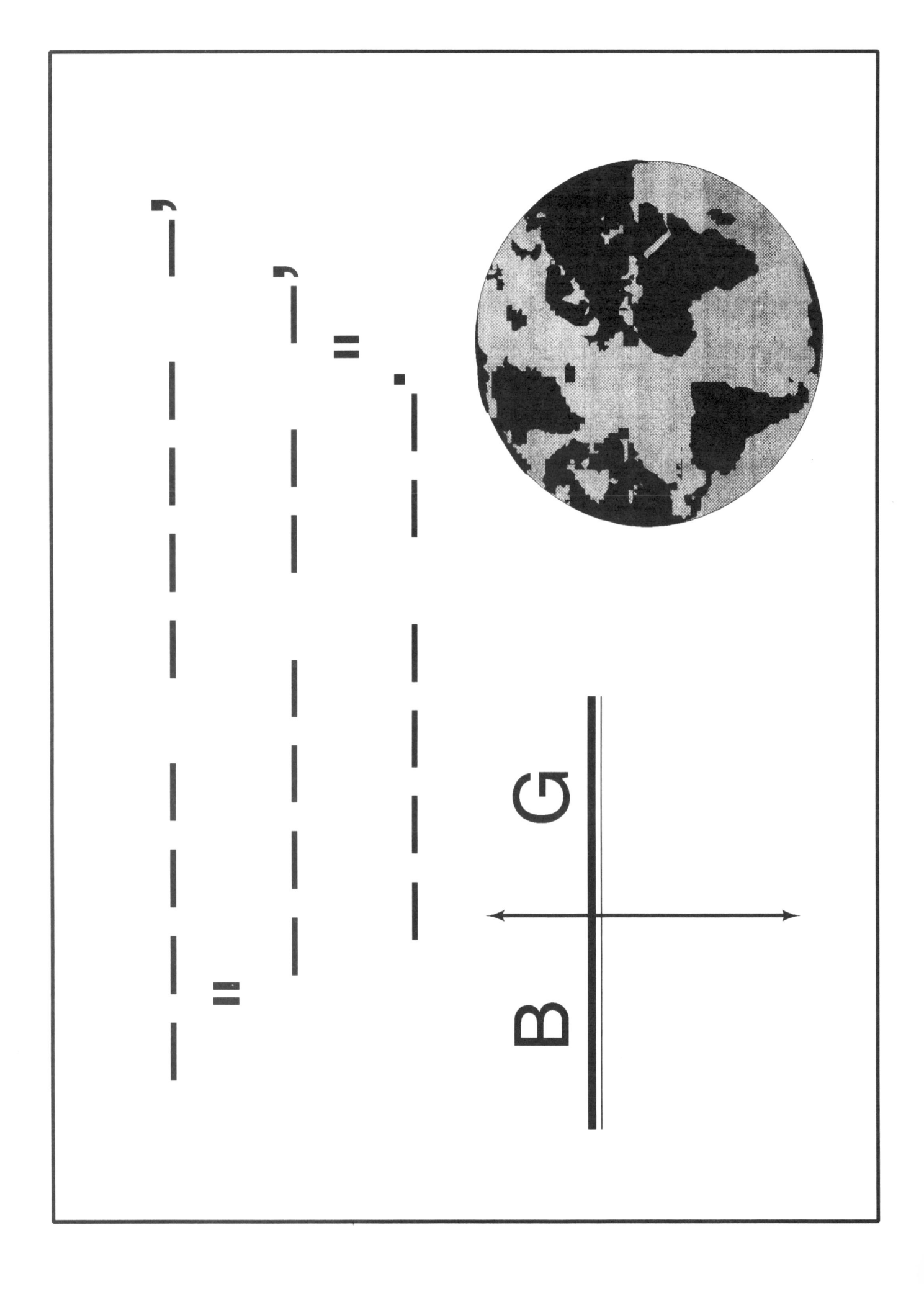

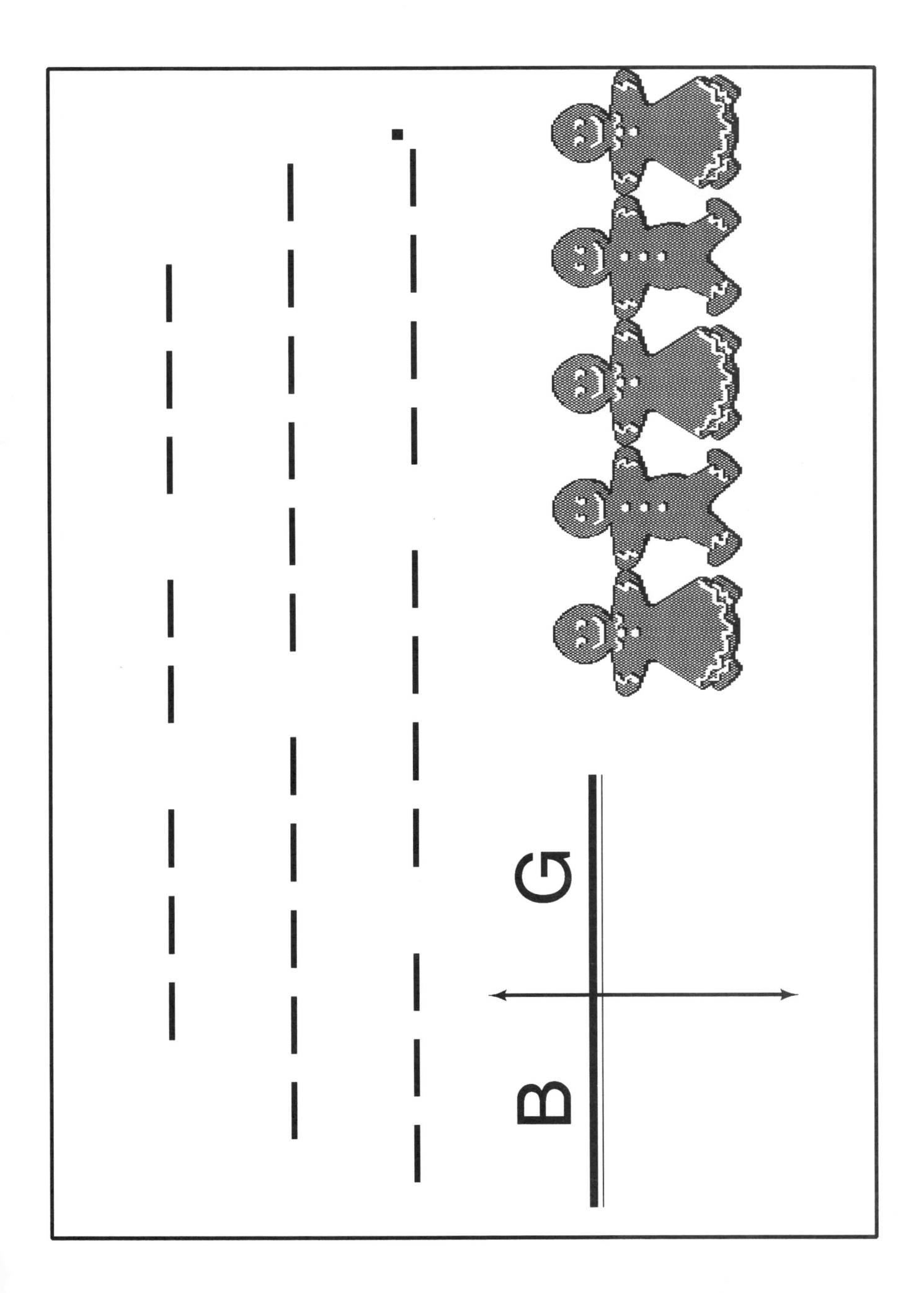

B | G

BIG

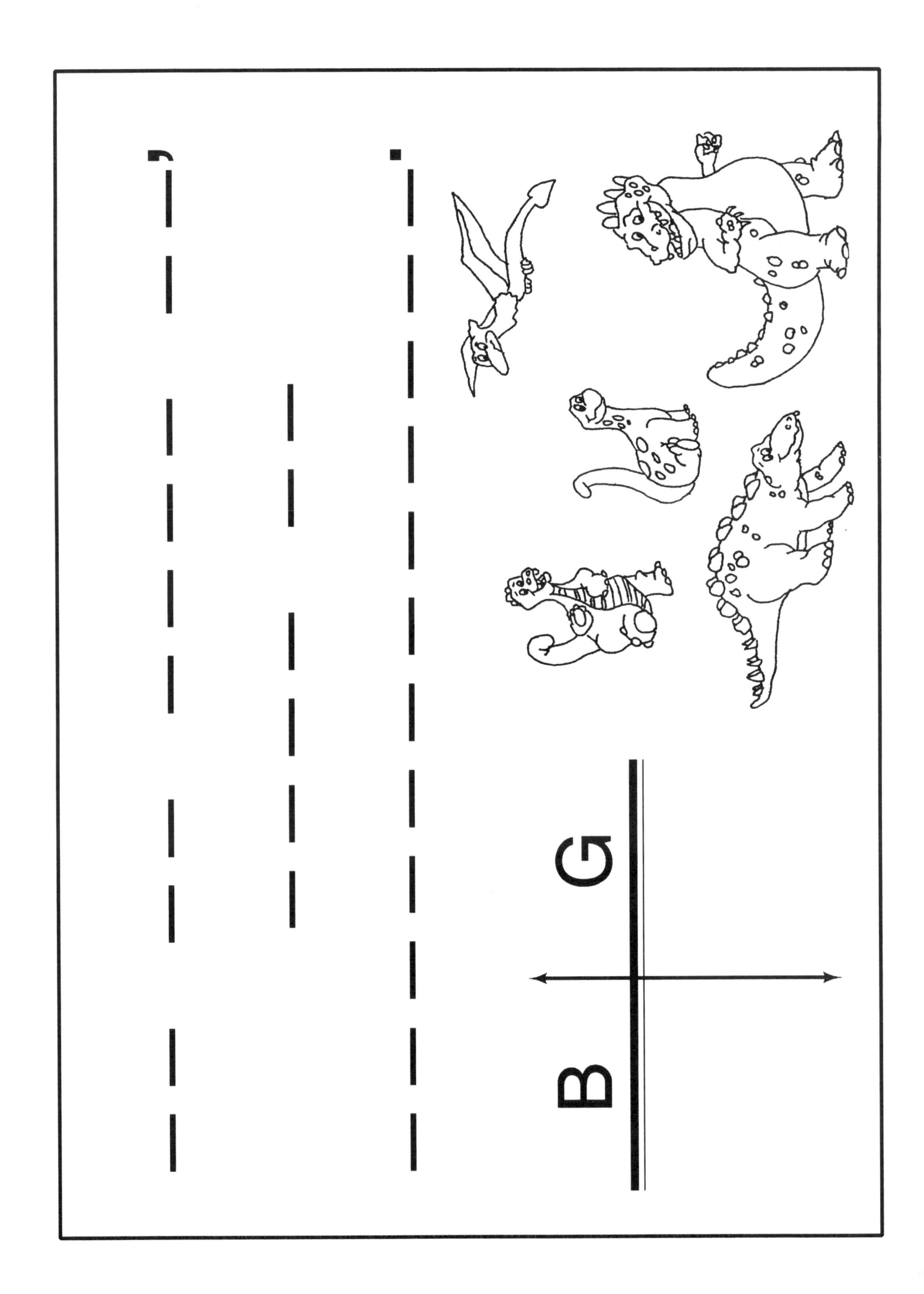

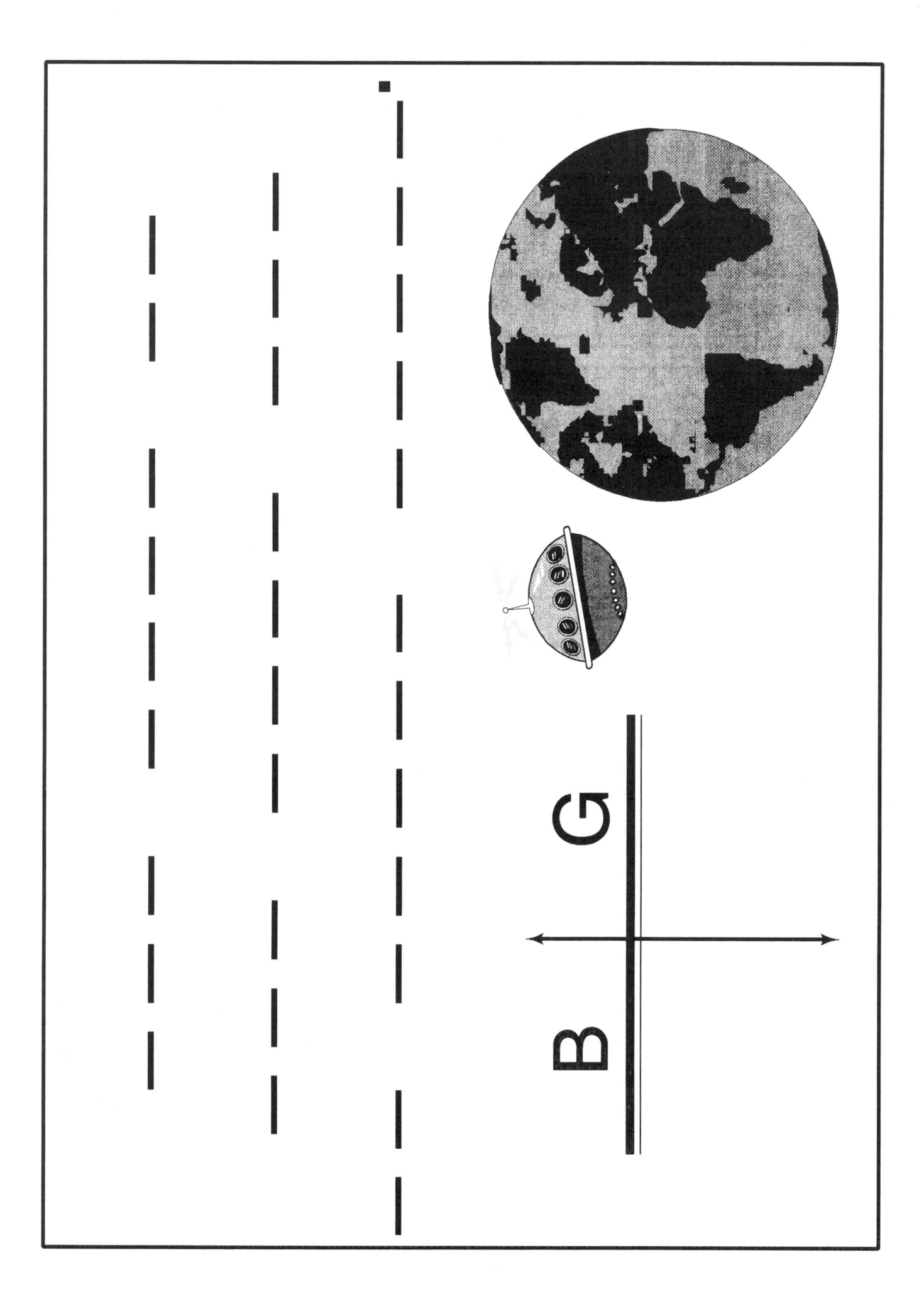

B G

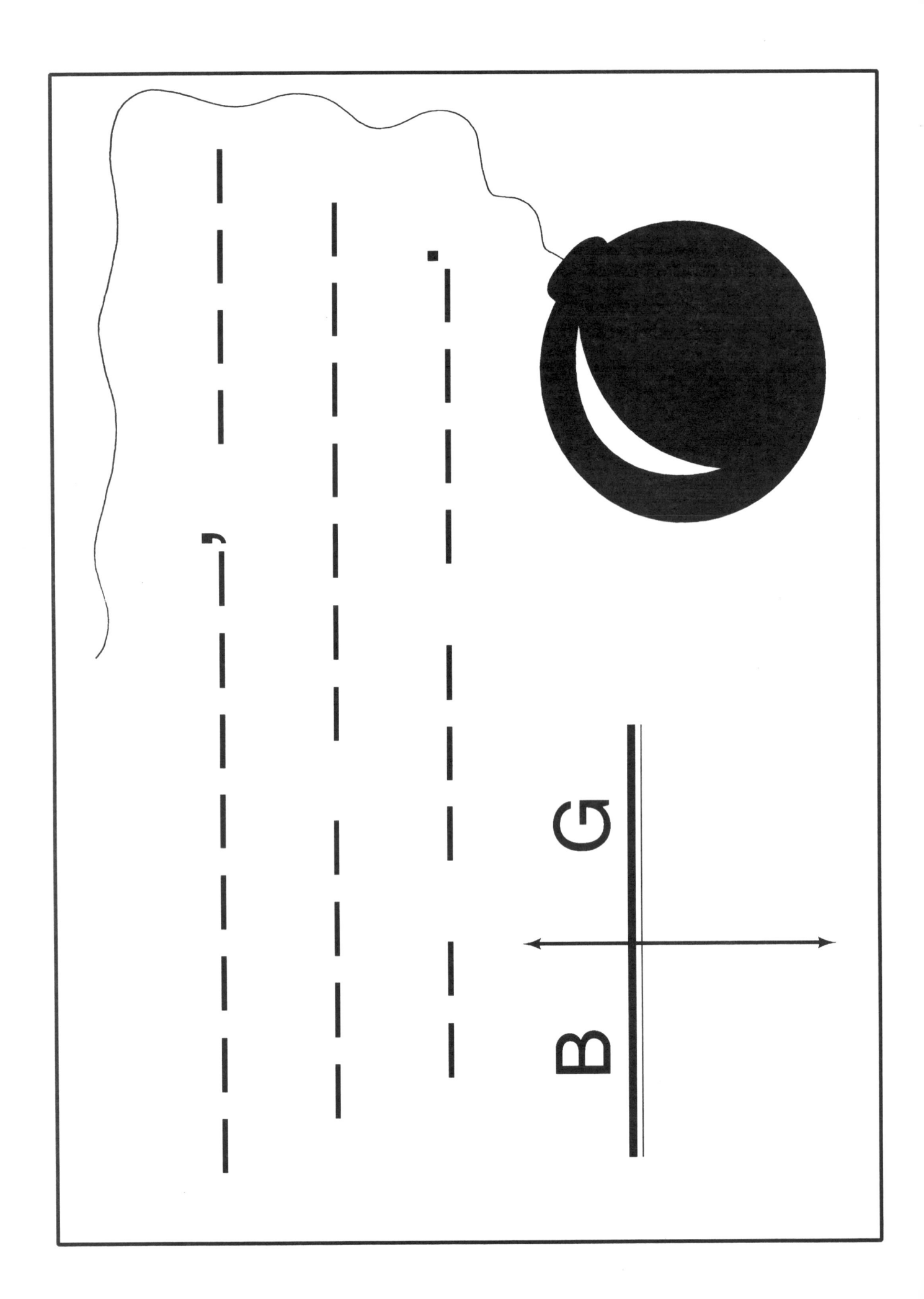

B G

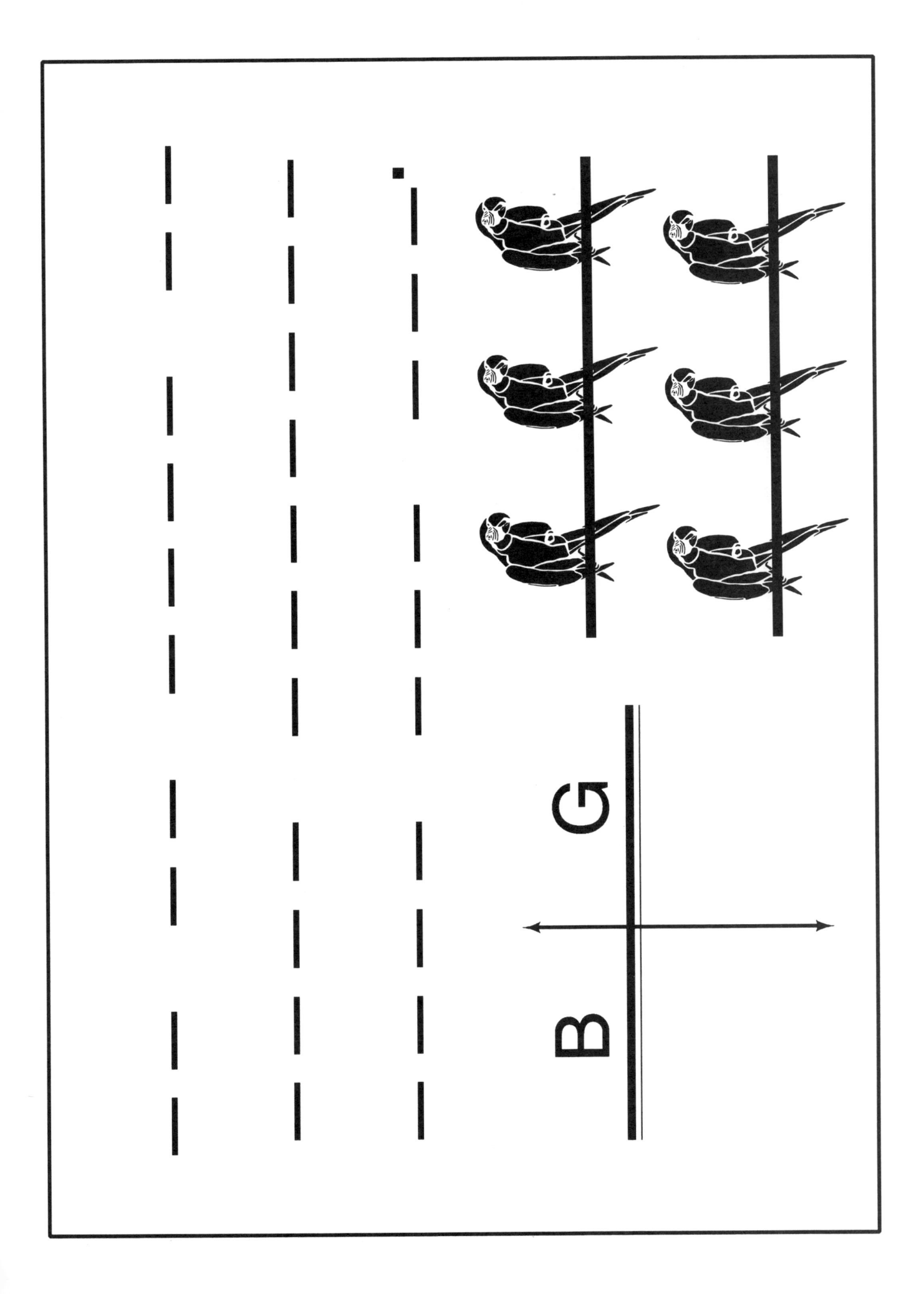

B G

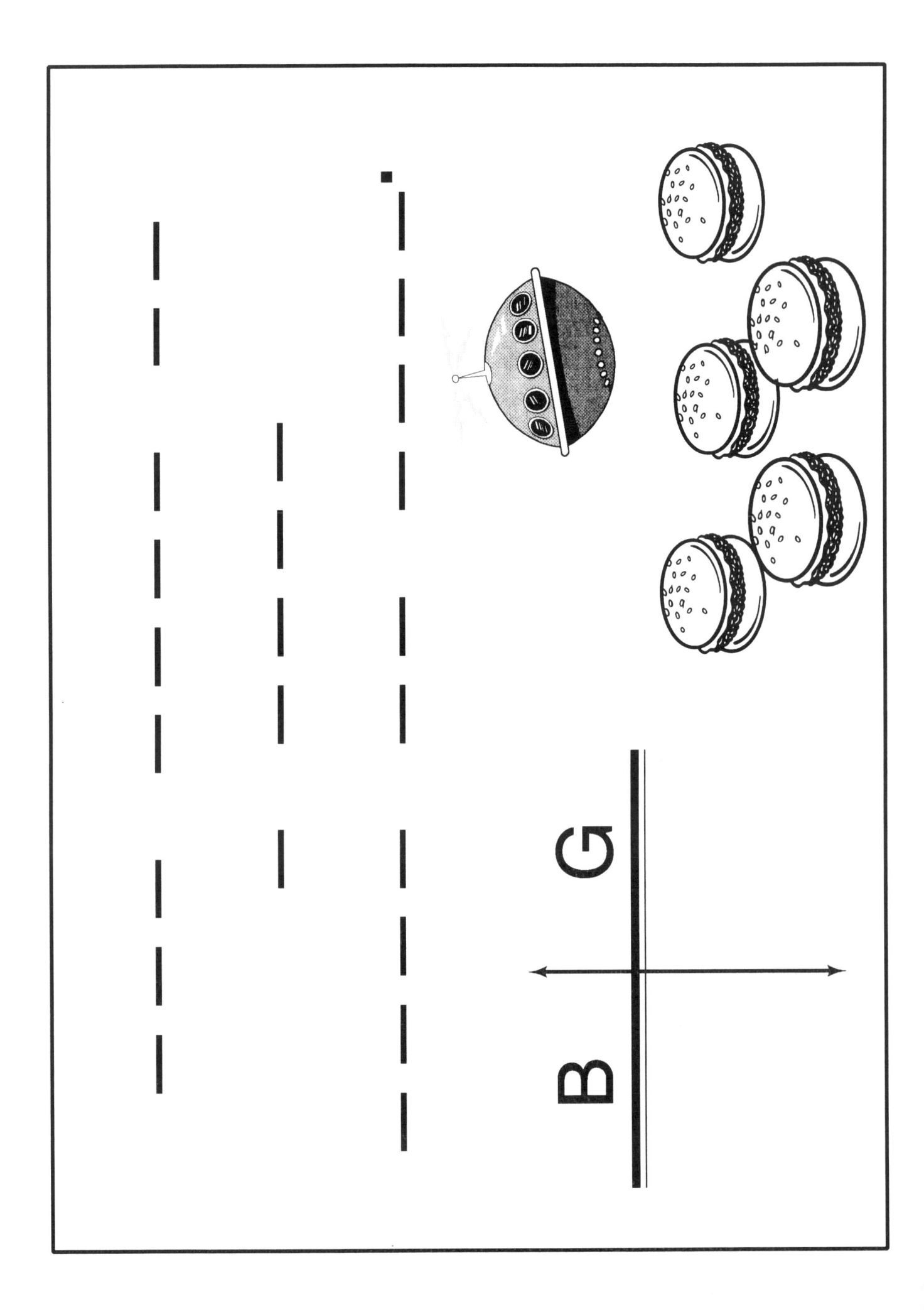

B | G

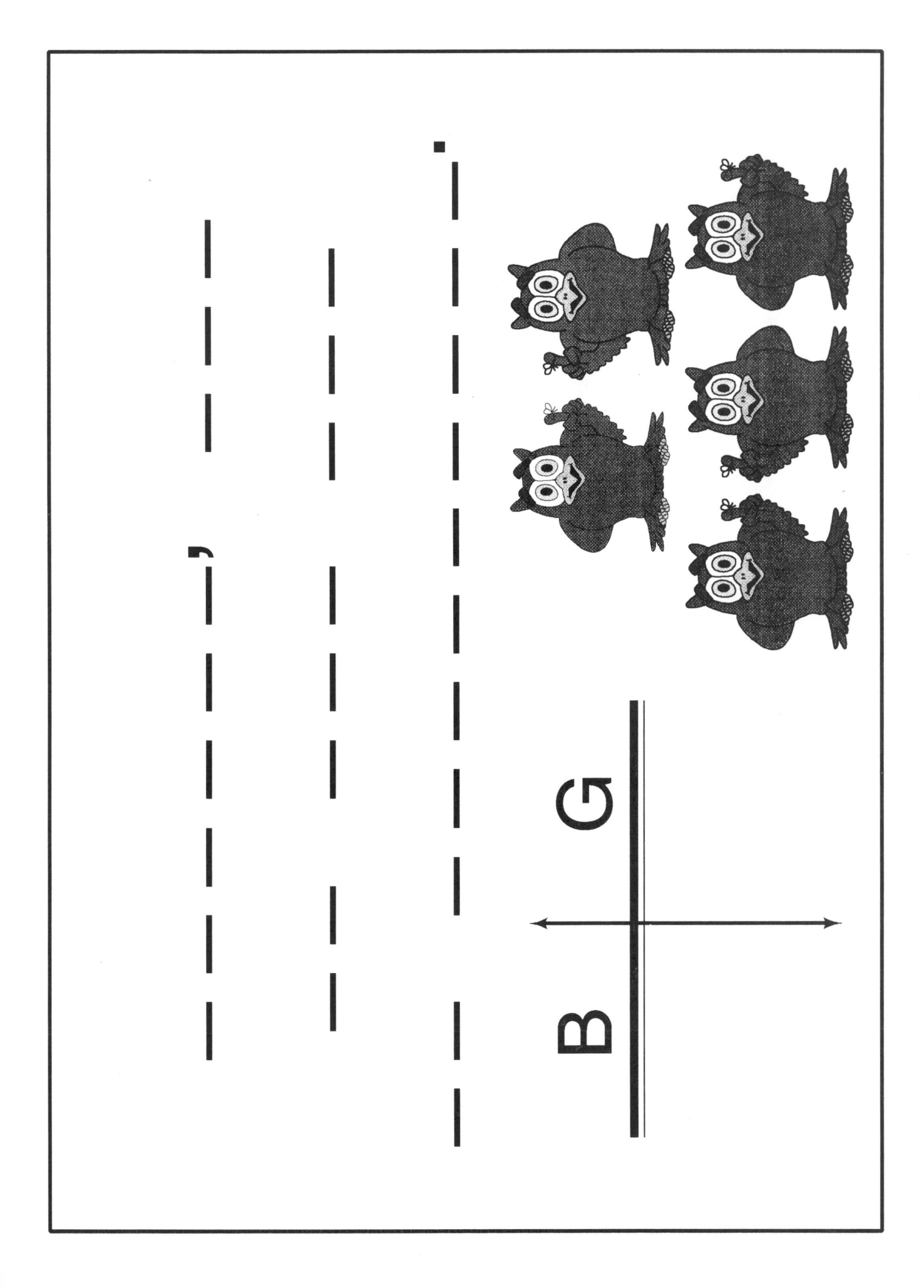

B | G

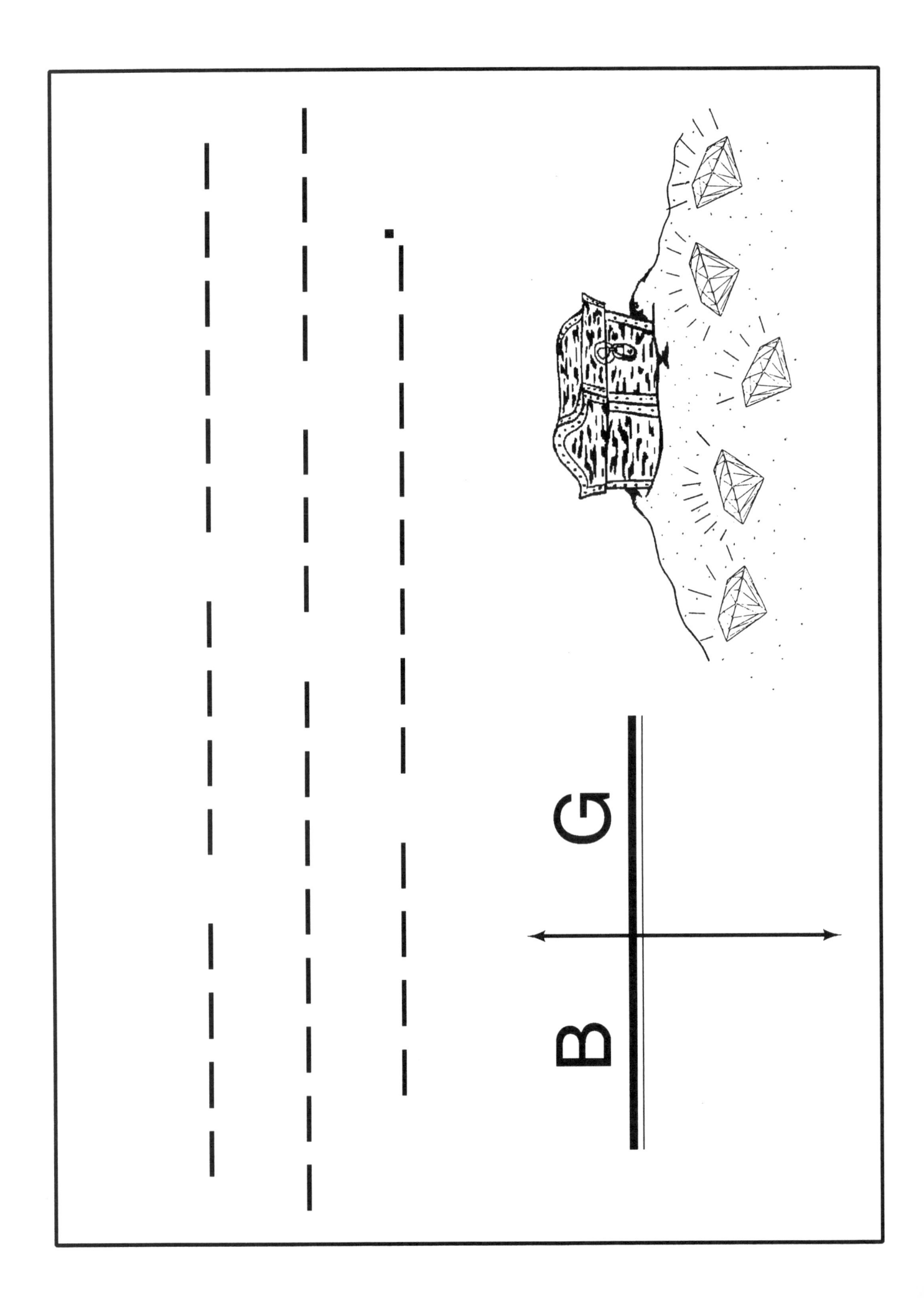

B G

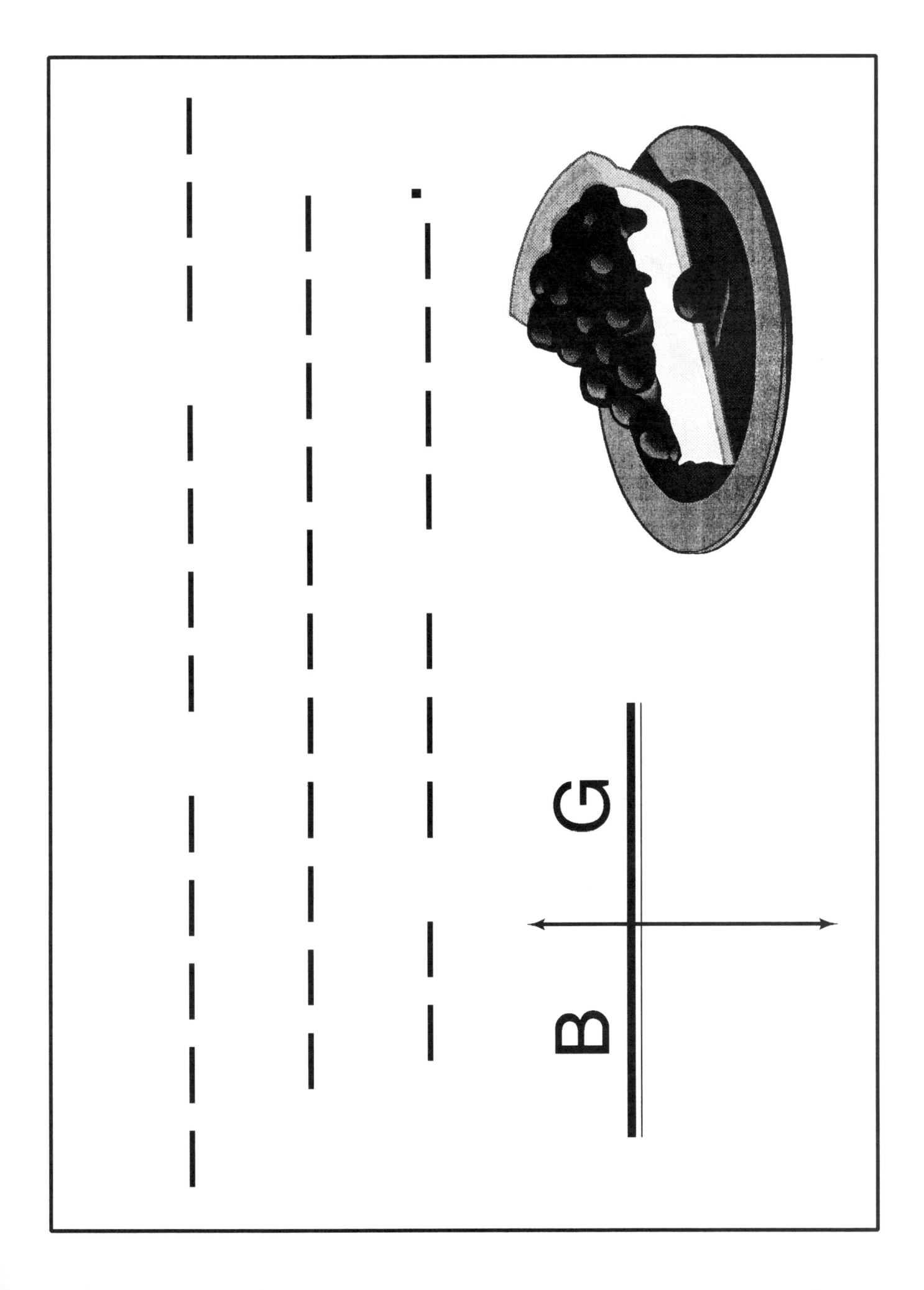

B G

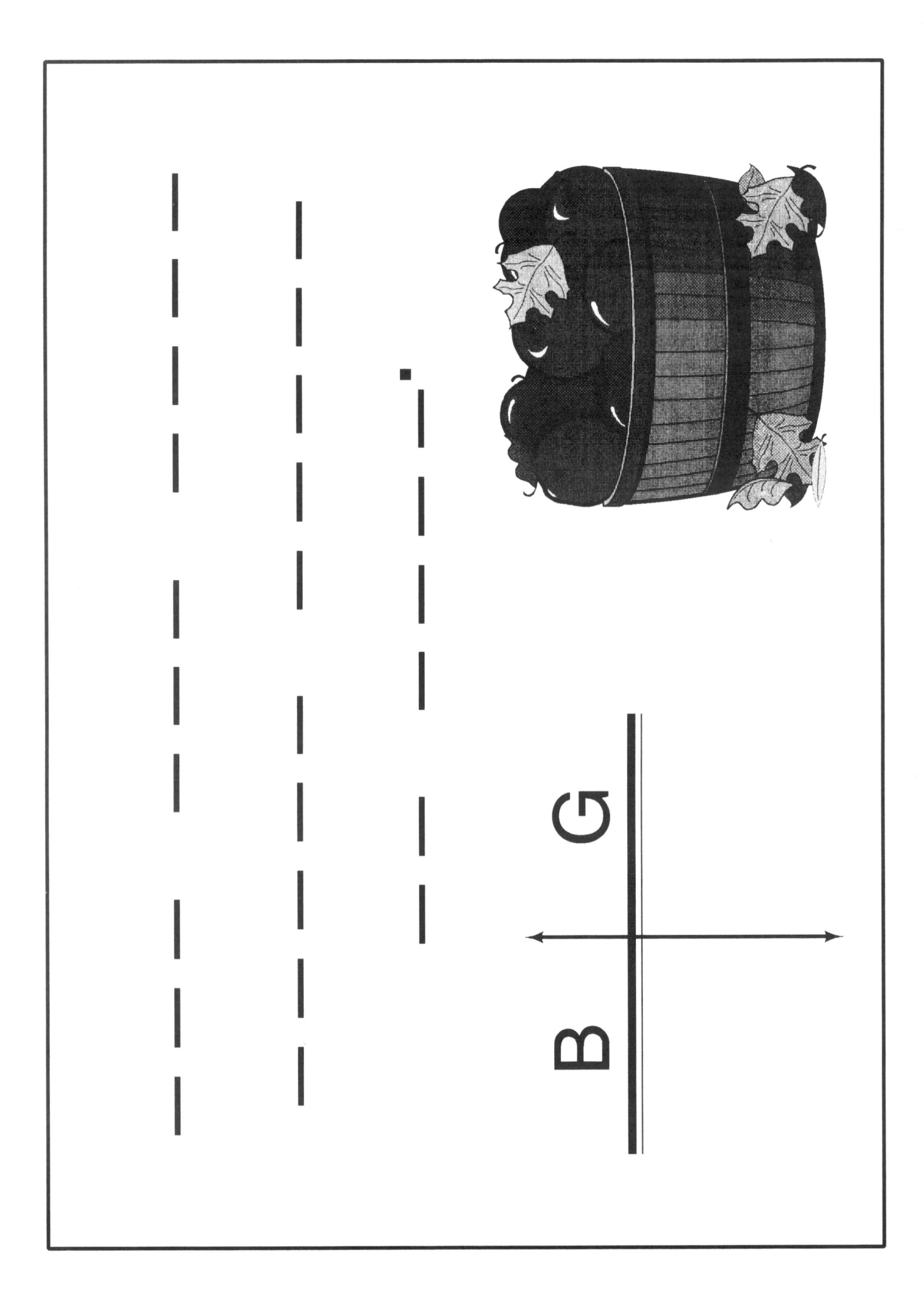

B G

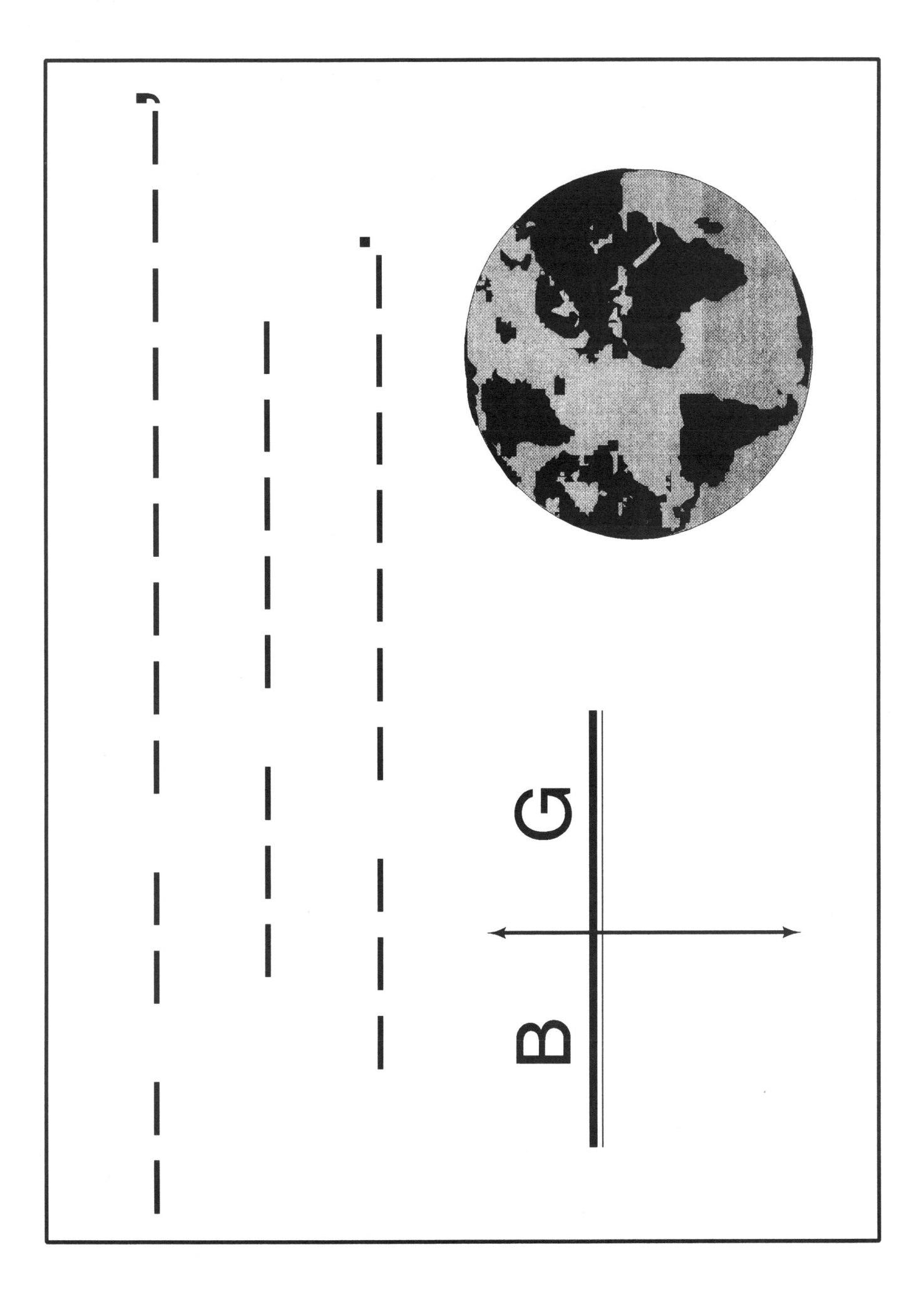

B G

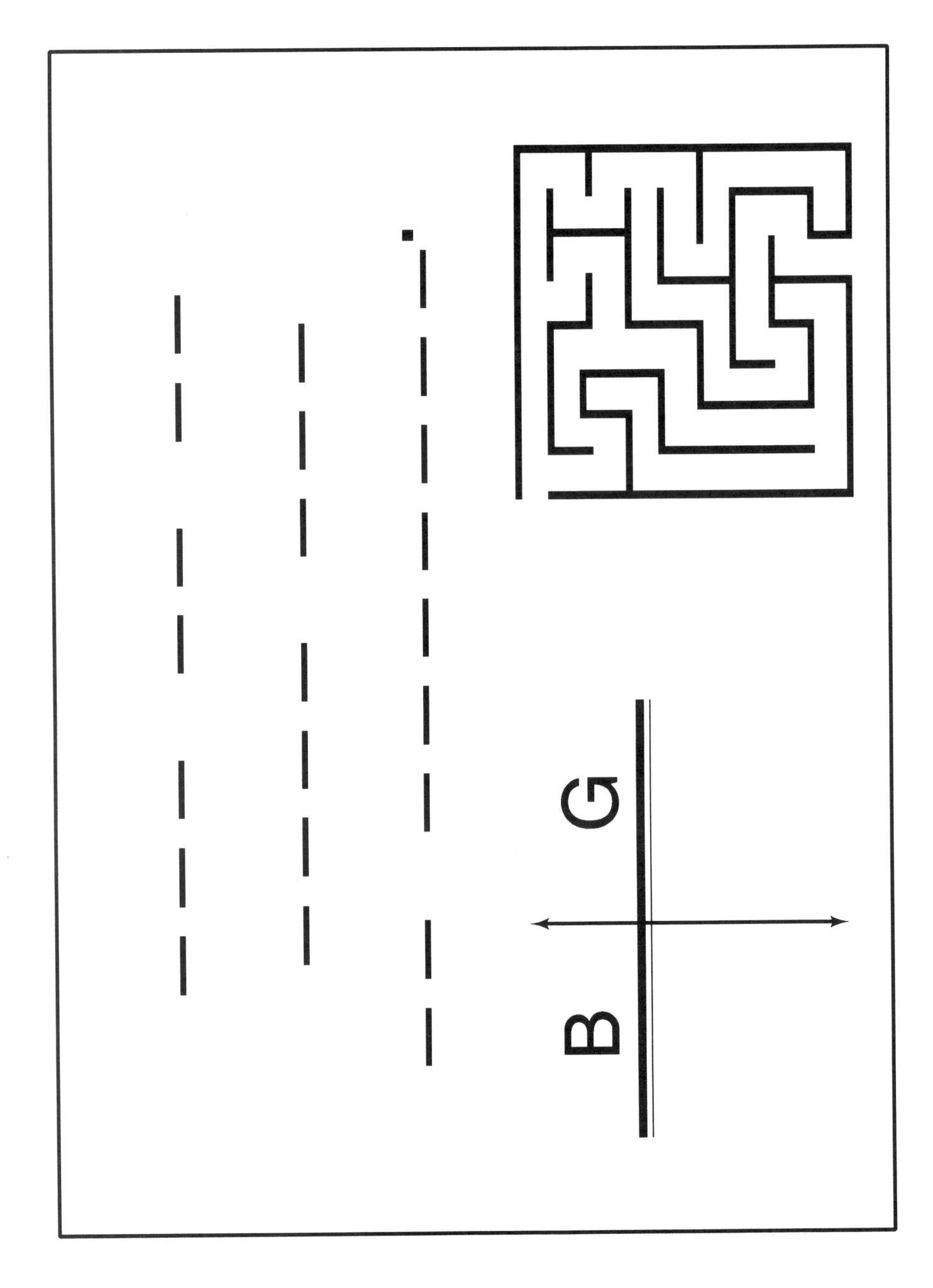

B G

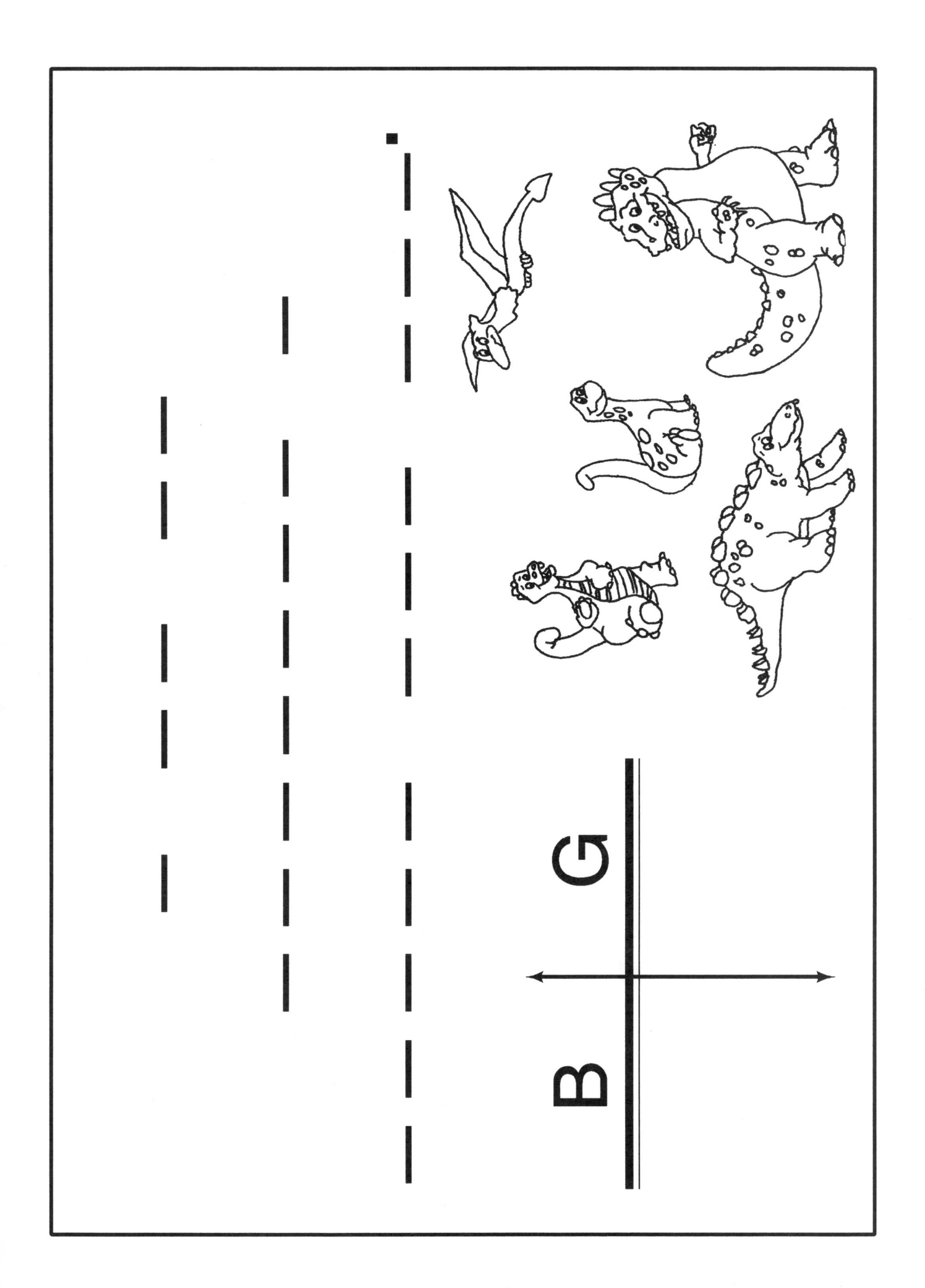

B G

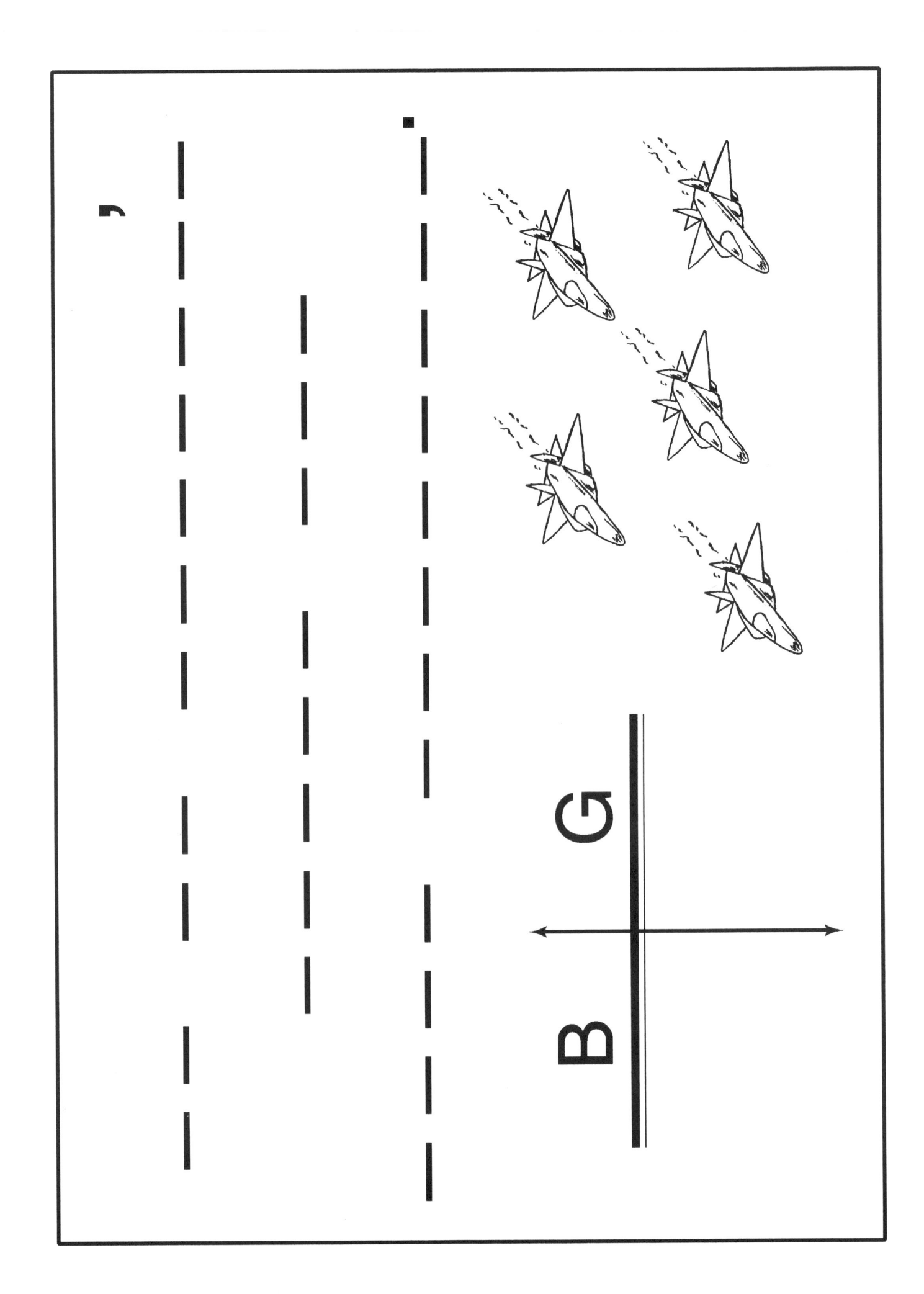

B G

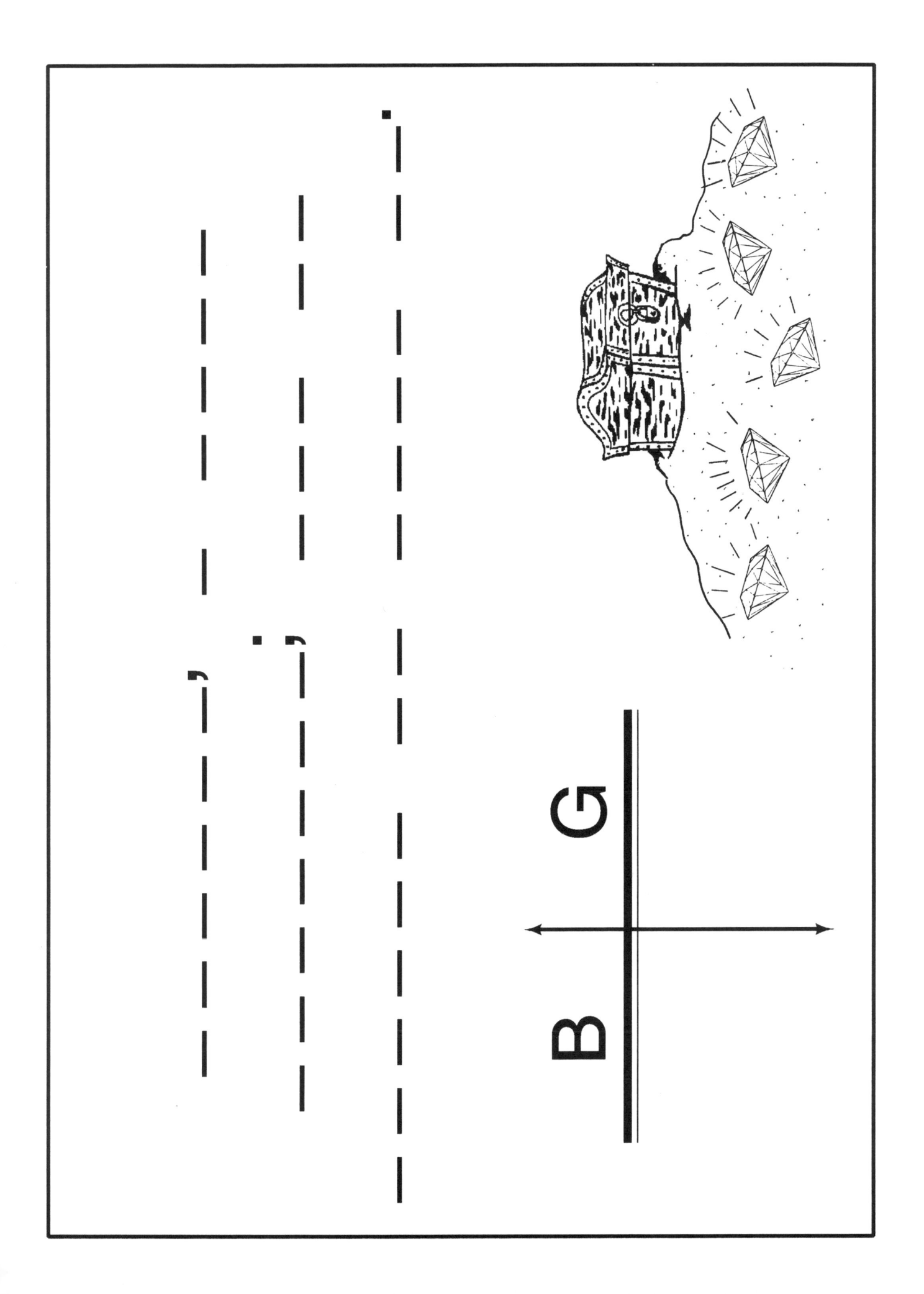

B G

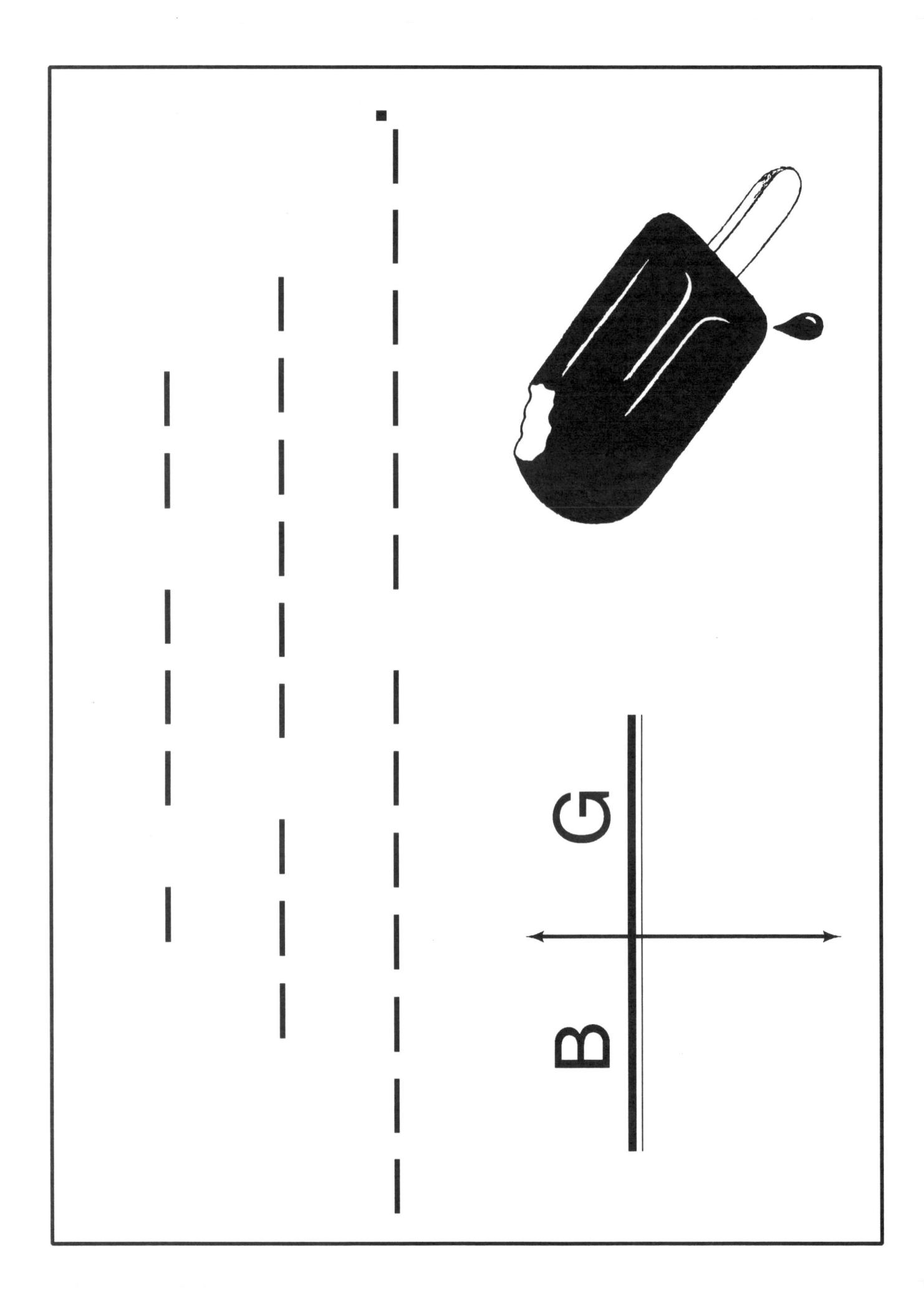

B G

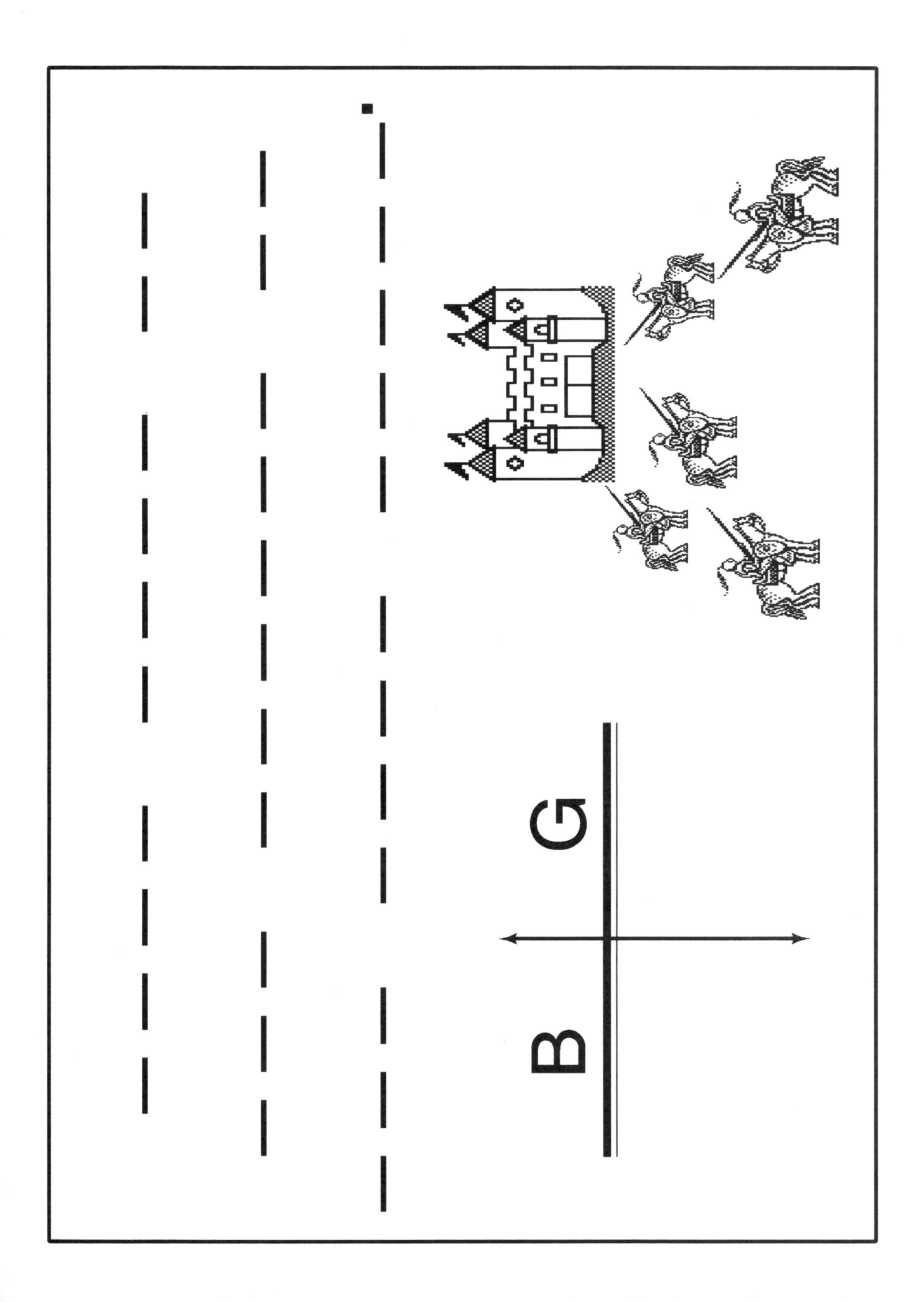

B G

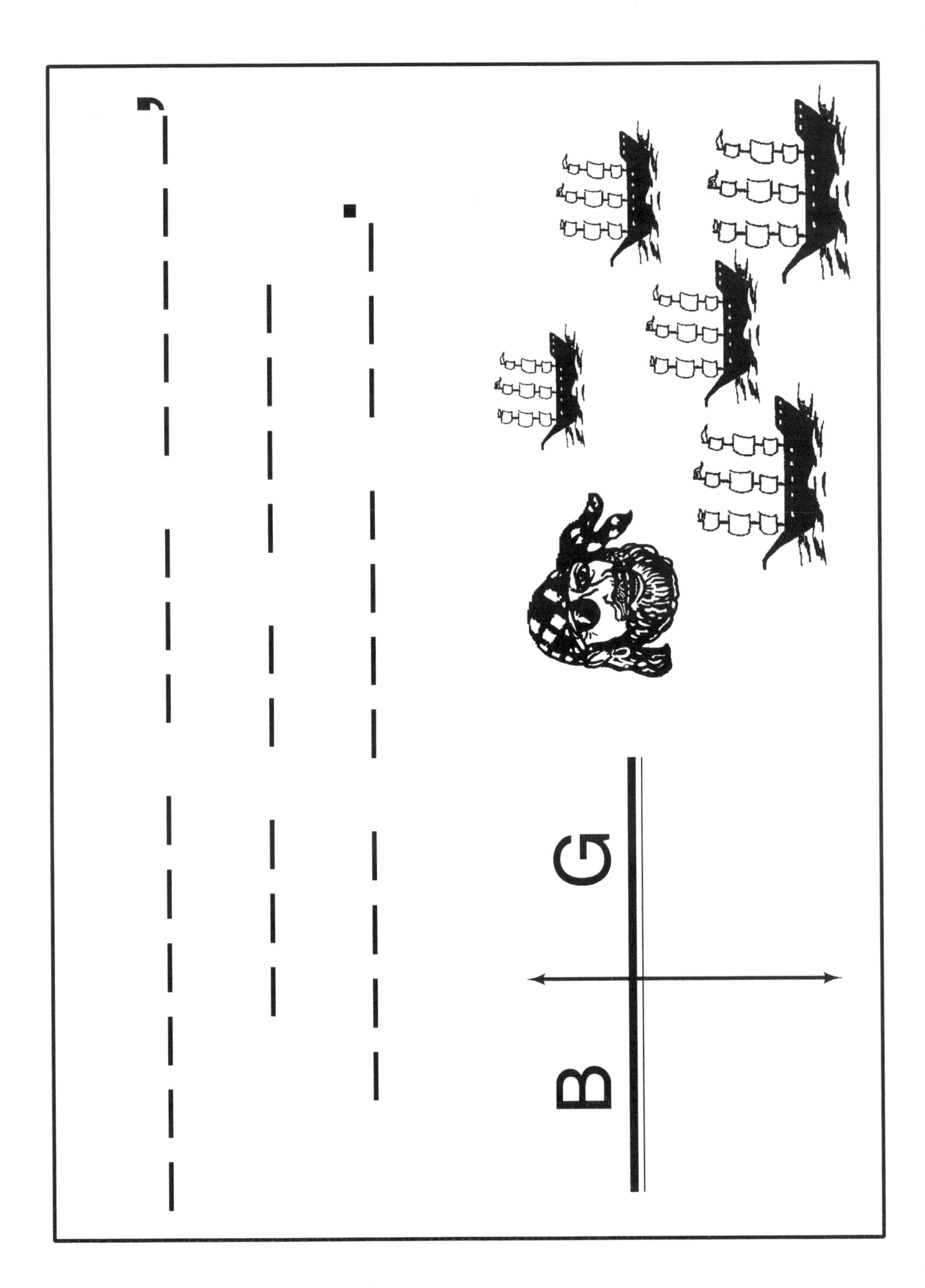

B G

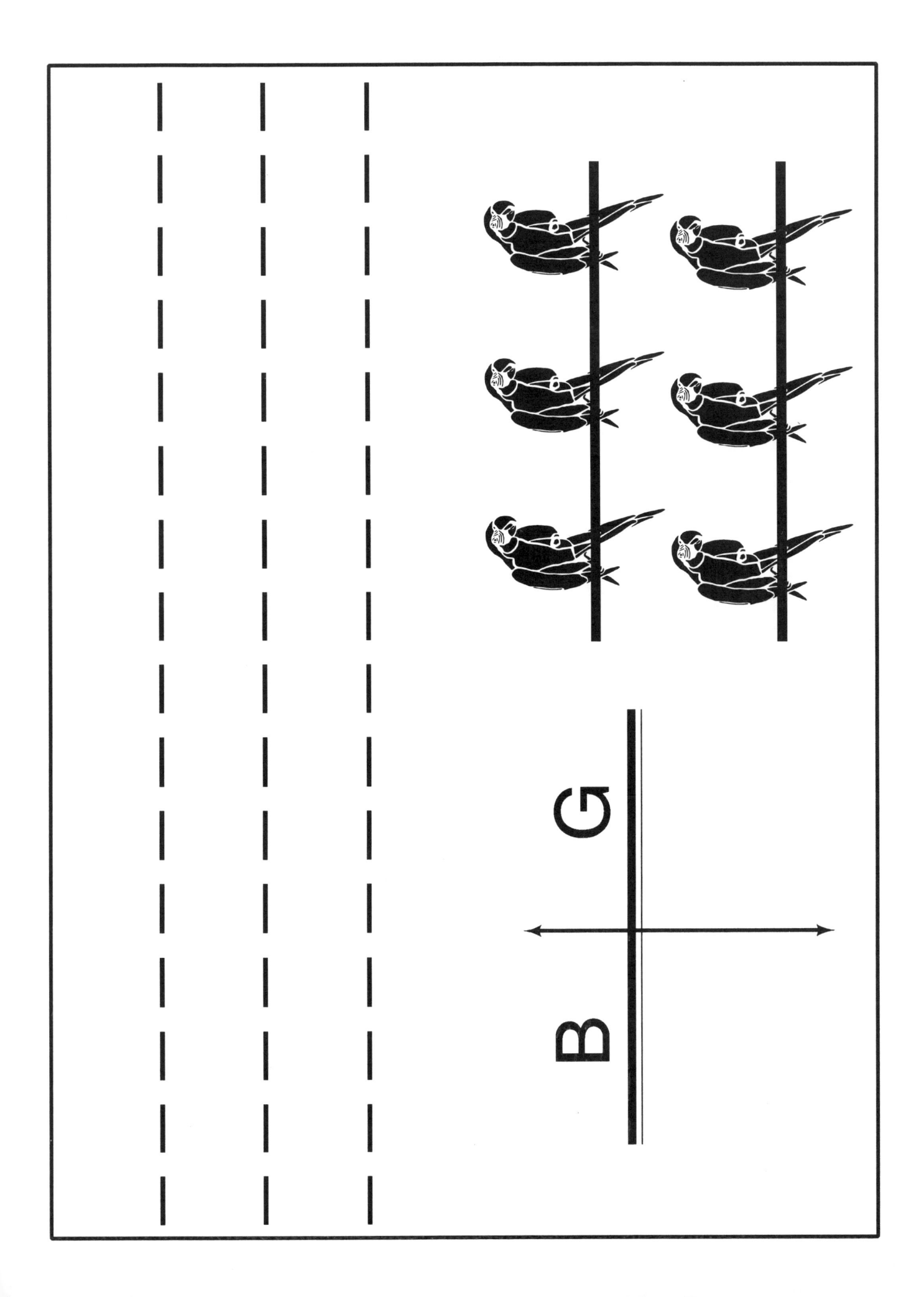

B G

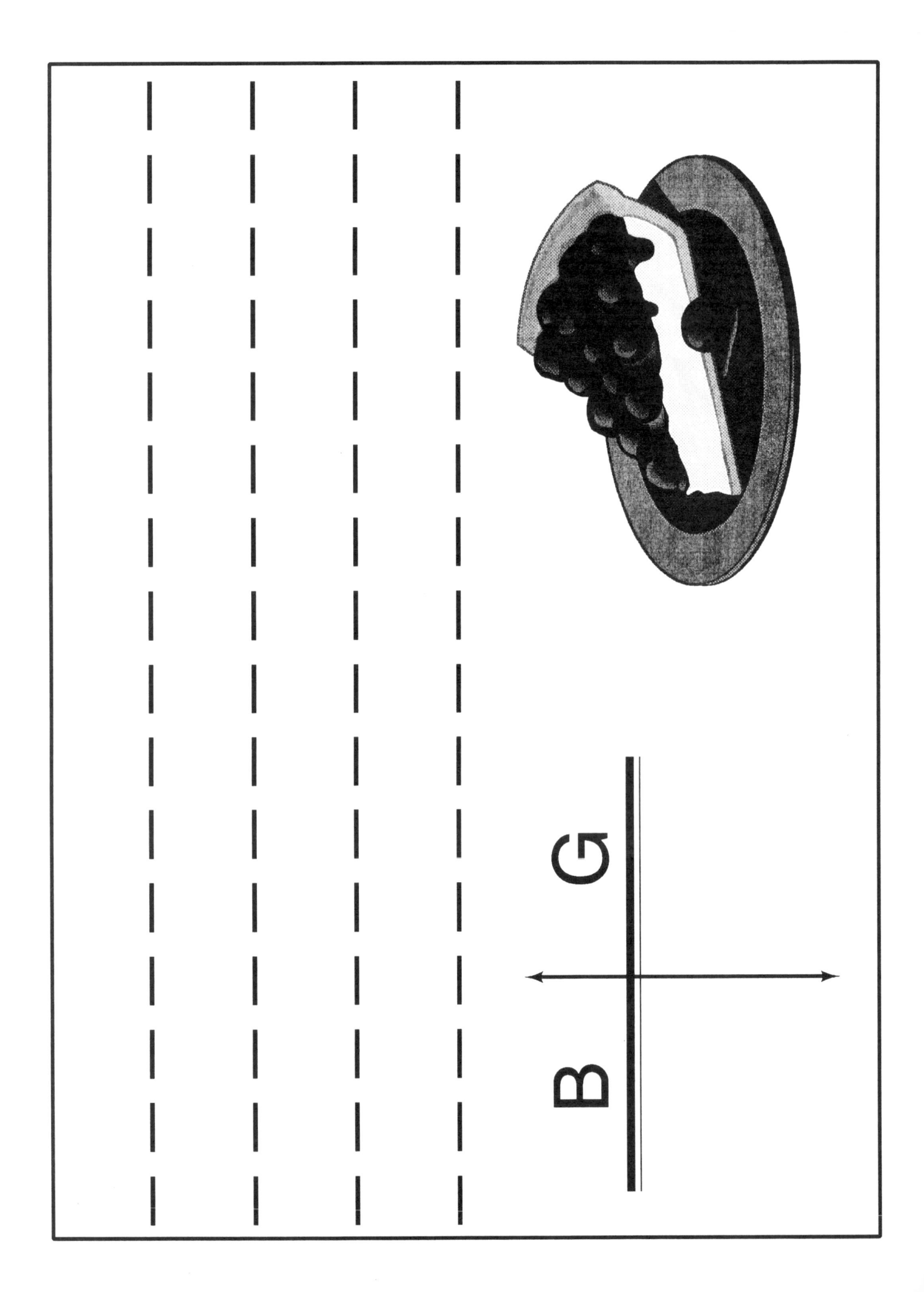

B G

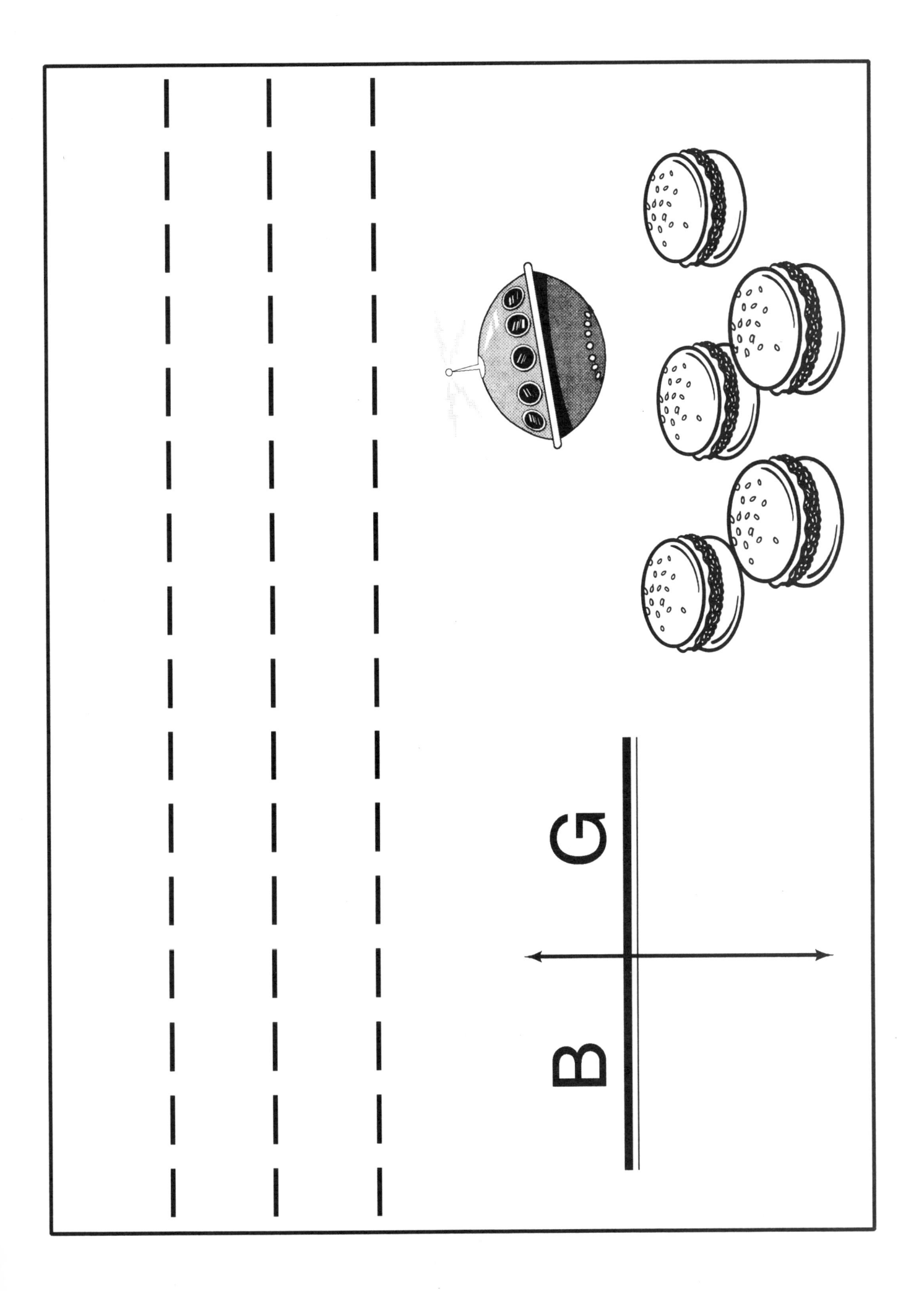

B G

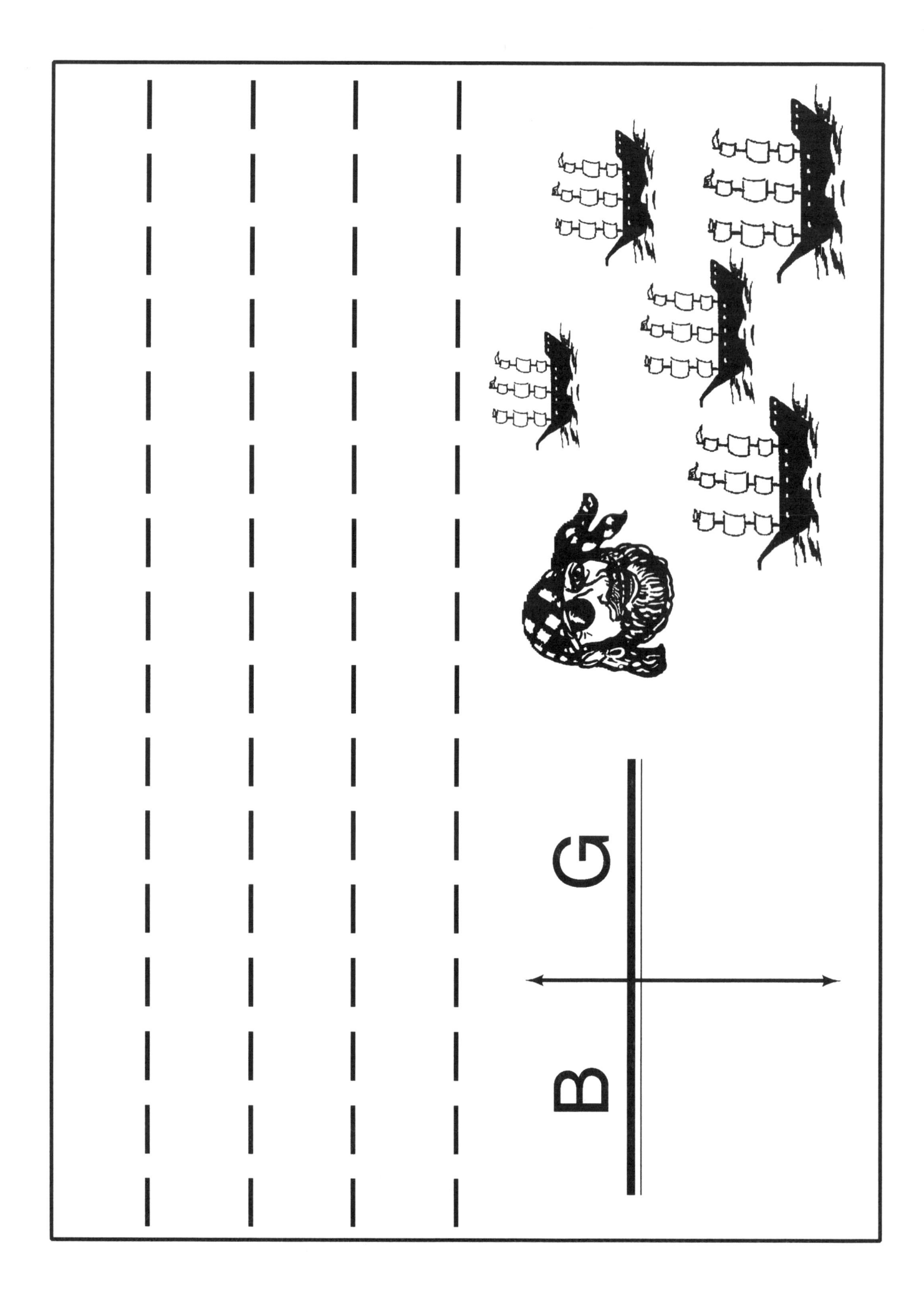

B G

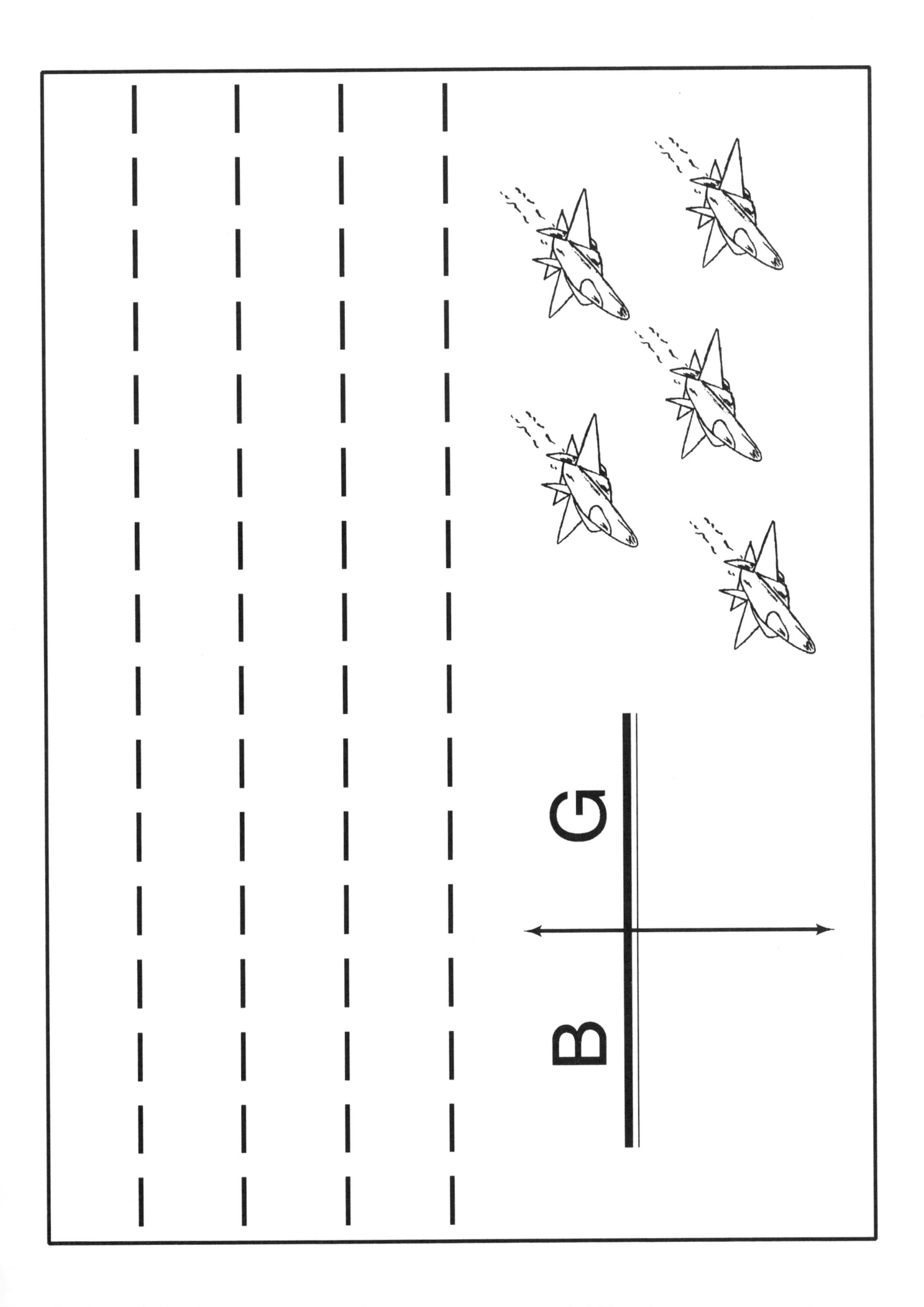

B   G

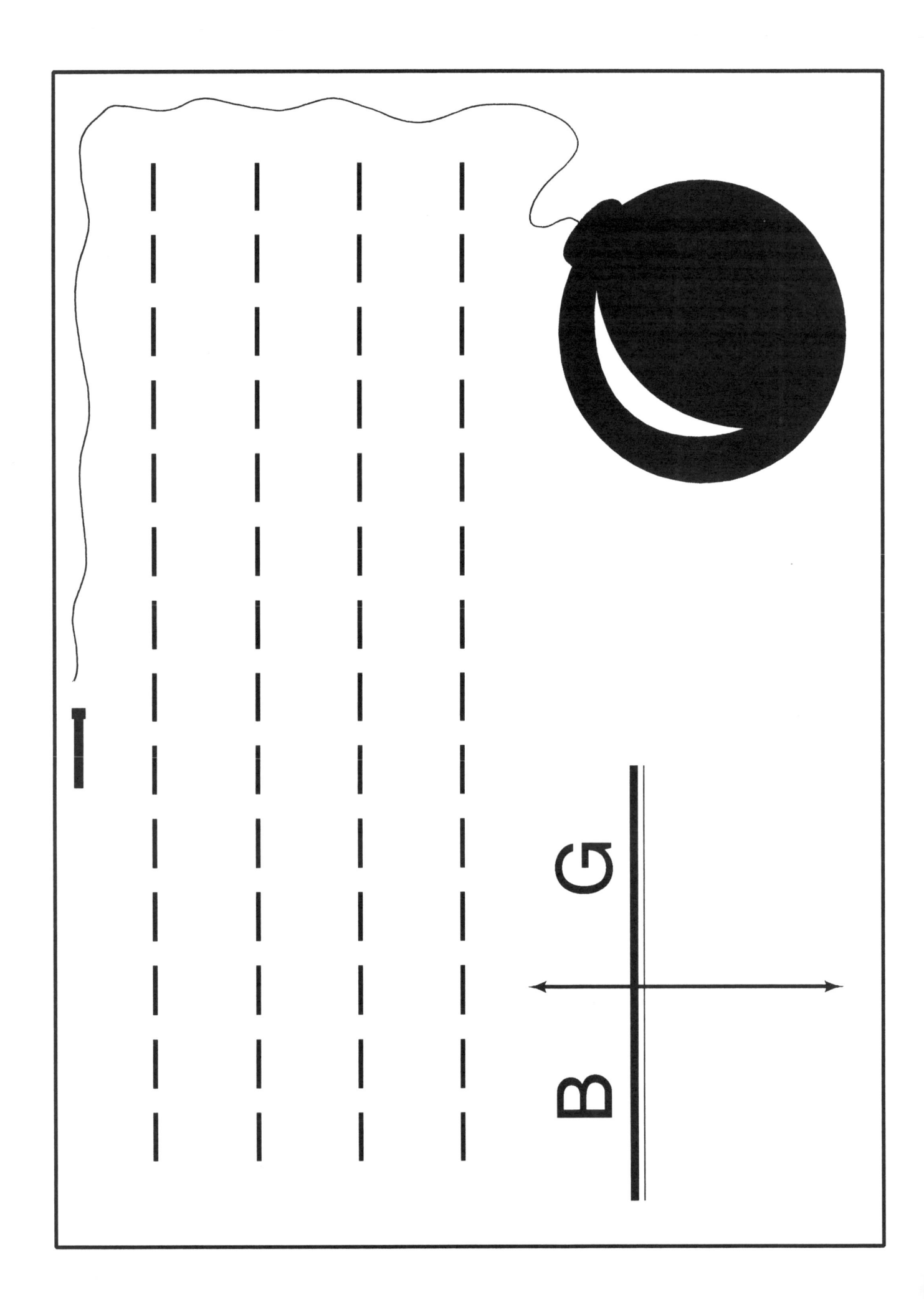

B G

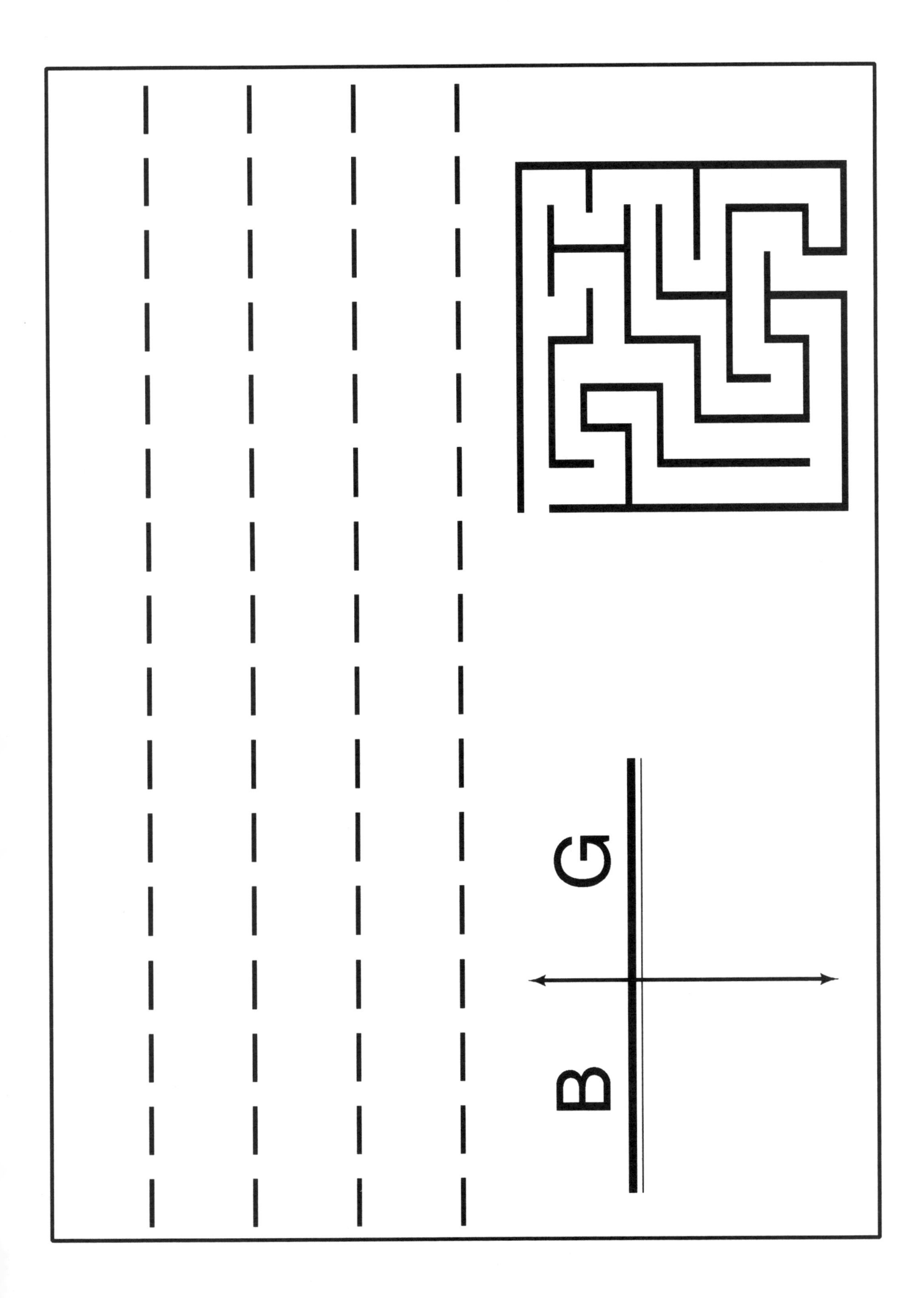

B G

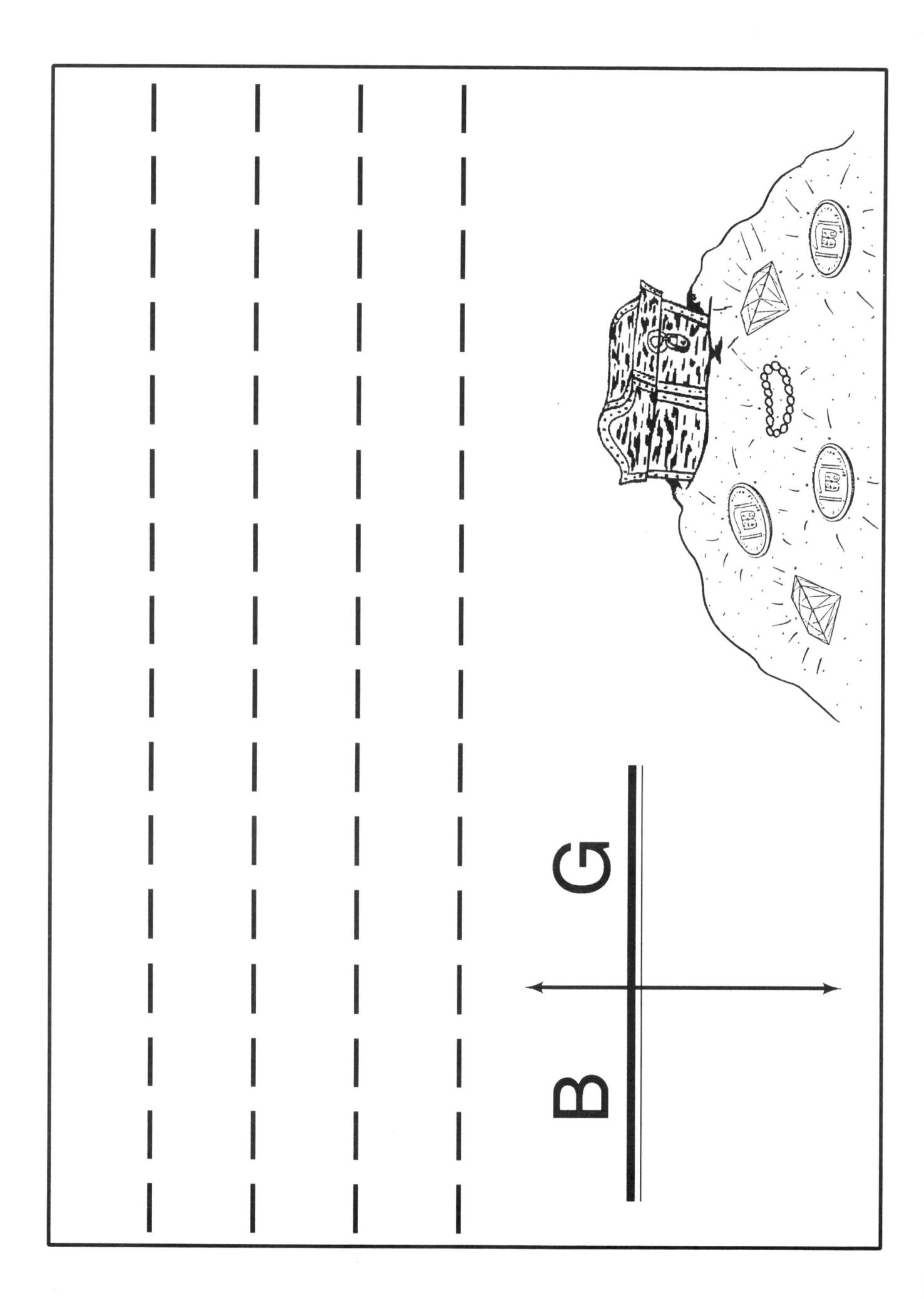

B G

Scripture Puzzles, Solutions, 1-8

#1
WE LOVE HIM, BECAUSE HE FIRST LOVED US.

I John 4:19

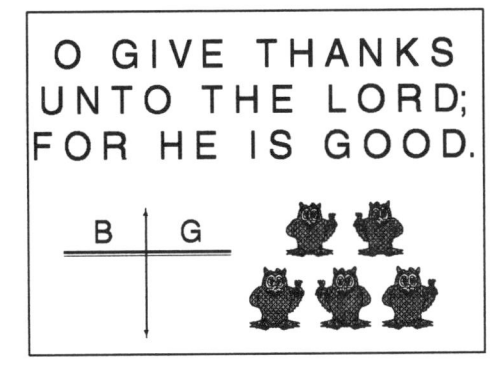

#2
O GIVE THANKS UNTO THE LORD; FOR HE IS GOOD.

Psalm 107:1

#3
THY WORD HAVE I HID IN MINE HEART.

Psalm 119:11

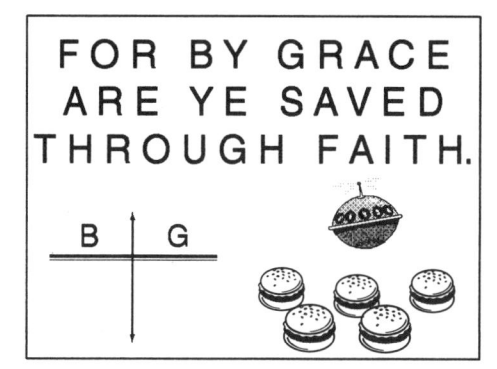

#4
FOR BY GRACE ARE YE SAVED THROUGH FAITH.

Ephesians 2:8

#5
SEEK YE THE LORD WHILE HE MAY BE FOUND.

Isaiah 55:6

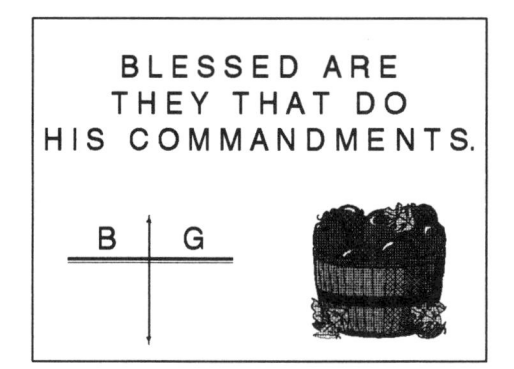

#6
BLESSED ARE THEY THAT DO HIS COMMANDMENTS.

Revelation 22:14

#7
AND YE SHALL BE WITNESSES UNTO ME.

Acts 1:8

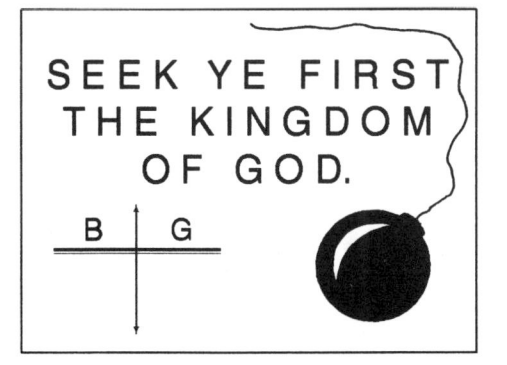

#8
SEEK YE FIRST THE KINGDOM OF GOD.

Matthew 6:33

Scripture Puzzles, Solutions, 9-16

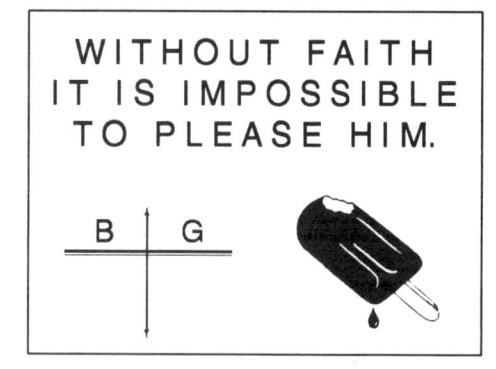

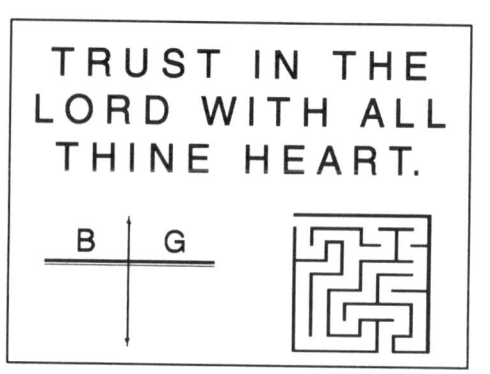

#9
WITHOUT FAITH IT IS IMPOSSIBLE TO PLEASE HIM.
Hebrews 11:6

#10
IN THE BEGINNING GOD CREATED THE HEAVEN AND THE EARTH.
Genesis 1:1

#11
ALL WE LIKE SHEEP HAVE GONE ASTRAY.
Isaiah 53:6

#12
TRUST IN THE LORD WITH ALL THINE HEART.
Proverbs 3:5

#13
CALL UNTO ME, AND I WILL ANSWER THEE.
Jeremiah 33:3

#14
THEN SAID I, "HERE AM I, SEND ME."
Isaiah 6:8

#15
BUT MY GOD SHALL SUPPLY ALL YOUR NEED.
Philippians 4:19

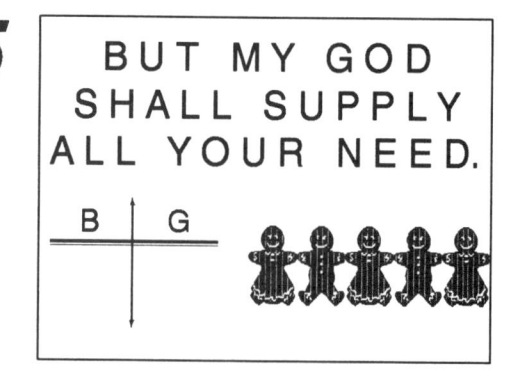

#16
IF YE LOVE ME, KEEP MY COMMANDMENTS.
John 14:15

Scripture Puzzles, Solutions, 17-24

#17 THE EYES OF THE LORD ARE IN EVERY PLACE.
Proverbs 15:3

#18 CHILDREN, OBEY YOUR PARENTS IN THE LORD.
Ephesians 6:1

#19 IT IS GOOD TO SING PRAISES UNTO OUR GOD.
Psalm 147:1

#20 THY WORD IS A LAMP UNTO MY FEET.
Psalm 119:105

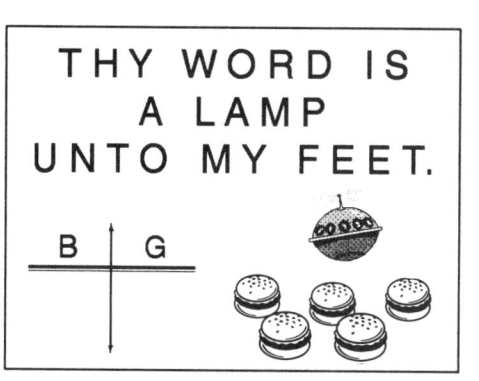

#21 BEHOLD, NOW IS THE DAY OF SALVATION.
II Corinthians 6:2

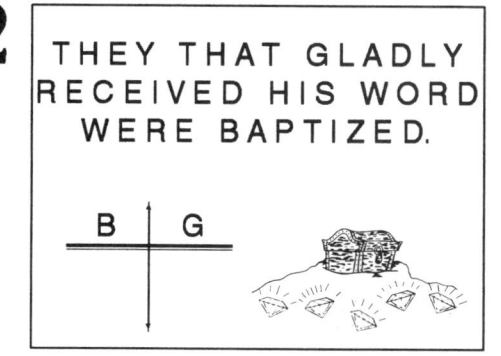

#22 THEY THAT GLADLY RECEIVED HIS WORD WERE BAPTIZED.
Acts 2:41

#23 LYING LIPS ARE ABOMINATION TO THE LORD.
Proverbs 12:22

#24 LET HIM THAT STOLE STEAL NO MORE.
Ephesians 4:28

Scripture Puzzles, Solutions, 25-32

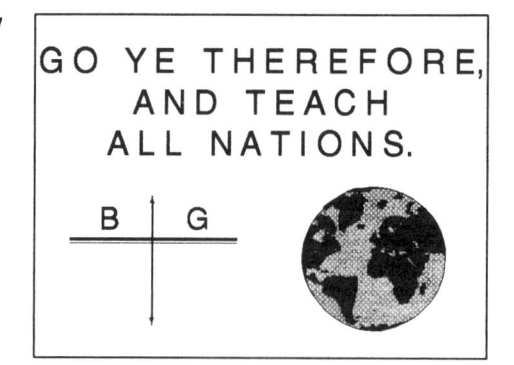

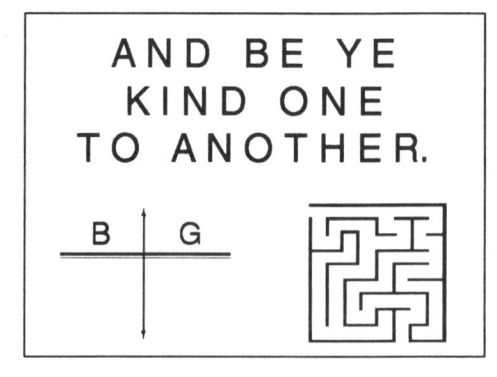

#25 GO YE THEREFORE, AND TEACH ALL NATIONS.
Matthew 28:19

#26 AND BE YE KIND ONE TO ANOTHER.
Ephesians 4:32

#27 I GO TO PREPARE A PLACE FOR YOU.
John 14:2

#28 IN MY FATHER'S HOUSE ARE MANY MANSIONS.
John 14:2

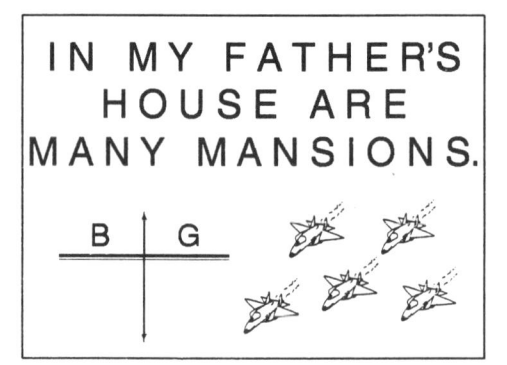

#29 BEHOLD, I COME QUICKLY; AND MY REWARD IS WITH ME.
Revelation 22:12

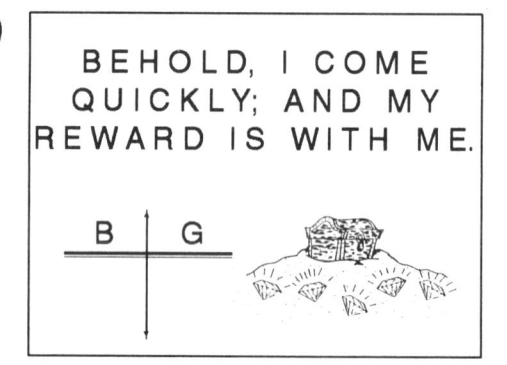

#30 I CAN DO ALL THINGS THROUGH CHRIST.
Philippians 4:13

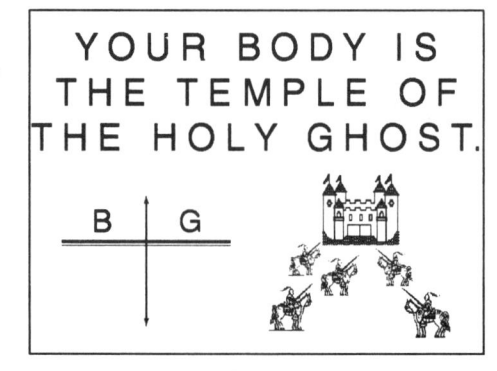

#31 YOUR BODY IS THE TEMPLE OF THE HOLY GHOST.
I Corinthians 6:19

#32 RESIST THE DEVIL, AND HE WILL FLEE FROM YOU.
James 4:7

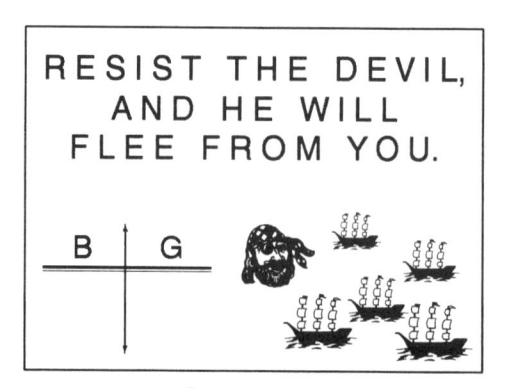

A Final Word

Remember when you first started teaching? You couldn't wait for Sunday to come. The thrill of presenting the eternal truths of God's Word to eager young students was exhilarating. It was fulfilling and rewarding to realize that you were molding young lives for the Master. You could hardly get enough.

But what about today? Do you still find yourself looking forward to Sunday with eagerness and anticipation? Or does the thought of preparing for class fill you with dread and apprehension?

As a teacher of children for the past twenty-three years, I've experienced my own ups and downs. Teaching can be such a joy — and yet, how quickly it can move from my list of delights to my list of duties. It's easy to grow weary in the work; it happens to all of us.

Why not step back, take a deep breath, and brave a self-evaluation for just a few moments? If you've lost the joy of teaching, chances are you're no longer giving it your very best. Come on, now — be honest with yourself.

Perhaps this book can help. Get started right away using the games and puzzles you find here. If you're anything like me, the challenge of "something new" can be quite stimulating. You'll find yourself looking forward to class time again, eager to see how "your kids" are going to respond to that new *Operation Spy Trap* game, or that new Scripture puzzle. And you'll find your newfound enthusiasm spreading to other aspects of class as well. It's fun to teach when you're excited about it.

So why not get started on the overhead games and puzzles right away? Make several different ones on your copier today, and use the first one in class this week. Your class time will begin to sparkle with new life, and you and your students will look forward to it each week.

Ask the Lord to recharge you with new energy and enthusiasm for the ministry of teaching! He deserves your very best!

> *You'll find your new-found enthusiasm spreading to other aspects of class as well. It's fun to teach when you're excited about it.*

ABOUT THE AUTHOR

Ed Dunlop has worked in children's ministries full-time for over twenty-three years. He is the author of another book for Christian educators, *Teaching With Bible Games*.

Ed and his family travel most of the year. As a children's evangelist, he conducts kids' crusades in local churches. He also conducts teacher-training seminars, speaks at junior camps, and presents visualized drug and alcohol programs in public elementary and junior high schools. He uses ventriloquism, gospel magic, blacklight effects, balloon sculptures, and a variety of other visual media in his presentations. He holds memberships in the North American Association of Ventriloquists and the Fellowship of Christian Magicians.

A graduate of Pacific Coast Baptist Bible College, Ed has written magazine articles and novels for middle readers, including an adventure story entitled *Escape to Liechtenstein*. He recently completed a how-to manuscript about children's church.

Ed, his wife, Janice, and their three children, Rebecca, Steven, and Phillip, reside in Ringgold, Georgia.

ORDER FORM

MERIWETHER PUBLISHING LTD.
P.O. BOX 7710
COLORADO SPRINGS, CO 80933
TELEPHONE: (719) 594-4422

Please send me the following books:

_____ **Let's Play a Bible Game! #CC-B183** — $12.95
by Ed Dunlop
Scripture puzzles and games for the overhead projector

_____ **Teaching With Bible Games #CC-B108** — $10.95
by Ed Dunlop
20 "kid-tested" contests for Christian education

_____ **The Official Sunday School Teachers Handbook #CC-B152** — $9.95
by Joanne Owens
An indispensable aid and barrel of laughs for anyone involved in Sunday school activities

_____ **No Experience Necessary! #CC-B107** — $12.95
by Elaine Clanton Harpine
A "learn-by-doing" guide for creating children's worship

_____ **Storytelling From the Bible #CC-B145** — $10.95
by Janet Litherland
The art of biblical storytelling

_____ **Celebrating Special Days in the Church School Year #CC-B146** — $9.95
by Judy Gattis Smith
Liturgies and participation activities for children

_____ **Where Does God Live? #CC-B189** — $9.95
by Ted Lazicki
Fifty-eight children's sermons for worship

_____ **Something for the Kids #CC-B192** — $9.95
by Ted Lazicki
Fifty-two "front row" sermons for children

_____ **You Can Do Christian Puppets #CC-B196** — $10.95
by Bea Carlton
A basic guide to Christian puppetry

These and other fine Meriwether Publishing books are available at your local Christian bookstore or direct from the publisher. Use the handy order form on this page.

NAME: _____

ORGANIZATION NAME: _____

ADDRESS: _____

CITY: _____ STATE: _____ ZIP: _____

PHONE: _____

❑ Check Enclosed
❑ Visa or MasterCard # _____

Signature: _____ Expiration Date: _____
(required for Visa/MasterCard orders)

COLORADO RESIDENTS: Please add 3% sales tax.
SHIPPING: Include $2.75 for the first book and 50¢ for each additional book ordered.

❑ *Please send me a copy of your complete catalog of books and plays.*